A CULTURAL HISTORY OF LAW

VOLUME 4

A Cultural History of Law
General Editor: Gary Watt

Volume 1
A Cultural History of Law in Antiquity
Edited by Julen Etxabe

Volume 2
A Cultural History of Law in the Middle Ages
Edited by Emanuele Conte and Laurent Mayali

Volume 3
A Cultural History of Law in the Early Modern Age
Edited by Peter Goodrich

Volume 4
A Cultural History of Law in the Age of Enlightenment
Edited by Rebecca Probert and John Snape

Volume 5
A Cultural History of Law in the Age of Reform
Edited by Ian Ward

Volume 6
A Cultural History of Law in the Modern Age
Edited by Richard K. Sherwin and Danielle Celermajer

A CULTURAL HISTORY OF LAW

IN THE AGE OF ENLIGHTENMENT

Edited by Rebecca Probert and John Snape

BLOOMSBURY ACADEMIC
LONDON • NEW YORK • OXFORD • NEW DELHI • SYDNEY

BLOOMSBURY ACADEMIC
Bloomsbury Publishing Plc
50 Bedford Square, London, WC1B 3DP, UK
1385 Broadway, New York, NY 10018, USA
29 Earlsfort Terrace, Dublin 2, Ireland

BLOOMSBURY, BLOOMSBURY ACADEMIC and the Diana logo are
trademarks of Bloomsbury Publishing Plc

First published in Great Britain 2019
Paperback edition published in 2023

Copyright © Bloomsbury Publishing Plc, 2019

Rebecca Probert and John Snape have asserted their right under the Copyright,
Designs and Patents Act, 1988, to be identified as Editors of this work.

Cover image © DeAgostini/Getty Images. United Kingdom - circa 2002: The rake's progress,
the tavern scene, by William Hogarth (1697–1764). London, Sir John Soane's Museum

All rights reserved. No part of this publication may be reproduced or transmitted in
any form or by any means, electronic or mechanical, including photocopying, recording,
or any information storage or retrieval system, without prior permission in writing
from the publishers.

Bloomsbury Publishing Plc does not have any control over, or responsibility for,
any third-party websites referred to or in this book. All internet addresses given in this book
were correct at the time of going to press. The editor and publisher regret any inconvenience
caused if addresses have changed or sites have ceased to exist, but can accept
no responsibility for any such changes.

A catalogue record for this book is available from the British Library.

A catalog record for this book is available from the Library of Congress.

ISBN:	PB set:	978-1-3503-6891-0
	HB:	978-1-4742-1265-6
	PB:	978-1-3503-6868-2
	ePDF:	978-1-3500-7926-7
	eBook:	978-1-3500-7925-0

Series: The Cultural Histories Series

Typeset by Integra Software Services Pvt. Ltd.
Printed and bound in Great Britain

To find out more about our editors and books visit www.bloomsbury.com
and sign up for our newsletters.

CONTENTS

LIST OF FIGURES	VI
NOTES ON CONTRIBUTORS	VIII
SERIES PREFACE	X
Introduction *John Snape and Rebecca Probert*	1
1 Justice: Popular Ideas and Actions in the Long Eighteenth Century *Steve Banks*	15
2 Constitution: Handel's *Solomon* and the Constitution at Covent Garden *John Snape*	33
3 Codes *Rebecca Probert*	53
4 Agreements *Timothy J. Dodsworth*	71
5 Arguments: Reputation and Character in Eighteenth-Century Trials *Dana Rabin*	89
6 Property and Possession *Julia Rudolph*	107
7 Wrongs *Ruth Paley*	127
8 The Legal Profession *James Oldham*	145
NOTES	160
BIBLIOGRAPHY	172
INDEX	194

LIST OF FIGURES

JUSTICE

1.1	A Perjuror in the Pillory.	24
1.2	The Ducking Stool in Leominster Church.	25
1.3	Hudibras Encounters the Skimmington.	27
1.4	A Stang Riding with a young man acting as substitute.	29
1.5	Plough Monday celebrations.	31

CONSTITUTION

2.1	George Frideric Handel in 1749.	38
2.2	The Judgement of Solomon.	44

CODES

3.1	Harlot's Progress, plate II.	55
3.2	Harlot's Progress, plate V.	56
3.3	Fleet marriage.	65
3.4	The Elopement.	66

AGREEMENTS

4.1	A country Post Office.	72
4.2	Scene in a London Coffee House.	74
4.3	Lloyd's Coffee House, London.	76
4.4	The East Offering its Riches to Britannia.	78
4.5	Marriage à la mode: plate I, The Marriage Settlement.	83
4.6	The Marriage Contract.	84

ARGUMENTS

5.1	Portrait of Sarah Malcolm.	90
5.2	Elizabeth Canning and Mary Squires.	103
5.3	Mary Squires.	104

PROPERTY AND POSSESSION

6.1	Sir Robert Clayton.	108
6.2	Moore's estate mortgage.	110
6.3	Mr and Mrs Andrews.	114
6.4	First Stage of Cruelty.	117
6.5	Rake's Progress, plate III.	119
6.6	Rake's Progress, plate V.	120
6.7	Prodigal Son.	121

WRONGS

7.1	A perspective view of the execution of Lord Ferrers.	129
7.2	The execution of the idle apprentice.	131
7.3	The pillory at Charing Cross.	132
7.4	Reward Notice.	134
7.5	Jonathan Wild.	138
7.6	Plan and detail of the slave ship *Brookes*.	142

THE LEGAL PROFESSION

8.1	Court of King's Bench.	146
8.2	Lawyers in Term.	153
8.3	Court of Chancery.	155
8.4	The trial of M. D'Eon by a jury of matrons.	157

NOTES ON CONTRIBUTORS

Steve Banks is Associate Professor of Law at the University of Reading. He works mainly on the role of violence in social ordering and in the field of British Legal History. Among his publications are *A Polite Exchange of Bullets: The Duel and the English Gentleman* (2010) and *Informal Justice in England and Wales, 1760–1914: The Courts of Popular Opinion* (2014).

Timothy J. Dodsworth is a lecturer at the University of Exeter and researches mainly in comparative contract law. He completed his Ph.D. on the underlying values of German and English contract law in 2015.

James Oldham is St. Thomas More Professor of Law and Legal History at Georgetown Law School. He is the author of *The Mansfield Manuscripts and the Growth of English Law in the Eighteenth Century*, 2 vols. (1992) and *English Common Law in the Age of Mansfield* (2004), both titles in the Studies in Legal History series published by the University of North Carolina Press in association with the American Society for Legal History. He is also the editor of volume 128 in the main series published by the Selden Society, *Case-notes of Sir Soulden Lawrence, 1787–1800* (2013).

Ruth Paley worked on the *History of Parliament* project, focusing on those peers and bishops who had significant interactions with the law. Her personal research interests are in the social history of the law with particular reference to the administration of criminal justice in eighteenth-century London.

Rebecca Probert is Professor of Law at the University of Exeter. Her research focuses on the history of marriage, bigamy, divorce and cohabitation and she is the author of numerous articles and books, including *Marriage Law and Practice in the Long Eighteenth Century: A Reassessment* (2009) and *The Legal Regulation of Cohabitation: From Fornicators to Family, 1600–2010* (2012), both published by Cambridge University Press.

Dana Rabin is an Associate Professor of history at the University of Illinois, Urbana-Champaign, where she teaches global history, British history, and the history of crime. She is the author of *Identity, Crime, and Legal Responsibility in Eighteenth-Century England* (2004) and *Britain and its Internal Others, 1750–1800: Under Rule of Law* (2017).

Julia Rudolph is Professor of History at North Carolina State University. Her major publications include *Revolution by Degrees: James Tyrrell and Whig Political Thought in the Late Seventeenth Century* (2002), ed. *History and Nation* (2006), and *Common Law and Enlightenment in England, 1689–1750* (2013). Her books and articles explore constitutional law, gender and criminal law, property theory, legal publishing, forensic science and conceptions of fact and, finally and most broadly, the long history of common law jurisprudence. Many of these themes inform her current research into mortgage, empire, and the history of political economy.

John Snape is an Associate Professor of Law at Warwick Law School, University of Warwick. A specialist in tax law, its history and in the history of property law and tax law ideas, he has written on Grotius, Locke (with Jane Frecknall Hughes), Montesquieu, and Hume. His books include (with Jeremy de Souza), *Environmental Taxation Law* (2006), (with Gary Watt) *How To Moot* (2nd edn, 2010), and the monograph *The Political Economy of Corporation Tax* (2011). He has recently edited (with Dominic de Cogan as co-editor), *Landmark Cases in Revenue Law* (forthcoming) and is currently working on a monograph about tax in corporate transactions. His work on Handel's *Solomon* combines his interest in the eighteenth century with a love of Handel's music that goes back many years.

SERIES PREFACE

The six volumes in *A Cultural History of Law* present a panorama of law's cultural significance over the span of several centuries, especially as it relates to the place of law in the arts and humanities. Each volume focuses on a distinct time period from antiquity to modernity and in each volume a chapter is devoted to one of eight legally significant themes: "Justice," "Constitution," "Codes," "Agreements," "Arguments," "Property and Possession," "Wrongs" and "The Legal Profession." The collection does not seek to provide encyclopedic coverage, but rather to present cultural case studies that highlight how particular cultural artifacts express and explore the key legal—and inevitably the key political and social—concerns of their time. The authors have picked flowers from their field of expertise—a play, a painting, a mosaic, a book, a film—which bring into close focus the cultural and legal flourishing of the time. The volume editors are internationally distinguished scholars with a passion and deep appreciation for the law and culture of their chosen period. Together with the experts that they have assembled to contribute chapters on the eight themes, they are reliable guides not merely to the facts about each period but to the feel of each period. Every volume has an ethos and a style that immerses the reader in the distinctive quality of its era. The series is indebted to the archivist's concern to discover and catalog historical materials, but what sets it apart is its concern to show how the materials of history are materially meaningful. In this way, our retrospective of more than 2,000 years continues to have relevance for lawyers and for all culturally concerned citizens today.

Sometimes we find that artifacts have lost the cultural meanings that first produced them. Likewise, we sometimes we find that artifacts are culturally meaningful today in ways that they were not at the time of their creation. Take the example of Magna Carta—The Great Charter of King John of England sealed at Runnymede on the Thames in 1215. Today, in the United States in particular, Magna Carta has been hoisted to totemic heights in the cultural imagination. It might therefore seem strange to us that William Shakespeare's play *King John* makes no reference at all to this great artifact. The reason for its omission is that for Shakespeare and his early modern contemporaries, the most dramatic historical event in the reign of King John was his surrender of the crown to the papal legate and his receiving it again as a papal vassal. The modern significance of Magna Carta is largely a post-Enlightenment invention and its principal promoters were the great myth-makers who framed the American constitution and created the idea of the United States. It is some proof of this that the Magna Carta memorial which stands at Runnymede today was erected by the American Bar Association. The small-scale temple, like the much larger Jefferson Memorial in Washington DC, has become a place of secular pilgrimage; a sanctuary to the values of political freedom and human rights under law.

In 2015, to mark the 800th anniversary of the sealing of Magna Carta, sculptor Hew Locke's "The Jurors" was installed at Runnymede. It comprises twelve bronze chairs, each of which (according to the official narrative) "incorporates symbols and imagery representing concepts of law and key moments in the struggle for freedom, rule of law and equal rights." In this respect, it performs a similar function to the eight bas-relief panels by sculptor John Donnelly Jnr that adorn the great bronze doors of the United States Supreme Court in Washington DC. Shakespeare would have appreciated the performative purpose of these "solemn temples" but he would surely be surprised to see today how much has been made of Magna Carta. The rise of Magna Carta as an artifact of cultural history would certainly have amazed the landed aristocrats who first compelled King John to set his seal to the charter in the culturally Christian, monarchal, and feudal context of the High Middle Ages. The narrative accompanying "The Jurors" alerts us to the license that the sculptor has taken with the history of law. We are told that it is "not a memorial, but rather an artwork that aims to examine the changing and ongoing significance and influences of Magna Carta." It is, in short, a cultural reworking of an artifact that owes its great status to creative cultural appropriation. The actual provisions of Magna Carta that survive in law are impressively few, but the three survivors are perhaps all the more significant for their small number. Much is still made of the survival of the right to trial by jury. Rather less is made, nowadays, of the provisions that preserve the "liberties of the English Church" and the "privileges of the City of London." One of the most important contributions we can make to the appreciation of history is to show where cultures are selective in what they present as fact. The artifacts of history are always presented in the cabinets of culture.

The word "fact" comes, in fact, from the Latin *facere* ("to make") and it can be helpful to think of historical facts as things that are produced by the action of culture and as things which, in turn, produce cultures. Even where a society is collectively in error in its understanding of historical fact, a commonly held mistake inevitably becomes part of the cultural history of that society. The story becomes the history. One of the mistakes we often make, as the shifting status of Magna Carta indicates, is to suppose that the modern commentator can claim a monopoly in the present moment to determine "true" history from "false." Today's official history is only ever the history of the present. The past had its own histories. Cultural history allows an appreciation of the cultural stories that give meaning to societies in time and across time. From a cultural perspective, myths can be more meaningful, and in that cultural sense more "true," than many a cold matter of fact.

Another great and oft-repeated mistake that this book series seeks to remedy is the supposition that law can be meaningfully separated from the culture in which it exists. In *Law as Culture*, Lawrence Rosen observes that law:

> never stands apart from life—some refined essence of professional inquiry or arcane speech. Rather, it forms the conscious attention we give to our relationships. Like art and literature, through law we attempt to order our ties to one another ... However it is displayed, however it is applied, we can no more comprehend the roles of legal institutions without seeing them as part of their culture than we can fully understand each culture without attending to its form of law.[1]

There is an historical aspect to this understanding of law as culture. Pierre Legrand writes, for example, that:

> French law is, first and foremost, a cultural phenomenon, not unlike singing or weaving. The reason why the French have the *chanteurs* they have lies somewhere in their history, their Frenchness, in their identity. Similarly, the reason why the French have the legislative texts or the judicial decisions they have, say, on a matter of sales law, lies somewhere in their history, their Frenchness, in their identity.[2]

There are obvious limits to the mechanistic metaphor by which we talk of cultural history as something manufactured or fabricated. Human hands fashion historical artifacts, but legal artifacts grow out of a culture in a way that makes it hard to know where the artifact starts and the culture ends. It might be better to take the "culture" metaphor seriously and to suggest that laws grow out of a society organically and that the artificial intervention of human hands are like those of the gardener—taming, tending, and ordering wild growth. Thus the cultural history of law becomes something like a horticultural history. This is not such a strange thought when one considers that the English word for the "court" of law is derived from the Latin *hortus* (garden). Malcolm Andrews has suggested that "one could write an illuminating, if oblique, history of a nation's cultural development by examining its changing conception of the garden's scope, design and function."[3] The gardening metaphor may be especially useful in helping us to understand the cultural history of law, given the complex relation between natural justice and artificial laws in human society. Dress is another artificial creation of human craft which, as a cultural outworking of the complex relation between nature and human ordering, serves well as a way to understand the artificial and creative nature of law's contribution to culture. Laws are produced in society in much the same way that gardens, dress, and other products of complex cultural systems are produced in society. When we have completed our journey through the six volumes of this series we may conclude that the chief legislator across the ages has been no parliament nor any body of the people politically represented, but that the great lawmaker has always been the deep, rich, and creative power of human culture.

Gary Watt, Professor of Law, University of Warwick, UK

Introduction

JOHN SNAPE AND REBECCA PROBERT

> The gamesters and lawyers are jugglers alike,
> If they meddle your all is in danger.
> ...
> Your pockets they pick, and they pilfer your house,
> And give your estate to a stranger. (Gay [1728] 1986: 78)

There is a tendency for law and for lawyers to be seen as unsympathetic, remote from everyday concerns. Lawyers may be seen, at worst, as corrupt and, at best, as no more than amoral agents of their clients, existing simply to further, through technical skill, a particular sectional interest. Recent media discussion of the way in which specialist lawyers and other professionals are said to manipulate tax laws, to serve the interests of multinational corporations, without any regard for the wider public good, may prove a classic instance of this.

Eighteenth-century writers were no less critical. Take, for example, *The Beggar's Opera* ([1728] 1986) from which the epigraph to our introduction is taken. With a text by John Gay (1685–1732) and to music, largely adapted from popular tunes by John Christopher Pepusch (1667–1752), the "ballad opera" is peopled by picaresque characters. Almost all of them are bad, and they argue for a moral equivalence between their immorality and the morality of polite society, notably that of members of the legal profession. Peachum, a "thief-taker," compares his business to that of a lawyer. "A lawyer is an honest employment, so is mine. Like me too he acts in a double capacity, both against rogues and for 'em" (Gay [1728] 1986: 43).

Gay portrays lawyers exactly as members of criminal society perceive them to operate. However, implicitly he is also suggesting what the criminal law ought to, or should, be. Just. Not corrupt. Not manipulable by unscrupulous people. The possibility that laws might be improved is another characteristic of law during the Enlightenment. Satire on the ways of lawyers and the law was of course not new. What was new in this period was that it was accompanied by fresh ideas about the conduct of lawyers and the possibilities of making law better.

This appetite for change and improvement was linked to a broader theme of the Enlightenment. As John Robertson has written, the Enlightenment can be thought of as "a distinct intellectual movement of the eighteenth century, dedicated to the better understanding, and thence the practical advancement, of the human condition on this earth" (Robertson 2015: 13). For some people, the focus on earthly conditions was linked not just to Whiggish ideas of progress but also to an emerging secularism; for many, it seemed possible to think of the here and now separately from an afterlife.

In this Introduction, we outline something of the Enlightenment, of the society and politics that gave rise to it, of the law and lawyers shaped by it, and how Enlightenment culture suggested possibilities for change. First, we survey the various ways in which law and culture were thought about. These demonstrate the sheer scope of what law, in an eighteenth-century context, was taken to comprehend. Next, we sketch aspects of English society and politics during the period 1680–1820. This second part outlines the broad context within which people thought about lawyers and law. In the third part, we focus on the law itself, to show how improvements actually began to take shape. In the final part, we consider some of the cultural prompters to such changes.

The focus of the book is England and its laws in the fourteen decades that make up the period under consideration. Yet it should not be overlooked that not only did English ideas of law come to dominate the British Isles, but they also were exported to Britain's colonies. They brought Britain into conflict with native populations and with rival colonial powers. Nor of course was England isolated from debates and cultural developments in other countries, as we shall see from the vibrant exchanges between scholars across Europe and the newly fledged United States.

CULTURE, HISTORY, LAW, AND ENLIGHTENMENT

When we think of culture, we tend to think of what Raymond Williams has called "a thing in itself," of "the general body of the arts" (1960b: xvi). This is an eighteenth-century conception. Previously, culture either denoted a personal disposition to self-improvement or simply "the 'tending of natural growth'" (Williams 1960b: xvi). "High culture," so John Brewer writes, in the sense of the arts "as a whole, with theatre, music, literature, and painting [being] given a special collective identity" (1997: xvi) also belongs to the eighteenth century. So, too, does "low culture" as well as "other forms of self-expression," such as pornography. The law was not only the subject of commentary in both high and low culture but also part of the culture. The ritual procession of judges on circuit was a form of "public display and theatre" (Lemmings 2003: 47), while officer holders were "expected to disseminate the letter of the law in print and speech and a complex of performances" (Griffiths, Fox and Hindle 1996: 3).

Now, when we think of history, this encompasses not just large-scale political history but women's history, "black history," economic development and everyday life stories. The eighteenth century sowed the seeds of this too. David Hume's *History of England* (1754–1762), so Mark Salber Phillips argues, was admired for extending the scope of history writing beyond political and military events to arts, manners and commerce (Phillips 2013). During the eighteenth century, through the work of a large group of writers, of whom Sir William Blackstone (1723–1780)[1] is merely the most famous (Rudolph 2013), law itself became the subject of historical inquiry. Blackstone, as Lemmings has observed, was writing history with a purpose, being "concerned to constrain parliament against 'wantonly' interfering with standing rules of law, in his case by educating lawyers and parliamentarians to appreciate the historical rationality of previous legal development and therefore avoid disrupting it" (Lemmings 2011: 135). His *Commentaries on the Laws of England* (1765–1769) attempted to provide a reasoned exposition of the law as a whole, rather than simply listing topics and relevant cases. It became one of the key texts that an educated English gentleman might be expected to have read (Lobban 1991).

Again, when we think of law, we think of the rules created by government by which we are bound in our daily lives. Eighteenth-century people also thought of law in that way. But they thought of it, too, as having a range of other meanings. The central case, the rules created by governments, they classified as "positive law" (Montesquieu [1748/1750] 1949: 5). That was the everyday reality. Other types of law were divine law, natural law, and the law of nations. Each of these provided yardsticks by which existing positive law could be evaluated. Divine law would tell us what the Deity thought was the right thing to do. Natural law would tell us what we would need to do to flourish as human beings. The law of nations would tell us, not only what one prince could expect of a treaty with another prince, but what other nations considered to be the right thing to do in situations comparable to ours. Today, we would think of these disciplines as theology, economics, anthropology, and international relations, but their eighteenth-century analogs were regarded as types of law. Indeed, the language of laws and rules was used even more widely, encompassing the physical laws elaborated by Sir Isaac Newton (1643–1727),[2] or the rules of harmony, with which composers such as Johann Sebastian Bach (1685–1750) had to comply. This was why Baron de Montesquieu (1689–1755) wrote that "Laws, in their most general signification, are the necessary relations arising from the nature of things" (1). The yardstick that natural law provided suggested a surer basis for public policy and legislation than historical precedent or the whim of a prince. This was not the natural law of Aristotle or of St. Thomas Aquinas but a secular development that was ultimately identified with "political economy." This approach is, of course, most closely associated with Adam Smith (1723–1790) and his *Wealth of Nations* (1776). It is therefore understandable that, at the end of the period covered by this volume, Jeremy Bentham (1748–1832) and John Austin (1790–1859) were concerned to rein in the scope of law, in order to detach positive law from these other associations, especially natural law.

Turning to the concept of "the Enlightenment," it is worth bearing in mind that although educated eighteenth-century people knew they were living in "enlightened times," they did not think of them as constituting "The Enlightenment." The expression is not even a century old (Robertson 2015). It also conceals what was in fact a range of "enlightenments." What characterized the Enlightenment in England was empiricism and pragmatism. Montesquieu and another visitor to England, one François-Marie Arouet (the self-styled "Voltaire") (1694–1778), noted the grip of Protestant Christian English people on their material possessions and on their sense of order. Voltaire singled out John Locke (1632–1704), the most distinguished of empirical philosophers, who by then had been dead just over two decades, for special praise (Voltaire 1733). Meanwhile Bernard Mandeville (1670–1733), a Dutch medic and satirist living in London, became notorious. Mandeville had suggested, in *The Grumbling Hive* (1705), that individual self-interest might be nothing less than the very basis of prosperity (Goldie and Wokler 2006). This idea is satirized in *The Beggar's Opera*, when Lockit tells his daughter Lucy: "If you would not be looked upon as a fool, you should never do anything but upon the foot of interest" (Gay [1728] 1986: 97). But such satire did not carry the day. Mandeville's thought was developed and transformed much later on, by Smith, into the new kind of natural law mentioned above. Society does not thrive on benevolence, Smith wrote, but on individual self-interest. When the "butcher, the brewer, or the baker" supplies us with provisions, he is not being benevolent but looking to his "own interest" to make a living. So, when we negotiate with each of these people, we do not "talk to them of our own necessities"—as a beggar would do—but of the "advantages" to the tradesman in question." (Smith [1776] 1976: I, 26–27). Self-interest, though, includes the desire for the esteem of other people. Seeing the satisfaction of the customer tempers the commercialism of the tradesman (Smith [1790] 1976).

The distinctiveness of that type of empirical enlightenment thinking, with its emphasis on individual behavior, rather than on government, is brought into sharp relief against the later Prussian Enlightenment, or *Aufklärung* (Robertson 2015). Smith's theory convinces if everyone gets on with their work in a responsible manner. In Prussia, however, a more collective sense was in evidence. By 1784, when Immanuel Kant (1724–1804) had responded to a newspaper advertisement with the essay entitled, "An Answer to the Question: 'What is Enlightenment?'" ([1784] 1991: 54), Enlightenment was coming instead to be associated with "freedom to make *public use* of one's reason in all matters" (55). This is what we today call "public reason" and it is the idiom of articulate public debate. "Intellectual immaturity," wrote Kant, is "self-incurred." It "is the inability to use one's own understanding without the guidance of another." For Enlightenment, what is required is courage to think for oneself and to argue one's views. "The motto of enlightenment [he wrote] is therefore: *Sapere aude!* Have courage to use your *own* understanding!" (54).

British Enlightenment thought had an empirical and self-interested quality that contrasted with the community-focused and deliberative thought of the *Aufklärung*. The latter was taken up by John Rawls (1921–2002). The former, typified by Locke, Hume (1711–1776) and Smith, has since attracted Friedrich August von Hayek (1899–1992), Robert Nozick (1938–2002) and, most recently, Amartya Sen. These living traditions of Enlightenment thought should be regarded as illustrating the Enlightenment as a philosophical and argumentative disposition for today.

ENLIGHTENMENT SOCIETY AND POLITICS

Enlightenment society in England struggled to achieve stability. In late 1688, the Stuart king James II had fled to France with his wife and son, confronted by the presence on English soil of William, Prince of Orange, and a Dutch army of the order of 15,000 men (Jardine 2008). In the event, the Dutch and English armies never joined battle (Morrill 2000). Parliament rationalized James' flight as an abdication that had left the English throne vacant (Langford 2000). They invited William and his wife Mary (James' elder daughter), to rule jointly as James' successor. These events became known as "the Revolution" or, to the "Whigs," "the Glorious Revolution." The Bill of Rights 1689[3] set out the terms of the Revolution settlement. It was followed, in 1701, by the Act of Settlement,[4] designed to provide for the succession of a Protestant heir (Hoppit 2000). James' younger daughter, Anne, duly became queen on William's death in 1702. Despite her eighteen pregnancies, Anne died without any living children in 1714, her oldest surviving child, William Duke of Gloucester, dying aged eleven, in 1700 (Somerset 2012). Then, pursuant to the 1701 Act,[5] the crown passed to George I, the Elector of Hanover. George was the great-grandson of James I, the first of the Stuart monarchs of Great Britain. James' daughter Elizabeth had married the King of Bohemia and her daughter Sophia had in turn married Ernest Augustus of Brunswick-Lüneburg. His claim to the throne was, however, even more remote than that brief genealogy might suggest, since there were over fifty men and women before him in the line of succession (Landgraf and Vickers 2009). They, however, were all Catholic: George's claim was based on the simple fact that he was the first Protestant in the line of succession.

George reigned until 1727, when he was succeeded by his son, George II. These periods were characterized by Whig government, and Whiggism was associated with progress. However, in part because the succession had been so contrived, in part because the 1701 Act had not originally applied to Scotland (Hoppit 2000), the Stuart claim to the throne would not die. Adherents to the Stuart cause were called "Jacobites" (from the Latin for James). They were twice defeated after 1700: first, in 1715, when a Jacobite army traveled as far south as Preston in Lancashire before surrendering to government troops (Hoppit 2000; Lenman 1984); and, secondly, at Culloden, in 1746, when their destruction was followed by terrible reprisals at the hands of government troops under the command of the Duke of Cumberland, the king's younger son (Langford 2000). Thus secure on his throne, George II reigned until 1760, when his grandson succeeded him as George III. George III invited the "Tories" back to court, even though many of them had supported the Stuart cause. The subsequent relative stability was marred by periodic difficulties in raising and enforcing taxes, consequences being the American War of Independence of 1775–1783 and the Declaration of Independence of 1776. George III's "violent paroxysms" of mental illness became so serious in 1811, after the death of his youngest daughter, that Parliament passed an Act[6] enabling his son George to rule as Prince Regent (Uglow 2015).

None of this took place in a stable Europe. The Continent was scarred by military conflict throughout the early decades of the eighteenth century. Britain's main adversary was the absolutist France of Louis XIV. The so-called War of the Spanish Succession (1702–1713) saw a series of astonishing victories for Britain and her allies, most notably, Blenheim (1704), Ramillies (1706), Oudenarde (1708) and (possibly, though this is disputed) Malplaquet (1709). Britain's part in these military successes meant that Europe and the world became fascinated by English customs and manners. That fascination was what successively brought Voltaire and Montesquieu to London (Rahe 2009). There, in the early decades of the eighteenth century, visitors found a voluble, vigorous, diverse, often unruly, civil society. London, in 1700, was just about the biggest city in Western Europe, slightly larger than Paris and more than twice as big as Venice or Madrid (Hoppit 2000). Beyond Westminster (where the two houses of Parliament raucously, and often corruptly, debated the interests of the Church of England, the aristocracy, the landed gentry, and—increasingly—urban merchants) were coffee houses, learned societies, publishers of books and pamphlets, and theaters (Porter 1991). This was the London that made such an impression on a very young Benjamin Franklin (Goodwin 2016). It contributed to a distinctive, largely secular, view of the world. By the end of the eighteenth century, so Faramerz Dabhoiwala argues, London was also the center of a frank and "public discussion of sex," even influencing "the cities of the far-away North American colonies" (2012: 343). Philosophical works by the doyens of what was to become known as the "Scottish Enlightenment," Smith and Hume, were published in London, as well as in Glasgow, Edinburgh, and Dublin. Andrew Millar (1705–1768) and William Strahan (1715–1785) were their wealthy publishers. As the anti-Catholic Gordon riots of 1780 showed (Langford 1989), London was not exempt from serious civic violence, yet it nurtured a stable, commercial society. What was true of London was, to an extent, true also of provincial towns. Birmingham's "Lunar Men"—who included such luminaries as Erasmus Darwin (1731–1802), Matthew Boulton (1728–1809), James Watt (1736–1819), Josiah Wedgwood (1730–1795) and Joseph Priestley (1733–1804)—were exemplars of a commercial, technological, but also politically radical, philosophical disposition (Uglow 2003). The fundamental strength of British society, and its parliamentary government, made possible a relatively high burden of taxation, which culminated in 1799 in the introduction of income tax (Lenman 1984; Hilton 2006).

The closing decades of the eighteenth century and the opening ones of the nineteenth were also dominated by Anglo-French military struggle paid for by Britain's parliamentary state. Revolutionary and Napoleonic wars lasted intermittently from 1793 to 1815. What the revolution that unfolded in France between 1789 and 1799 eventually presented, was a challenge to Britain's political society greater even than French absolutism. When

Maximilien Robespierre (1758–1794) spoke in favor of progressive taxation in August 1789,[7] this was as threatening to the stability of British society as had been Louis XIV's absolutism (McPhee 2012). Britain's military and naval success, at Aboukir Bay (1798), Copenhagen (1801),[8] Trafalgar (1805), Salamanca (1812), and Waterloo (1815) were all possible because of the United Kingdom's social and political stability and the concomitant feasibility of relatively high levels of taxation. This success seemed all the greater because of the key role of the United Kingdom's statesmen (notably Lord Castlereagh (1769–1822)) in the creation of a new European order after Napoleon's defeat and exile, at a series of congresses at Vienna, Troppau, Laibach and Verona (1814–1824) (Bew 2012). Between these protracted periods of strife, British forces had been engaged: with the French in India (1751/1752); again with the French in India, Europe and North America in the Seven Years War (1756–1763) (Pocock 2002); and with British colonists in the American War of Independence. In the American context, ironically enough, the colonists' success was achieved by their imposing British values, notably the security of property and its concomitant ban on taxation without parliamentary representation, on the British themselves.[9] So, eighteenth-century ideas of law were Enlightenment ones, sure enough, but, as a character in one of the eighteenth century's most-admired operas sings, ideas forged in *un Mondo in guerra*, in a "world at war" (Haym 1724: 18).

British values, ultimately so widely exported, centered on the legal institution of property. This was no more or less than an individual's right to set up the justice of his claim to material possessions in defiance of a government, whether king or popular despotism. It was Locke who had set out a philosophical doctrine that argued for the essential justice, by descent from the first human beings, of eighteenth-century landed wealth (1690; Dunn 1984). Locke's was not primarily a theory about distributive justice, about inequalities between rich and poor, but one designed to show that property in land could be a just entitlement and not necessarily the fruit of peculation. Locke gave philosophical depth to the Hanoverian dispute with the Jacobites, by showing that Jacobite insistence on the Divine Right of Kings made property unstable. If property rights, far from being natural in origin, depended on the will of a monarch, whose property was secure? From property flowed liberty, especially freedom from arbitrary taxation. Even thinkers who did not share Locke's premises (especially Hume, Edmund Burke (1729–1797), and Smith) acceded to the truth of this broad proposition. Smith it was who wrote that the purpose of "civil government, so far as it is instituted for the security of property, is in reality … the defence of the rich against the poor, or of those who have some property against those who have none at all" (Smith [1776] 1976: I, 284–285, 401–402, II, 709–714). Toleration, too, was a crucial value. Locke had advocated religious toleration, except for Catholics, Muslims, and atheists, the former two being seen as owing their primary allegiance to a foreign prince (Locke [1689] 2003: 245).

The values expressed or implied in all this begin to look disconcertingly modern. Twenty-first-century libertarians, taking their cue from Nozick, still draw on the values just described. Then, as now, however, these values are controversial. They helped to set Jacobite against Hanoverian. Their failure to address distributional issues made them the touchstone for Revolutionary French opposition from 1793 onwards. They continue to animate debates in favor of small government. Then, as now, they tended to exclude the needs of the very poor from political consideration. Hence Thomas Paine's reaction in the *Rights of Man* (1791–1792) (Paine [1791–1792] 2008; Israel 2010). They also tended to exclude women from politics, hence Mary Wollstonecraft's (1759–1797) *A Vindication of the Rights of Woman* (1792), with its emphasis on female education, and

Frances Burney's (1752–1840) gentler assertion of female virtue through experience in, for instance, *Evelina* (1778).

When these values encountered those of other cultures, the latter were usually eradicated in the embrace.[10] Even "colonial slavery" was long seen as being consistent with them (Simpson 1986: 159). When, in 1779, Lieutenant James King, of H.M.S. *Resolution*, beheld the severed flesh of his commander, Captain James Cook (1728–1779), killed by Hawaiian islanders the day before, he wrote that " it is impossible to describe the horror which seized us" (King 1784: 68). Generations of indigenous peoples will have echoed that feeling when assessing the human consequences of the imposition of British values on First Nations. It is in this context that we should reflect on attempts to construct a "global" Enlightenment (Robertson 2015: 11). And yet, sensitive engagement with ancient cultures was also possible, as evidenced by the career of the barrister-philologist Sir William Jones (1746–1794), not only author of *An Essay on the Law of Bailments* (1781), but also a colonial judge and scholar of ancient India (Franklin 2011).

Values of liberty and property found expression in the conduct of lawyers and of those involved in the administration of justice. The Enlightenment disgorged many important legal thinkers. But Britain also generated the characteristic division of barrister and solicitor or attorney. William Garrow (1760–1840) was, so it is believed, the first barrister to conduct forensically methodical witness examinations in criminal cases (Beattie 2013).[11] Barristers began to be seen as the more prestigious branch of the legal profession (Baker 2002). Much justice was administered at a local level by justices of the peace, laypeople, often with a tradesman's background. Some lawyers, especially among the bar, began to be seen as philosophical, sensitive souls. *Mr Spectator*'s "young lawyer studying at the Inner Temple" was an important cultural and satirical figure early in the eighteenth century (Hoppit 2000). Daines Barrington (1727/8–1800), a barrister of the Inner Temple, visited Leopold Mozart (1719–1787) and his son, Wolfgang Amadeus Mozart (1756–1791) (aged nine), at their lodgings in London's Thrift Street, "to subject Wolfgang's talent to the test" (Gutman 1999: 199) and set up the test designed to afford "irrefragable proof" that this infant was a musical genius (Miller 2008).

There was a belief, occasionally shared by Whigs no less than Tories, that the 1688/1689 Revolution had encouraged disorder and criminality (Langford 1989). In fact, according to J.M. Beattie (1986a), criminal offenses stabilized at relatively low levels from the end of the seventeenth to the second half of the eighteenth. The subsequent growth in crime coincided with a massive growth in population. In Westminster, around 1750, the Fielding brothers (Henry and John) "were to the fore in the campaign to make the capital a law-abiding city" (Langford 1989: 161). Crime was confronted by a "ferocious but discretionary criminal code" (Langford 1989: 159). After a visit to Newgate prison, on Tuesday May 3, 1763, the Scottish lawyer James Boswell was so depressed that not even getting his barber to read to him out of Hume's *History of England* was enough to cheer him up (Boswell [1762–1763] 1974).

If security of property meant one enduring thing, though, it was prosperous commerce. When property in commodities is secure against both government and neighbor, commodities can be traded. It is not surprising that the maritime conflicts discussed above engendered a maritime "commercial empire" centered on London and other ports in the British Isles (Langford 1989: 168). That they were able to do so was the result of the close study of physical laws, especially the ability, after 1759, to measure longitude. Commerce, to the eighteenth-century mind, denoted trading relationships, for sure, but it also signified an advanced stage in humankind's progress, one that compared more than favorably with the feudalism of European princes and "societies discovered overseas" (Langford 1989: 2). Montesquieu, among others, extolled Britain's commercial empire (Spector 2011). Commerce was furthered by state power, by protectionism and military might (Langford 1989). Commerce, in turn, led to "luxury," at once the absence of any "limit to the enrichment of so vigorous a society" and yet also the potential "economic nemesis" of "a people unaware of the natural limits of expansion" (Langford 1989: 4). "Luxury," in short, "was the subject of endless controversy" (Langford 1989: 4).

Toleration, though valued by polite people, was not always a reality. The 1689 Toleration Act[12] "was one of the most important parts of the Revolution settlement," and it "severed" what had previously been "[t]he exclusive relationship between citizenship" and the doctrines of the Church of England.[13] However, a bill that was introduced into the House of Lords in 1753 to allow Jews to become naturalized subjects, provoked a wave of anti-semitism (Langford 1989). There were anti-slavery campaigns, based on Montesquieu, and an Act of 1807 banned the deportation of Africans by British merchants.[14] But eighteenth-century black history is not only about slavery. Many black men served as able seamen in the Royal Navy, where it is claimed that they were "entitled to the same consideration as any other man" (Rodger 1988: 161).

ENLIGHTENMENT LAW

The law we are speaking of here, as mentioned above, was what the eighteenth century regarded as positive law, such as might be embodied in judicial rulings and decrees (Spector 2015). Increasingly, though, it came to be contained in government legislation. In the seventeenth century the Stuarts had claimed, as the Bourbons continued to claim throughout the eighteenth, that a king could rule by Divine Right. To be sure, he had to observe certain fundamental laws, but he did not rely on the consent of the people for the authority of his decrees. He was accountable to God, not to man. His prerogative was the basis of this entitlement. What the 1689 settlement established for law in Britain was a "bottom-up" doctrine precisely the opposite of this. Positive law in the form of legislation would gain its authority from the consent of the elected representatives of those entitled to vote in parliamentary elections.[15] The king would be accountable to man, possibly also to God. This would be the ultimate guarantee of the security of property against the overweening ambition of the state, especially as regards arbitrary taxation. It is from this Hanoverian conception that much of the modern notion of "the rule of law," especially as championed by Hayek, derives.

As the eighteenth century progressed, the state that administered this system of law of became something similar to the political entity we know today. Wales had been annexed to England in 1536 (Colley 2014). The accession of James I, in 1603, had unified the Scots and English crowns (Colley 2014: 88). More importantly, the 1707 Act of Union[16] joined the Scottish Parliament to that of England and Wales, making Anne the first monarch of the Kingdom of Great Britain. The 1800 Act of Union then joined the crown of Great Britain to the crown of Ireland,[17] English kings having been kings of Ireland since 1541 (Colley 2014). The year 1798 had seen a violent Irish rebellion (Uglow 2015), to which the 1800 Act was a response designed to "heal and manage" underlying divisions (Tombs 2014; Uglow 2015). So the 1800 Act also saw the abolition of the Irish Parliament in Dublin. George III therefore became the first monarch of the United Kingdom of Great Britain and Ireland (the present day "United Kingdom of Great Britain and Northern Ireland" of course reflects more recent political developments and dates only from 1922) (Tombs

2014). The yardstick for the positive laws that this state created was natural law, first as "political arithmetick" and then as political economy. There must have been a strong sense that, as Alexander Pope (1688–1744) had put it earlier in the century:

> For forms of government let fools contest;
> Whate'er is best administered is best ... (1733–1734: 298)

Certainly, by the end of the eighteenth century, the United Kingdom's political arrangements, most importantly a highly centralized state, with a single Parliament that gave it unprecedented tax-raising powers, had a global reach. It is no accident that income tax dates from this period, nor that many of the century's most influential voices were involved in state administration. Paine and Robert Burns (1759–1796) were both excisemen and even Adam Smith was a commissioner of customs (Phillipson 2010).

Crucial to the stability of the state just depicted was a particular conception of the rule of law. It is fair to say that Britain's external and internal affairs were both guided by this conception. Britain's involvement in the War of Spanish Succession, for instance, asserted an elaborate legal justification (Hoppit 2000). While it would be anachronistic to speak of this legal framework as one of "international law," there was nonetheless a developing law of treaties, the virtues of which were well-recognized, not least by Hume (1739–1740). Internally, the rule of law was manifested by an emphasis on parliamentary procedure and, as mentioned, on property. In fact, as *The Beggar's Opera* and the label "the Robinocracy," associated with the administration of Sir Robert Walpole (1676–1745) attests (Langford 1989), government proceedings were probably corrupt (Hoppit 2000). Nonetheless, there were proceedings that led to the creation of legislation, motivated by some sense of the public interest. That was what motivated the Copyright Act 1710, the Licensing Act 1737, and the Clandestine Marriages Act 1753 ("Lord Hardwicke's Act"), to take just three examples (Langford 1989; Hoppit 2000; Probert 2009). The emphasis of the first of these on one sort of property right—intellectual property rights— remind us that the public interest was almost exclusively identified with property. Land enclosure was a movement ultimately justified by political economy, but one which, in the eighteenth century, had to be effected by Enclosure Acts, special statutes that awarded common land to neighboring estate holders in return for compensating the loss to the commoners. That some losses were incapable in financial compensation was recorded by John Clare (1793–1864), the laborer-poet from Northamptonshire, for example in "The Fallen Elm" or in "Remembrances" (Bate 2003). Though Enclosure Acts were infamous, their implementation nonetheless did tend to adhere to a fixed pattern involving local hearings before barristers sent from London, as commissioners, who would make enclosure awards and provide for the payment of compensation (Langford 1989). It was in relation to the Black Act, of 1723,[18] that E.P. Thompson reached the conclusion that "the notion of the rule of law" was "itself an unqualified good" (1990: 267). Given the skepticism of the Left to the rule of law, this is one of legal history's most unexpected yet justifiable conclusions. The identification of property rights with the public interest is well illustrated by *Entick v. Carrington*,[19] in which Lord Camden CJCP upheld the sacrosanct nature of property rights against so-called "general warrants."

The most striking features of the administration of criminal justice in eighteenth-century Britain are both its severity and the fact that, with the notable exception of Voltaire, contemporary thinkers did not much demur. While the Bill of Rights had formally banned the imposition of "cruel and unusual" punishments (Baker 2002: 512n),[20] conviction for a wide range of felonies would nonetheless lead to the death penalty. "For felony," the common law had long provided, "the convict's person was at the king's mercy" (Baker 2002: 512), although, where the convicted felon was female, she might "pray the benefit of her belly"—that is, claim to be pregnant—and have the death sentence deferred to save the child in her womb. That this plea was made relatively frequently was in some measure due to the fact that the government had increased the range of offenses carrying the death penalty (Baker 2002). Whig administrations introduced a succession of capital statutes to signal "a stern but rational rebuke" (Langford 1989) to certain offenses. The Riot Act 1715[21] rendered magistrates competent to preserve public order: "the continued assembly of twelve or more people together, after having been ordered to disperse by a Justice of the Peace, could be broken up by unrestrained deadly force" (Hoppit 2000: 48). Perhaps the most infamous reliance on this legislation was at Manchester in 1819, when, the Riot Act having been read, the local Justices unleashed, first the yeomanry, then the regular army, on a peaceful—though extremely large—assembly in St. Peter's Fields, gathered to hear a radical speaker (Marlow 1971). In a grim allusion to the Napoleonic battle four years earlier, the incident, which resulted in the deaths of fifteen people (including a little boy of two years) became known as "the Peterloo Massacre."

In addition to the 1715 Act, 1718 saw the passing of the Transportation Act,[22] which provided a legislative basis for banishment to Britain's colonies in America. The 1723 Black Act, already mentioned, instituted around fifty offenses, mainly against property, which carried the death penalty (Hoppit 2000). The years 1736 and 1745 each saw Smuggling Acts (Langford 1989; Langford 1991) that created and consolidated capital offenses regarding the wounding of customs officers and using weapons against them (Phillipson 1973). One critic of these laws was Smith, who thought that smuggling laws were against "natural justice" on the basis that the duties the smugglers were evading themselves breached free commerce between individuals (1776: II, 898).

In 1752, the Murder Act[23] made statutory provision for judges to sentence convicted murderers to death and for their bodies to be "dissected and anatomized" or, at the discretion of the judge, hanged in chains (Beattie 1986a). Anatomization and hanging in chains had been carried out in earlier ages but as a result of "executive decision" rather than the sentence of a judge (Beattie 1986a: 528–529). Such severe legislation was not the preserve of the Whigs. Later in the eighteenth century, the Tory administration of William Pitt the Younger (1759–1806) significantly increased "the coercive powers of the state," in a process that contemporary opponents called "Pitt's terror" (Hilton 2006: 65). Later still, Peterloo led to the so-called "Six Acts"[24] of 1819, under which—among other things—libel and blasphemy laws were made stricter, the permission of a sheriff or magistrate was required for meetings of fifty people or more, and pamphlets and newspapers were made practically unaffordable to many people by being subjected to stamp duty of four pence (Hilton 2006). Severe punishments did not seem, by themselves, to worry people. Judges did not recoil from imposing barbaric penalties left over from earlier ages. In 1746, following the failure of the 1745 Jacobite Rising, the conviction for high treason of Francis Towneley (a Lancashire gentleman) and eight fellow Jacobites, resulted in their hanging, drawing and quartering on Kennington Common, in front of a baying crowd. The nine were strangled, eviscerated and decapitated and, in Jacqueline Riding's terrifying description, the remains were burnt at the scene (Riding 2016).

> After completing his task, spattered in blood, the executioner cried 'God save King George!' and the crowd responded. By this time the air must have been heavy with the sickening aroma of roasting human entrails. (2016: 476)

In 1757, Lord Mansfield CJKB, an enlightened judge, "showed himself willing to impose" the fifteenth-century penalty of *peine forte et dure* (pressing to death with iron and stones) on a man who refused to plead to an indictment accusing him of robbing the Royal Mail (Poser 2013). People at large, including philosophers, had surprisingly little to say against all this savagery. Then, towards the end of the century and under the inspiration of Cesare Beccaria (1738–1794), Jean-Jacques Rousseau (1712–1778), and Bentham (Rosen 2014), Sir Samuel Romilly KC (1757–1818) argued for prison rather than the death penalty for many offenses. Pickpocketing was one of only two offenses in relation to which he succeeded (Baker 2002). Garrow, interestingly, was "implacably opposed to any" such "reform of the criminal law" (Beattie 2013).

An important effect of the 1707 and 1800 Acts of Union, somewhat understated, was that they made common customs areas with Scotland and Ireland (Colley 2014). This was a powerful stimulus to the development of modern commercial law, as was a quickly expanding overseas trade. The dark side of that law is highlighted by *Gregson v. Gilbert* (the *Zong*),[25] the case of the slave-ship insurance claim for the loss of slaves thrown overboard in a storm. Poser has traced Lord Mansfield's important positive role in developing commercial law (Poser 2013). These look like matters of contract law but they have important constitutional and administrative dimensions. Increased trade meant increased public revenues. Dudley Pope recounts the story of George III, who, "seeing the luxurious carriage of a Jamaica planter driving along a London street with liveried outriders, demanded of his Prime Minister: 'Sugar, sugar, eh? All *that* sugar! How are the duties, eh Pitt, how are the duties?'" (Pope 1972: 7n). This is why the government punished smuggling so severely. There were eventually limits to what could be traded. A desire to discourage trade in property in human beings is the true significance of *Somerset v. Stewart*,[26] a decision rightly hailed for the judge's humanity (Langford 1989). "The state of slavery [said Lord Mansfield] is of such a nature, that ... only positive law, which preserves its force long after the reasons, occasion, and time itself from whence it was created, is erased from memory: it's so odious, that nothing can be suffered to support it, but positive law."[27]

ENGLIGHTENMENT LAW IN ENLIGHTENMENT CULTURE

There are many late seventeenth- and early eighteenth-century eulogies of English law. Julian Hoppit, for example, quotes Henry Care in 1691. "In *France*," wrote Care,

> the meer Will of the Prince is *Law*, his Word takes off any Man's Head, imposeth Taxes, or seizes any Man's Estate ... But in *England* the Law is both the *Measure and the Bond* of every Subject's Duty and Alleigiance, each Man having a fixed Fundamental Right born with him, as to Freedom *of his Person, and Property in his Estate*. (1691: 1–2)[28]

Thus it was that, when a Jacobite army was moving south, in 1745, the Reverend Thomas Morell (1703–1784), the librettist of Handel's *Judas Maccabaeus*,[29] was penning the lines that, "The almighty Jehovah" would strength the hand of the Israelites "In defence of ... [their] nation, religion and laws" (Morell 1748: 3). This illustrates, too, the strong identification of British people with the chosen people of the Christian Old Testament (Colley 1992).

The British Constitution, with the centrality it accorded to property, was widely celebrated in literature and art. Human experiences, as depicted in culture, are recursive. Cultural phenomena both shape a constitution, and the legislation passed within it, and are themselves shaped by that constitution, that legislation. The way in which Jane Austen (1775–1817) treated the relationship between the propertied classes and the state (Evans 1987) is hardwired into the consciousness of middle-class English people even today. On their long, measured closure with the French and Spanish fleets at Trafalgar in 1805 (Howarth 1970), the officers and ratings of the British ships of the line were steadied for battle with the melodies of "Britons strike home" (Adkins 2004: 151), a song which—in one near-contemporaneous version—exhorts Britons to "Protect your KING, your LIBERTIES, and LAWS" (Anon. 1800 [?]), and "Rule Britannia," the original lyrics of which eulogize the commerce and freedom of Britain (Thomson 1740). We can note here a change of tone from *The Beggar's Opera* and the early years of the eighteenth century. "Rule Britannia" was also played by the band of "the Royton contingent" of the crowd at Peterloo (Marlow 1971).

Oliver Goldsmith's poem *The Deserted Village* (1770) depicted the perceived evils of enclosure, a process that, so the poet says, meant "wealth accumulates, and men decay" (Goldsmith [1770] 1984: 524). The landscapes of Thomas Gainsborough (1727–1788), so Langford reminds us, are "peopled with subdued, industrious peasants rather than the cheerful rustics of rococo art" (Langford 1989: 441). His painting of Holywells Park in Ipswich provides one example of this. Austen, be it noted, thought that unpretentious and non-extravagant estates, like Pemberley in *Pride and Prejudice*, were a credit to their holders (Duckworth 1971). What was true in relation to Great Britain's internal affairs was also true in relation to its external ones. James Gillray's cartoon of Pitt and Napoleon, dividing the world between them (entitled *The Plumb-pudding in Danger* (1805)), is an artifact of the cultural history of international law. It is much else besides but it is importantly that too. Gillray's earlier *Destruction of the French Colossus* (1798), in a related sense, portrays a British eighteenth-century understanding of divine law (Uglow 2015).

Yet debates remain as to the relationship between law and popular culture. The earlier idea of a stark split between elite and plebeian culture has been replaced by a more nuanced view of cultural gradations (Black 2001), but the gap between rich and poor was a deep one, and there was little in Enlightenment law or culture that attempted to bridge it. As David Lemmings has pointed out, "in its register of polite sensibility and secular reason enlightenment thinking might also entail the conscious detachment of government from its institutional exchanges with popular cultures" (2011: 13). He noted a similar exclusion of the poor from the courts, as the costs of litigation rose and proceedings became increasingly professionalized. And those that did litigate might have a different conception of law from those tasked with its administration: as Dana Rubin has commented, the law was "a site of struggle in which participants from different social backgrounds actively contested vying conceptions of right and custom" (2004: 24).

Neither lawyers nor magistrates generally emerge as humane or sympathetic characters in the novels of the period.[30] In Tobias Smollett's *Sir Launcelot Greaves* (1762), Mr. Gobble, a justice of the peace, is denounced as a contemptible: "without sentiment, education, or capacity" (Smollett [1762] 1973: 98).[31] Sir Launcelot Greaves deplores Gobble's inhumanity: "[W]hat avails the law? Where is our admired constitution, the freedom, the security of the subject, the boasted humanity of the British nation?"[32] In Henry Fielding's *Joseph Andrews* (1742), the hero is robbed, stripped, and left for dead in a ditch by the roadside. He is rescued by the passengers of a stage coach, one of whom is a lawyer. The lawyer wishes that they had ignored Joseph altogether but, having stopped, there would be a danger of being accused of his murder were Joseph to die. As the lawyer says, "no man could be too cautious in these matters," especially as there are some "very extraordinary cases in the books" (Fielding [1742] 2003: 90).³³ This is the opposite of the divine law illustrated by the parable of the Good Samaritan. In Austen's *Persuasion* (1818), Mr. Shepherd, "a civil, cautious lawyer" avoids giving his own advice, since he "would rather have the *disagreeable* prompted by any body else" (Austen [1818] 1975: 18) and he knows that Lady Russell will advise what he would himself recommend. The amorality of Fielding's lawyer and the calculation of Austen's both resonate with portrayals of lawyers today. Even more acerbic was Jonathan Swift in *Gulliver's Travels* describing lawyers as a group of men "bred up from their Youth in the Art of proving by words multiplied for the Purpose, that *White* is *Black*, and *Black* is *White*, according as they are paid" and as being "in all Points out of their own Trade … usually the most ignorant and stupid Generation among us, the most despicable in common Conversation, avowed Enemies to all Knowledge and Learning" (Swift [1735] 2005: 306–307, 309).

While the severity of the criminal code seemed to meet with little adverse comment from many moral philosophers, other writers depicted it with mounting abhorrence. Daniel Defoe (1660–1731), traveling through Halifax, noted with a *frisson* "the famous course of justice anciently executed there," namely a decapitating "engine" (Defoe [1724–1726] 1971). The day after visiting Newgate in May 1763, Boswell described his distress at witnessing the execution at Tyburn of the robber "Captain" Paul Lewis. Lewis, wrote Boswell, "was just a Macheath" ([1762–1763] 1974: 251), though, "unlike the hero of John Gay's play, there was no last minute reprieve for Lewis, who died only after several minutes of dangling from the cord's noose" (Zaretsky 2015: 81).³⁴ Public executions certainly excited great curiosity, not least because of the spectacle of the long journey followed by condemned prisoners between Newgate, which was in east London, and Tyburn, which was in the west (Linebaugh 1975: 67, 105). In *The Beggar's Opera*, Polly Peachum imagines Macheath's execution: "What vollies of sighs," she exclaims, "are sent from the windows of Holborn, that so comely a youth should be brought to disgrace!" (Gay [1728] 1986: 64). It might be mentioned, in this connection, that Macheath is of course a highwayman,³⁵ a class of criminal popularly regarded—at least in the early eighteenth century—as being somewhat glamorous and "polite." The reason for this was possibly that "[t]heir victims were by and large the relatively well off who could afford to travel on horseback or by coach, and they did not frequently have to resort to violence" (Langford 1989: 157).

It may come as a surprise that "public execution was defended as one of the rights of Englishmen, not less necessary than public trial" (Langford 1989: 298). When, in 1783, "Tyburn Tree" was transferred to Newgate, Samuel Johnson (1709–1784) deplored it. "[If] executions do not draw spectators they don't answer their purpose … The publick was gratified by a procession; the criminal was supported by it." (Boswell [1791] 1980: 1211). Anything else, he thought, would be French despotism. But London was expanding westwards and gibbeted corpses decaying close to the doorsteps of Berkeley and Hanover Squares hardly conduced human flourishing (Boswell [1791] 1980).

In any event, this was justice according to law. It was law's miscarrying that caused disquiet, as with "the justice with which Admiral Byng was dispatched in 1757" (Langford 1989: 298; Pocock 2002: 20–39). In Voltaire's *Candide* (1759), the eponymous hero reaches England and is shocked to observe the "extremely satisfied" crowd standing on the shore at Portsmouth to witness the execution by firing-squad of an admiral "on the quarter-deck of one of the ships of the fleet" (Voltaire [1759] 2005: 76). "What is all this?" asks Candide, "and what devil is at work in the world?" Someone explains to him that the admiral failed to engage the French "closely enough" (this was the Seven Years

War). When Candide rejoins that neither fleet was nearer the other, his neighbor assents. "Unquestionably so … but in this country it is considered useful now and again to shoot an admiral, to encourage the others" (76). Voltaire, famously detached, was nonetheless enraged by such miscarriages of justice (Robertson 2015). Again, the suspicion that what happened at Peterloo was a breach of natural or divine law, if not of positive law, prompted Percy Bysshe Shelley (1792–1822), in the *Mask of Anarchy* (1819, publ 1832), to visualize Lord Castlereagh as Murder itself and to place on the brow of Anarchy the words, "I AM GOD, AND KING, AND LAW" (Shelley [1819] 2009: 401). It is, however, important to remember that Peterloo, as Robert Tombs writes, "remains notorious in our history because of its rarity" (2014: 425).

The protection of property and thence commerce was the mainspring of the law's severity. The importance of commerce is well attested in Enlightenment literature. In *The London Merchant* (1731), a prose tragedy by George Lillo (1693–1739), and set in seventeenth-century England, commerce is held up as a noble occupation. To his good apprentice, Trueman, Thorowgood—the London Merchant—says:

> Methinks I would not have you only learn the method of merchandise, and practise it hereafter, merely as a means of getting wealth. 'Twill be well worth your pains to study it as a science. See how it is founded in reason, and the nature of things; how it has promoted humanity, as it has opened and yet keeps up an intercourse between nations, far remote from one another in situation, customs and religion; promoting arts, industry, peace and plenty; by mutual benefits diffusing mutual love from pole to pole. ([1731] 1928: 238)

This is, of course, a radically different view of commerce and of accounts from that presented in Gay's *The Beggar's Opera* (1728). Different again is Colman and Garrick's portrayal of the merchant, Mr. Sterling, a vulgarian manifest: "The chief pleasure of a country house is to make improvements, you know, my lord. I spare no expense, not I" ([1766] 1928: 291).

CONCLUSIONS

The period of almost a century and a half between 1680 and 1820 was one in which the whole range of our contemporary ideas about the nature and scope of law and culture, and of the ways of lawyers, were exhaustively explored. Culture came to be seen in the round and positive law was only the central instance of the various meanings of law. Sometimes these enlightened ideas were enforced by the barrage of artillery fire or the swift fall of the executioner's blade. More often, though, ideas of law were persuasively woven into the consciousness of men and women through countless books, pamphlets, philosophical tracts, and judicial decisions. Law is fundamental to the ordering of political societies, so this much should not surprise us. What might give us pause for thought, however, is the extent to which ideas of law were also embedded in "the pleasures of the imagination" (Brewer 1997): in plays; in the brushstrokes of pictorial art; in the meticulous lines scored by the engraver's stylus; in the speeches, arias and choruses of the dramatic stage; and, most notably perhaps, in wiles of the picaresque characters of the popular novel. All of the cultural and political artifacts thereby comprehended were central to that movement in the current of European ideas now thought of as the Age of Enlightenment.

CHAPTER ONE

Justice

Popular Ideas and Actions in the Long Eighteenth Century

STEVE BANKS

As a term, "justice" is a difficult abstraction; aspirational, ill-defined, often seeming to refer to a kind of balance that will only be achieved when the world is made "right." Historically, men and women have turned to a god for justice, aware that only a god is likely to be able to deliver it in its final definitive form—and often not in this world but the next. In the material world though, law has always made great claims in respect of its connection to justice. Indeed, law tries to occupy as much of justice's cognitive space as possible. Law tries to consume justice, to swallow it whole in order to legitimize itself and to claim that there is no justice to be done or found outside "The Law." Not for nothing do we in the United Kingdom (as in many other places) now have a governmental organization that grandly declares itself to be the Ministry of Justice.

In the eighteenth century, however, things were somewhat different. The state's capacity to act was severely circumscribed. Jennifer Davis observed of a later period that historians have "overestimated the extent to which the nineteenth-century state was either able or willing to intervene in the everyday affairs of its subjects" (1984: 314). What was true of the nineteenth century was even more true of an eighteenth century in which the state was quite unable to monopolize the justice business to the extent observable today. This chapter then considers what ordinary people meant when they spoke of justice in the long eighteenth century and considers how, in the absence of an all-powerful legal center, they tried to obtain it. As the chapter will observe, notions of justice were generally rooted in particular times, places, and privileges. The term "justice" was more often used in reference to very particular bundles of entitlements rather than employed as an all-embracing word expressing general notions of fairness or even personal rights. Injustice was said to have occurred when traditional entitlements had not been respected or when other legitimate expectations within a community had been ignored. To remedy injustice recourse was generally had to local mechanisms. Some of those mechanisms were official and some unofficial although, as we shall see, the barriers between the two were not always easy to define. In the absence of a monopolistic legal system those seeking their entitlements or wishing to uphold accepted social mores often relied upon lively traditions of self-help expressed through the customary rituals of popular justice.

A WORLD OF LEGAL PLURALISM

It is scarcely an exaggeration to say that there was no unified legal system in the long eighteenth century. What one observes, rather, are a series of jurisdictions, sometimes running parallel, sometimes overlapping, but often operating independently of each other. There was a central spine of higher civil and criminal courts but it was afflicted with many procedural complications. Not the least of these was the fact that there was a division between the common law courts and the courts of equity. Cases to be heard under the common law naturally went before the common law courts. However, it was not possible for formal rules of law to deal fairly with all imaginable circumstances. If application of the law might do a manifest injustice it was possible to seek a remedy instead in the courts of equity. The most notable of these was the Court of Chancery and there were times when there was rivalry between it and the common law courts which led in turn to some legal uncertainty and confusion. The position was additionally complicated by the fact that there was also an independent system of ecclesiastical courts. The church court system experienced a slow decline during the eighteenth century but this was uneven and in one particular area, Lancashire, there may in fact have been more ecclesiastical prosecutions than in the century before (Outhwaite 2006). This ecclesiastical system was riven with its own anomalies: even in 1832 there still existed some three hundred "peculiar courts," that is to say independent ecclesiastical courts outside of the jurisdiction of the parishes within which they were located.

For ordinary folk, contact with legal authority often came in the form of a Justice of the Peace (hereafter "JP") sitting either with a colleague or conducting business on his own—usually in his home. Of these JPs perhaps three things need briefly to be said. Firstly, that they exercised the most extraordinary personal discretion at the beginning of the eighteenth century.

> So powerful were the Justices that they were virtually independent ... neither the central government nor Parliament told them what to do, closely supervised their activity, or even insured that they act at all. (Landau 1984: 2)

Secondly, while there have been attempts to cast the whole legal system as the mere tool of the propertied classes, modern scholarship has shown that the common people frequently consulted and complained to JPs—for example after being assaulted (King 2004). As Peter King has observed, "Almost every aspect of social and economic life might generate a dispute, complaint or criminal accusation before a summary court" (2004: 128). Finally, far from being imperious and aloof, most magistrates were not at all indifferent to the mores of the community that surrounded them. In part this was due to simple pragmatism. If they had in theory a wide independence of action nonetheless JPs had to exercise caution insofar as they had rather limited resources with which to enforce their authority. Persuasion was often their best tool, and brute force of doubtful effect. In the majority of matters brought before them they acted not as unbending judges but rather as mediators or arbitrators. To quote King again:

> A huge variety of minor disputes—illegally obtained property, interpersonal violence, insults, wages, poor relief, dangerous driving, swearing, etc.—were all resolved by these magistrates without recourse to jury trial or summary punishment. (2004: 149)

Even in respect of criminal matters they generally strove to have the affair "compromised," that is, settled by a monetary payment to the victim.

Notwithstanding the wide remit of the JPs, there were still areas of jurisdiction that lay within the old manorial courts. Studies such as that of the Manor of Havering in Essex have shown that both the civil and in particular the criminal jurisdiction of manorial courts ebbed away during the seventeenth century in consequence of the emergence of the petty sessions and the expanding remit of the quarter sessions (McIntosh 1991). However, important agricultural questions remained within their purview, including water rights, questions over land transfer, and disputes over pasture. It was still said in 1809 that, "Manor courts are pretty generally held, even where the copyhold tenure is extinct, and their utility is experienced on many occasions, as the settlement of boundaries and preventing of litigations, appointment of constables etc" (Marshall 1818: 215). Matters were settled according to customary practice rather than common law and there were important variations between manors. Thus Lloyd Bonfield has observed that in these courts, "law in its modern sense may be absent, regardless of how judgments are articulated" (1989: 530–531). Similarly, Christopher Harrison has remarked that, "I have yet to come across a court leet record which exactly replicates the contemporary lawyer's view on what these courts did" (1997: 46). Legal plurality was further evidenced by the operation of special situational or occupational courts. Within the royal forests, for example, forest law prevailed, and this was enforced through gatherings of the forest wardens at verderer's courts. Tin miners were allowed to govern their own industry and offenses within it were prosecuted in front of gatherings of fellow miners in special stannary courts.

Custom remained an important determinant of legal outcomes and the writer Oliver Goldsmith declared that, "nothing could be more certain than that numerous written laws are a sign of a degenerate community, and are frequently not the consequences of vicious morals in a state, but the causes" ([1759] 1934: 415). However, although written law and custom could, and often did, inform each other, the written law could only go so far in acknowledging the diversity of customary practice and "from the middle of the sixteenth century onwards, that conflictual relationship between custom and central law was given a new expression with the growing strength of a variety of central equity law courts based in Westminster" (Wood 1997: 54). There was genuine perplexity when courts began to challenge customary entitlements and declare that they were no longer, nor indeed ever had been, lawful.

JUSTICE FOR THE COMMUNITY: CUSTOM AND ENTITLEMENT

In *The Rights of Man* (1791–1792), Tom Paine famously espoused privileges conferred by the mere circumstance of common humanity. However, when rights were referred to in the past they were often what we might better refer to as "entitlements," claims that were unashamedly particular to the claimant. Entitlements were vested in membership of a particular community and the enjoyment of a particular social situation; their very value lay in the fact that others could not enjoy them. As E.P. Thompson remarked, local economies were "parochial and exclusive: if Weldon's rights were ours, then Brigstock men and women must be kept out" (1991: 179). Justice then, was often a matter of recognition of entitlement; it was situational and referenced the traditions of communities that did not change much during the first half of our period.

The slow pace of change can be partly attributed to the fact that up until 1750 there was only a very gradual increase in population. There were about 5.3 million people in England and Wales in 1700 and fifty years later that number had only risen to about 5.9

million. It was thereafter that the population growth accelerated, with the total reaching 9.3 million by 1801 (Razell 1965). Traditional norms were maintained by the limitations on physical movement around the kingdom: most people were tied to the land and the agricultural seasons. In addition, perhaps a further 7.5–10 percent of the labor force was bound in non-agricultural apprenticeships (Wallis 2008). The restricted mobility that resulted suited state policy very well. A fear of masterless men and women moving about at will had influenced government from Elizabethan times onward. So the Statute of Artificers of 1563 had given the Justices power to impose yearly employment contracts upon unemployed workmen and laborers[1] and those wishing to learn a craft were forced into seven-year apprenticeships.[2] Once under contract, workers were bound and there were ten acts between 1720 and 1792 that prescribed whipping and incarceration for those in particular occupations that had left their employment early. These culminated in the Master and Servant Act (1823), which made any breach of any employment contract a summary offense liable to three months imprisonment.[3] Some magistrates applied the penalties with enthusiasm (Hay 1998). Those without employment were also constrained; in their case by the Act of Parish Settlements (1662) which obliged parishes to assist their own paupers but also instructed them to remove back to their own parishes those paupers whose places of legal settlement were elsewhere. It was possible to change parishes (most commonly, at least for women, by marriage) and legal settlement could be acquired by forty days' residence, but parish officials tended to treat new arrivals with some suspicion until it was established that they were not likely to become a burden upon the local poor rate (Fideler 2006). The importation of large numbers to staff major enterprises was potentially of great concern since should the enterprise fail then the charge upon the local poor rate might become prohibitive. However, the judges intervened to declare that workers who moved into a parish to work for such an enterprise would not acquire rights of settlement there and thus could be returned to their originating parishes if need be.[4] In the meantime, vigorous steps were taken to remove vagrants. There were Vagrancy Acts in 1700, 1714 and 1744 and between 1776 and 1778 there were some 14,789 vagrant removals in Middlesex alone (Hitchcock, Crymble, and Falcini 2014). The overall effect of poor law and master and servant legislation was to affirm that everyone belonged to a particular parish and to ensure that only a minority were free to move around as they pleased.

Many, though, had no expectation of moving away from their parish. There was a strong sense of local attachment. "Every man and woman and child old enough to understand anything looks upon his parish as being partly his"[5] wrote the journalist William Cobbett in the early nineteenth century, and the same view had prevailed in earlier decades as well. Emotional attachment ran in tandem with material benefits such as poor relief, the benefit of charitable bequests and the largess of doling customs. Many benefited from access (by law or custom) to local commons and wastes. Even those apparently well within the cash economy often depended upon grazing animals, gathering firewood, picking berries and so on. They also cultivated their own plots. J.M. Neeson's study of twenty-three unenclosed parishes in Northamptonshire in the late eighteenth century has shown that 53 percent of the population owned at least some land, and at Wigston Magna in Leicestershire in 1765 some 99 out of the 200 families owned a plot of between one and fifteen acres (1993; Hoskins 1957). Much of the cultivation and harvesting was necessarily done in collaboration with others. Membership of the parish brought not only economically quantifiable benefits it also served to ignite moral claims. As Bernard Capp observes, great value was placed upon acts of neighborliness, reporting and rescuing stray animals, lending tools, visiting the sick, and so on; without acts of mutual support many households could not have survived (2003: 27).

To many people then, their parish was their nation entire. As with a nation, collective practices, especially festive practices, reinforced the mental and geographic integrity of the parish. For example, annual perambulations around the parish boundary ensured that the boundaries were secured (Underdown 1985a). Where no boundary markers existed the old committed to the young the memory of where the borders lay so that the neighboring parish could not quietly encroach. Encroachment was a recurrent concern since practices were as much dedicated to exclusion as inclusion. The poet John Clare referred to those living outside his parish of Helpston in Northamptonshire as being, "out of the world," living at "the world's end" (Snell 2003: 5). These were "foreigners" needing to be kept at bay and as such were subject to the same prejudices as foreigners anywhere. Foreigners were deficient, dishonest, their women sexually lax and so on (Grose 1787). Villagers often met and fought each other (Stevenson 1979). They took particular delight in disrupting each other's festive practices, so for example, thirteen men stole the maypole from the parish of Gresford in 1686 and found themselves presented at Denbighshire Quarter Sessions as a result.[6]

One must not exaggerate the insularity of these communities, since they were not hermetically sealed. There were often strangers passing through. Sometimes these might be men and women peddling goods—and this trade was both routine and necessary. Considerable, sometimes even remarkable, distances were covered by those heading for hiring fairs, taking up offers of employment, seeking relatives, or even traveling to give evidence at the assizes. In addition, large companies of drovers, harvesters, and fruit pickers traveled seasonally in the course of their employment. Furthermore, there was considerable mobility within particular occupational groups, soldiers, and sailors being perhaps the most obvious but also within skilled occupations such as mining.

Notwithstanding all the above, many people were born, lived, and died within the same parish or migrated only as far as a parish nearby. Marriage was a common reason for relocation but Kevin Snell's study of sixty-nine rural parishes has revealed that in 1700 some 55 percent of all marriages were endogamous, that is to say between partners from the same parish. According to Snell the figures declined to 50 percent by 1750 but then increased again to 70 percent by 1829. The increase may be accounted for by changes in recording after the Marriage Act (1753) but it has been suggested elsewhere that parish communities may have been getting more insular after 1750 not less. This seems to have been particularly so in Wales, where some parishes vehemently refused to allow outsiders to settle and forced migrant workers to carry evidence of their place of legal settlement (Suggett 1996). In such parish communities there was a strong sense that their own particular prerogatives were in potential danger from outside and their calls for justice generally had a historical and retrospective quality. They were advanced when something which had been held in the past, had been lost and needed to be regained, or when something was currently threatened that needed to be preserved. The well-being of the community was strongly associated with success in preserving traditional rights and customary practices.

Similar instincts also governed labor. A great change was heralded in the history of ideas when by the end of the eighteenth century a new rhetoric of justice had emerged, one that referenced justice in terms of future expectation. It began to be argued that novel change was capable of delivering outcomes that were more just than ever they had been before—it became, in short, possible in the minds of men and women to progress.

However, it took a long time before such ideas prevailed. Labor was self-interested and fragmented and groups such as skilled craft laborers often remained rather more committed to turning the clock back to an idealized past than to hurrying it forward into an uncertain future. While the Statute of Artificers of 1563 seems to us to have been very proscriptive, for skilled labor it contained useful provisions insofar as it empowered the magistrates to set wage rates and gave them powers to prevent casual labor trespassing upon the privileges accorded to the apprenticed trades. However, in our period downward pressure upon wage rates was felt across many trades as the old distinctions and hierarchies of labor were increasingly disregarded and as, in broad terms, the economy became more laissez-faire. Skilled workers then regularly agitated for a reinvigoration of the Statute of Artificers since it seemed to offer the best hope for preserving their privileged status. One such group, the journeymen millers in Kent, did so in 1811 when they appealed to Kings Bench asking them to compel the setting of the prescribed wage rate. The court knew well, however, the way the wind was blowing. The millers did not succeed and in 1813 the wage-fixing provisions of the statute were repealed. The ability of employers to depress wages was greatly facilitated by the ease with which they were able to circumvent or simply disregard the rules that governed apprenticeships. So here again, the agitation was for a reinvigoration of the old regulations. Where labor was well organized and resolute such agitation was not always in vain. London silk weavers were able to secure some concessions in the Silk Weavers Spitalfields Act (1773) that, although it penalized those who combined to raise wages, reinvigorated some of the earlier restrictions under the 1563 statute. Masters were limited to taking on two apprentices and fines were to be levied upon those who tried to employ labor from outside the craft.[7] This, though, was a rare success: in general the tide was firmly against the protection of craft interests.

Men and women in many situations came under increasing pressure as the eighteenth century progressed. Broadly, what one observes during this time is a move towards a more unified economy, with, among other things, a repudiation of price-fixing and market restrictions in favor of a deregulated and national market in foodstuffs. As mentioned this was accompanied by a dismantling or discarding of the apprenticeship provisions which protected the skilled crafts. In addition, whereas customary practices had recognized multi-layered interests in land, there was an increasingly legalistic approach adopted which saw land arrogated to the exclusive use of the freehold proprietor. Developments in this last were piecemeal and often contested (not always unsuccessfully so), but the prioritization of interests was apparent. One reason advanced to the Board of Agriculture in 1794 for the enclosure of land was "The use of common land by laborers operates upon the mind as a sort of independence"; once that was removed "the labourers will work every day in the year (and) their children will be put out to labour earlier" (Sharp 1988: 118). The general consequence of change was that "the daily lives of the great majority of eighteenth century Englishmen and women were carried on against a backcloth of mounting economic insecurity within a rapidly developing capitalist market system" (Randall 2006: 1).

In attempting to preserve their prerogatives, men and women turned to the resources at hand, seeking justice in a spirit of opportunism and calculation rather than undue subservience. Sometimes they addressed themselves to their local magistrates and the common law courts, sometimes they referred to manorial or occupational courts, and sometimes they resorted to extralegal collective action. I say extralegal rather than illegal because groups rarely relied on force alone. Often they operated in the contested space between the common law and customary practice, legitimizing their actions by offering their own vision of what the "true law" was, or, at the very least, ought to be.

An excellent illustration of this multi-faceted approach is provided by the contest over the right to "glean" or gather the leftover grains remaining at the end of the harvest. Gleaning was a rule-based activity. It could not start until harvesting had been completed and gleaning times were signaled by starting and finishing bells rung from the church—a connection that was seen as strong evidence that the activity was legitimate (Morgan 1975: 59). Gleaning "Queens" were appointed, senior women who superintended the rest, expelling those who disobeyed (Porter 1969). However, some farmers, especially those who wanted to feed the leftovers to their livestock, challenged the practice in the courts. The matter was considered by *Steel v. Houghton*, a civil action for trespass brought by James Steel against Mary Houghton for gleaning on his land.[8] While one judge concluded that the general right of gleaning was "too notorious to be denied," the others decided that such a right could not be compatible with an owner's exclusive enjoyment of his land. Thereafter, there was no general right to glean at common law—but it was not unlawful when sanctioned by particular manorial regulations, or by byelaws or where it could be convincingly demonstrated that it had been practiced in a locality "time out of mind." What followed from the judgment, though, was in effect a contest of interpretation that can be observed through the medium of Peter King's study of the Essex petty sessions of Lexden and Winstree and Colchester between 1785 and 1808 (King 1989). Both sides mobilized to test the implications of the judgment. As he notes, the gleaners "were in a particularly militant and assertive mood that year ... [they] were exceptionally well-coordinated and mobilised" (121–122). They were also armed with a strong sense of right. In 1785 an Epping widow had asserted that, "she had as much right to glean as he [the farmer] had." Another woman in 1789 responded to a challenge from a farmer that "it was not his property but belonged to her" (120). The day after she brought thirty people to the field to prove it.

Farmers tried both to prosecute the gleaners and to use their laborers to expel them by force. Fifteen gleaning disputes came to the Lexden and Winstree petty sessions between 1785 and 1808. However, two-thirds of the prosecutions were actually brought by the gleaners for assault. Most disputes were settled informally but where judgment was given the gleaners prevailed. They did not hesitate to turn to law when it suited them, to test the law when it seemed uncertain or to break the law when that might serve. A Suffolk farmer who turned his fields over to his hogs learned this to his cost in 1772 being "met in a dark narrow alley by several men in disguise, who pulled him from his horse, and beat him in a most inhumane manner then dragged him through a little river ... saying they had stopped him oppressing the poor anymore" (Goodwyn n.d.: 20).

Collective action to defend customary economic rights, for instance to fix prices and prevent the undue commoditization of foodstuffs, has been well documented elsewhere (Storch 1982; Seal 1988; Thompson 1971; Wells 1977). Sometimes the adherence to older practices can seem rather irrational. For instance, from 1670 onwards the government tried to introduce an agreed national measure for bushels of corn, sending out specimen "Winchester" bushels of eight gallons to every chartered market (Randall 2006). However, in areas where a bushel had traditionally been larger, consumers and dealers simply refused to accept the Winchester measure.[9] So in Tewkesbury in 1768 a crowd destroyed their Winchester bushels alleging that the maltsters and bakers, "bought by the large measure and sold by the small one."[10] The fear was that whereas the older measures were traditionally "heaped" (i.e., a little more was offered than legally required) the change might encourage the introduction of a level measure.

It was not only the poor who resisted change. So too did those who defined themselves primarily by their parochial patriotism. Many of the clergy had an interest in protecting the traditions and privileges of the parish and were active in doing so. For example, it was the rector of the church at Bainton in Yorkshire, William Territ, who in 1748 led the attack upon the illegal enclosures erected by the local Lord of the Manor (Tate 1967). Less energetically, there were clergymen who intervened in the press to declare that practices such as gleaning were biblically sanctioned and, to do justice to them, there were farmers who thought so too. It may be an important explanation for the persistence of many popular rights and customs through the eighteenth century that during the course of it the clergy became increasingly important in the magistracy. There were only fifty-one clerical magistrates in 1702 but by 1761 this had grown to 932 (Landau 1984). It was not, however, only those magistrates who were clergymen who can be observed intervening upon the side of the crowd in times of dearth to regulate prices or try to enforce almost abandoned market regulations. One imagines that the responses of many such men to the changes taking place must have been uncertain and contradictory. Dror Wahrman has written of the "basic cultural dilemma" faced by office holders at this period as men who "had one foot in community and the other outside it" (1992: 48). Such men had to choose between "an emerging wide-ranging 'national society' and an alternative polymorphous communal-provincial culture" (Wahrman 1992: 43). Norma Landau (1984) for her part has divided the Justices of the time into "patrician paternalists" who looked to Westminster and the central government and "patriarchal paternalists" who looked primarily to the needs of their local community.

It is then misleading to construct easy binary opposites between a supposedly unified, folksy plebeian culture and the rational and unsympathetic instrumentality of the free market governing elite. At the elite level there were some deeply attached to traditional social and economic structures and as Andy Wood has noted, "as equity law courts impinged on local customary law, the defenders of custom transcribed and codified local laws which had hitherto existed only in 'common report' and speech" (1997: 54). However, just as the responses of elites were varied and nuanced, so too one must not forget that there were diverse and contradictory interests within plebeian culture itself. As Adrian Randall reminds us:

> Such institutions and offices as were developed to maintain and protect custom for one set of inhabitants might be used to deny custom to another set. In such cases, a language of custom was frequently deployed against the poor. Skilled workers or artisans often turned customary rules against poorer waged laborers. (1991: 200)

The assertion of class-based unities came later, for the moment the demand from the more organized laboring groups was for recognition of both privilege and time-honored difference.

JUSTICE WITHIN THE COMMUNITY: PERFORMANCE AND PUNISHMENT

If occupational groups and communities mobilized strategically to prevent trespasses upon their broad interests, the vigor of the times and their own sense of entitlement also enabled them to react energetically to individual offenses committed within their own bailiwick. Malefactors were often dealt with without any interference from authority. Thus a man who attempted sexual indecency in Lincoln's Inn in 1701 was peremptorily beaten up by the porters and watchmen.[11] Similarly, when a pickpocket was apprehended in Covent Garden in 1721:

> The Mob tumbled him about most miserably in the Dirt, so that afterwards they thought fit to wash him; accordingly he was first carried to the Pump in the Marketplace and there, having pulled off his fine Wig, he received their blessing on his naked head ... afterwards they carried him to the horse pond in Hart Street, and made him divert the Company with ducking under water.[12]

Another pickpocket in 1749 was ducked and beaten so severely in Whitechapel that he was "left for dead."[13] Reports of such popular punishments are often rather whimsical and understate the violence involved, for example, a weaver in Bristol was ducked in 1733 by his compatriots but also, "had the misfortune to have one of his eyes beat out."[14]

Women were treated with equal severity. A woman who had stolen children's clothes was tied to a boat's stern and almost drowned at Hungerford in 1737.[15] When another woman tried to sell an unknown sea fish as a salmon at Bridlington in 1764 she was severely dunked in the sea by the women who had mistakenly purchased it.[16] When a further woman tried to a steal yarn at Keswick market in 1777 she was "led around the Market place by the Bell-man, who, at intervals, proclaimed, 'This is the woman who stole the yarn.' She was afterwards delivered up to the mob, who drove her a mile out of town."[17]

The Keswick example demonstrates that the boundary between official acts and those punishments that were not only unofficial but also potentially unlawful was a shifting and porous one. Often no such boundary was acknowledged. One can readily imagine that victims rarely had the courage to complain lest further punishment be invited and that therefore it was only occasionally and after the fact that it became necessary to consider whether the action taken had been lawful or not. It would be immediately apparent today that there is a fundamental structural difference in the types of punishments that a mob might inflict as opposed to the state's justice system. Not so in the eighteenth century. Both employed rather similar instruments insofar as shame and public display were key components in the punitive response. To illustrate, the very essence of the pillory was that punishment was determined by public disapprobation. Those convicted of "unnatural" offenses could suffer horribly whereas by contrast, exposing popular figures could backfire on the authorities (Figure 1.1). Similarly, given the turbulent and volatile nature of the crowd and the slender mechanisms for law enforcement one can also readily imagine that the vigor with which a public lashing was conducted depended much upon the sympathies of the onlookers.

Any methodological differences between formal and informal sanction disappeared entirely when it came to dealing with certain troublesome women. While a ducking remained a common informal response to many kinds of wrongdoing it could still be officially sanctioned for scolds and the like. In 1731 there:

> Was erected at Oxford, at the charge of the Corporation, a very handsome ducking stool, to cool the tails and stop the mouths of several of the female sex, observed very sonorous of late, and to that end a young lad, dressed in woman's cloaths, hansell'd it; and was afterward exposed to the view of a very numerous assembly.[18]

A ducking was ordered by magistrates in Leominster in 1809 but there may be examples that are later still (Piggott 1869) (Figure 1.2).

Martin Ingram (1997) has observed how very difficult it is to differentiate between lawful and customary justice and unlawful crowd violence. This is particularly so because

FIGURE 1.1 A Perjuror in the Pillory. John Waller is pelted to death at the pillory in 1732: Newgate Calendar, 1824. Source: Mary Evans Picture Library.

respectable persons were sometimes involved in both. In 1716, a piece of street theater—a "mock groaning"—took place at Westonbirt in Gloucestershire to shame a tenant farmer accused of having attempted sodomy with a laborer. The play involved a scandalous mock baptism and the farmer's landlord demanded that the performers be punished. An investigation by the local clergyman ran out of steam, however, once it was discovered that all ranks of local society had participated, including the largest local employer and a churchwarden (Rollison 1981).

This then begs the question as to how often did crowds engage in punitive practices believing, rightly or wrongly, that the presence of a person of some authority in their midst legitimized their proceedings? We simply cannot know. However, we do know that it was popularly believed that certain traditional observances were thought to have the power to legitimize activities that would otherwise be unlawful. It was with some difficulty that an emerging state labored to convince groups that such beliefs were erroneous and that they were not entitled to penalize malefactors in the way that tradition allowed. The struggle to suppress the persecution of witches serves as a case in point. The very possibility of actual witchcraft was denied in the Witchcraft Act (1736) but, famously, Ruth Osborne died after being swum as a suspected witch at Tring in 1751. What is of interest for our purposes is that far from being a covert affair, the intention to swim

FIGURE 1.2 The Ducking Stool in Leominster Church. Source: Mary Evans Picture Library.

both her and her husband was declared several days in advance by town criers in Hemel Hempstead, Leighton Buzzard and Winslow.[19] This reflected the common supposition that acts of popular justice were lawful if the intention to perform them was declared in advance in three parishes (Banks 2014). Ruth's death was very likely unintended but it forced the authorities to respond, which they did with the exemplary hanging of one of the participants.[20] Many acts of so-called popular justice seem, however, to have been ignored or lightly penalized so it must be open to question as to whether the authorities would have intervened with such vigor in the absence of a fatality. There were further, very public, attempts to swim or assault witches in 1770,[21] 1808,[22] 1845[23] and 1876.[24] One gets the sense that few of the participants thought not only that what they were doing was morally reprehensible but that it was really, truly, unlawful.

There was one particular form of customary justice whose legitimacy was still being earnestly asserted by crowds into the twentieth century. Shaming processions through offended communities, with or without the malefactor in question being present, were invariably accompanied by a crowd announcing the affair to all and sundry by making "rough music," beating on pots and pans, blowing horns, and generally offending the eardrums in any way possible. In southern England the term "skimmington" (which refers to a species of large wooden ladle) was generally employed to refer to such parades, while in the North "stang riding" was preferred (a stang being a long wooden pole upon which offenders might also be mounted). Each involved the parade of a person or an effigy generally either mounted on a pole of this kind or upon a beast of some kind, usually a horse or donkey, although there were many regional variants in both terminology and practice.

The flexibility of the form allowed it to be deployed in many different contexts; for instance, rough music often played a part in the enforcement of labor discipline. Striking silk weavers staged a particularly violent parade in Southwark in 1771 that led to the death of a man who had informed upon them.[25] Parades of blacklegs were staged at Tiverton in 1749 (Minchinton 1951), Stroud in 1825[26] and Bristol in 1826 (Gorsky 1994). However, it is in the arena of moral offenses that processional justice was most important. It was taken for granted that communities had the right to recognize and penalize the moral derelicts of those living among them and they were particularly interested to notice inappropriate sexual and gender behavior.

Concern that wives might seek to wrest dominion from their husbands seems to have been one of the great anxieties of the age. In Jonathan Swift's, *The Cudgel'd Husband*

> As Thomas was cudgel'd one day by his wife,
> He took to his heels and fled for his life:
> Tom's three dearest friends came by in the squabble,
> And saved him at once from the shrew and the rabble.

One might imagine that the authorities might have saved him for, as we have seen, in places the ducking stool was still available to chasten scolds, but in general punitive measures seem to have fallen into desuetude (Underdown 1985b). In *Last Instructions to a Painter* Andrew Marvell complained in 1667 of "Masculine wives, transgressing Nature's law" and of the limited remedies available to a husband since, "No concern'd Jury for him Damage finds, nor partial justice for her Behaviour binds." In 1730, gentlemen (one presumes only gentlemen) were invited to attend the Oratory at the corner of Lincoln's Inn Fields where there would be a comic oration delivered, it was ambitiously claimed, "in the style of Demosthenes" and entitled *A Defence of Hen-Pecks or All the World and his Wife*.[27] In more pejorative tones a publication in 1639 had hectored upon "the several languages that Shrews read to the Husbands, either at Morning, Noon, or Night" and offered new tricks to tame them (Taylor 1639).

To most men, however, it seemed that the blame for a shrewish wife must lie with a husband who had failed to assert the appropriate authority. Grose's *Classical Dictionary of the Vulgar Tongue* even defined the practice of "riding skimmington" as:

> A ludicrous cavalcade in ridicule of a man beaten by his wife. It consists of a man riding behind a woman with his face to the horse's tail, holding a distaff in his hand, at which he seems to work, the woman all the while beating him with a ladle, a smock displayed on a staff is carried before them as an emblematical standard, denoting female superiority, they are accompanied by what is called the rough music, that is frying pans, bulls horns, marrow bones and cleavers. (Grose 1787)

Just such an event was portrayed in a late sixteenth-century frieze from Montacute House in Somerset. A man who has been helping himself to ale is belabored by his wife and is then paraded by his neighbors.

Such mocking processions had much in common with the judicial ridings of medieval and early modern London that were once employed by the authorities against economic and moral offenders (Ingram 1997). Ruth Mellinkoff (1973) reports that forcing a miscreant to ride backwards as a humiliation was a very ancient practice, recorded in the ninth-century chronicle of Theophanes and probably being referred to by Nicolaus of

JUSTICE

Damascus in the first century—when he mentions a donkey ride as a punishment for adultery.[28] Such ridings became common in European and Eastern culture and were often accompanied by symbols intended to represent or suggest the offense in question. Parodies of the cowering behavior of a submissive husband were enacted not simply to mock him but in order to ensure that others took note. William King's poem *Monarch* observed:

> When the young people ride the Skimmington,
> There is a general trembling in a town.
> Not only he for whom the person rides
> Suffers, but they sweep other doors besides;
> And by that hieroglyphic does appear
> That the good woman is the master there. (2004: 256–257)

Whatever the apprehension caused in the hearts of others, the reputational damage to the principal party was severe. In *Mason v. Jennings* (1680) a hackney driver complained that a rival had ridden skimmington against him. The consequence was that his customers supposed that he was a man who allowed himself to be beaten by his wife and thereafter they refused to take his carriage.[29] Right into the early twentieth-century victims of rough music might be refused service in local shops or find it difficult to secure regular employment (Bickley 1902). In a mobile and atomized society it is hard today to comprehend the difficulty of functioning in a society that had closed ranks against oneself. George Porteous committed suicide in 1736 rather than endure it and other instances are not unknown.[30]

Grose's definition of a skimmington was not quite accurate insofar as he refers to a woman riding alongside the victim. It is pretty clear that this was in fact a man dressed in women's clothes. In Hogarth's 1725 print *Hudibras encounters the Skimmington* (depicting a scene from Samuel Butler's satirical poem) the woman in question seems pretty clearly to be a man. (Figure 1.3). In Cheshire in 1790:

FIGURE 1.3 Hudibras Encounters the Skimmington. William Hogarth, 1725. Source: Mary Evans Picture Library.

A man dressed in female apparel was mounted on the back of an old donkey, holding a spinning wheel on his lap and his back towards the donkey's head. Two men led the animal through the neighbourhood followed by scores of boys and idle men, tinkling kettles and frying pans, roaring with cows' horns and making a most hideous hullabaloo. (Axon 1884: 300)

Not only did a man, dressed up, serve for the shrewish wife, but also on occasions the submissive husband would be substituted by an effigy or else by a neighbor. The substitute would declare, often in very poor doggerel verse, the nature of the offense, the identity of the offender and, for their own sake, that they were merely impersonating the real culprit. In the chapbook, *The Pindar of Wakefield* a group of young men determine to chastise a downtrodden new husband and so they,

Put a Boy drest in women's apparel like the woman, and a man like her husband, and put them both on a horse: All in the Town and the Countries thereabouts having notice of this new iest, came to see it. Thorow the Towne thus they rid, the woman beating the man, and scolding at him terribly.[31]

The tale is of course fictional but young men arrogating to themselves the right to penalize offenses reappears in contemporary descriptions often enough. Adam Fitz-Adam's parish was famous for:

Delighting in what is called rough music, consisting of performances on cow-horns, salt-boxes, warming pans, sheep-bells, etc. etc. and intermixed with hooting, hallowing, and all sorts of hideous noises, with which the young wags of the village serenade their neighbors on several occasions, particularly those families in which (as the phrase is) the grey mare is the better horse. (Fitz-Adam 1756: 192)

Shrewish wives were not the only moral offenders of concern. Adultery was a particularly egregious offense. The state of the sources makes it difficult to make bald statements with any great confidence but at least by the mid-nineteenth century it had become rather rare for hands to actually be laid on moral offenders. Effigies and substitutes were much more commonly employed (Figure 1.4). However, adulterers seem to have remained at most risk of actually being seized and roughly handled. When we learn that in 1761 a journeyman weaver and the lewd woman he had taken up with were paraded and then given, "a very severe ducking" I think we can be sure it was very unpleasant indeed.[32] This was an area in which occupational groups as well as parishes were also active, for instance the wool combers of Tiverton exercised the privilege of "cold staving"—parading and then ducking into the river Exe—any of their number suspected of this offense (Snell 2003).

A further offense, which was to appear much more prominently in the later history of rough music, was that of wife beating. In July 1748 *The Remembrancer* recorded that:

Last week there was a Skimmington rode through Islington on the following Occasion, viz. a Tradesman in that Town, for some Offence given by his Wife, ordered a Man to take her on his Shoulders, which he did, and there held her, while the Husband whipped her with Rods until the Blood ran down to her Heels; on which the Wife had a Warrant against him, and carrying him before a Justice of the Peace was, after Examination, sent to Prison, to which Place he was conducted through the Peltings, Hissings and Blows of Two-Thirds of the Women in the Town.[33]

FIGURE 1.4 A Stang Riding with a young man acting as substitute. Engraved by E. Kaufmann from a drawing by George Walker, "The Costumes of Yorkshire," 1814 (2nd edition 1885). Source: Mary Evans Picture Library.

In the later nineteenth century rough music practices were to become synonymous in many districts with the punishment of wife-beaters, whereas punishments of scolds and submissive husbands fell away. In the long eighteenth century it seems to have been somewhat the other way around. The aforementioned case was clearly an extreme one but raises interesting questions: at what point did necessary chastisement of a shrewish wife become unacceptable violence? At what point could a husband be characterized as unduly submissive? There must, in short, have been interpretive moments when an act, which could have been characterized in different ways, became affixed with a particular label that made it worthy of notice by those interested in the practices of community justice.

Or rather perhaps, worthy of notice at that particular time. The lad who frolicked in women's clothes at the inauguration of Oxford's ducking stool reminds us of the close relationship between revelry and many species of punishment. Festivity was often located within transgressive time and space in which norms were suspended. One thinks of the Lords of Misrule or the Molly Dancers also donning women's clothing in order to pursue their violent exactions. The liberty the symbols of festivity ignited seems to have operated in two different but connected ways. First, it allowed a crowd to cast off habits of obedience and thus empowered collective resistive action: the attacks on the turnpikes at Ledbury and Chippenham in 1727 were led by men in women's clothes (Malcolmson 1980) and those who gathered to attack enclosures in Northamptonshire in 1765 did so under the pretext of taking part in a football match.[34] Secondly, by constituting the community, by bringing it into being as it gathered, it empowered collective judgmental action.

A great many shaming processions and other punitive rituals occurred during festive time and broadly speaking that time can be divided into two different categories. There were individual celebratory events that sometimes inspired collective responses and then there were annual festivities such as Plough Monday and of course November 5 during which some form of mischievous action was to be routinely expected. If we look at individual celebratory events, it was a marriage that was most likely to excite a kind of counter-demonstration that expressed some disapprobation. So for example, when in 1737 an eighty-year-old married an eighteen-year-old it caused,

> A great Hudibrastick Skimmington composed of the Chairmen, and others of that Class, to the great Disturbance of the new-married Couple, and their Friends and Relations, who were all assembled on so joyful an Occasion.[35]

Similarly targeted were those who had remarried such as the Exeter saddler who was subjected to rough music in 1817.[36] Skimmington bands became the subject of much objection and were satirized in Essex Hawker's comic opera *A Country Wedding and Skimmington* in 1729. These skimmington bands interest us because they blended both justice rituals and the doling customs observable in many communities. A wayward marriage not only ignited disapproval but also inspired a sense of entitlement and gave rise to an expectation of a monetary compensation. Accordingly, a band appeared and a skimmington was staged. The victims were not expected to resist but to submit with good grace and fund the food and drink which turned the affair away from chastisement and into celebration. This being done the relationship between the parties could be restored to some form of equilibrium. And this was true not just in the case of dubious marriages. There were many instances of transgressions of the less egregious sort, which were good-naturedly forgiven by the crowd once the victim had submitted to his or her correction and once the crowd had secured the funding for a really good dinner. However, even during the course of these apparently rather mild instances of rough music failing to conform to expectations could be unsafe. The claims advanced were, to the claimants, real enough and revelry concealed implicit threat within it. So for example, violence might easily break out at those weddings where the guests resisted the attempts at extraction and in 1802 the arrival of a fiddler and friends at a marriage bidding caused general rioting in the course of which one man was shot dead.[37]

The remunerative and celebratory elements in popular justice practice beg the question as to the extent to which those practices were primarily aimed at punishing fault and meting out justice and to what extent what we observe was in fact primarily a celebratory system that was predicated upon the existence of punitive impulses. The answer is that both statements are true to varying degrees. There were instances clearly inspired by a very real and deeply felt sense of outrage. On the other hand there were also celebrations that simply required that some suitable victim be identified for chastisement. On Plough Monday (the first Monday after January 6) for example, a plow would be blessed in church and taken to the homes of wealthier inhabitants by bands of young men, the Plough Bullocks. The purpose of the process was to solicit doles of food and beer. However, Plough Monday (Figure 1.5) simply would not have been Plough Monday unless someone had resisted the exactions and consequently had his land and path plowed up as punishment. Equally November 5 could hardly proceed without a suitable guy. Of course Guy Fawkes was available but how much more delightful it was to parade the effigy of a known individual and enjoy the benefits of a

FIGURE 1.5 Plough Monday celebrations. Unattributed engraving, 1826. Source: Mary Evans Picture Library.

really big bonfire. At Castle Cary Guy Fawkes was rarely burned and instead the village decided among themselves annually who was most unpopular—in 1768 they burnt Mr. Justice Creed (Woodforde 1999). Of course, national figures might suggest themselves—Lord Bute was regularly burned in effigy during the demonstrations that induced him to step down as Prime Minister in 1763.

Identifying appropriate social enemies is of course the very stuff of politics. Patriotic groups employed bonfire culture to solidify sentiment against appropriate targets. There were, for example, many burnings of the disgraced Admiral Byng such as that at North Shields in 1756.[38]

In the early nineteenth century there was a nationwide campaign to immolate images of Tom Paine. The burning of effigies of the pope endures at the famous Lewes bonfire today. Shamings were only effectual because of the existence of common understandings of what shame was and what ritual activities "meant." However, it is apparent that if there was a bedrock of common understandings, nonetheless shaming rituals were part of a communication system that could be expropriated by those wishing to write their own narrative upon the public sphere. Any group could try to constitute themselves as the voice of the community. So criminal gangs (and pressed seamen) utilized rough music against informers, as did interest groups wishing to protest about a particular piece of legislation. A public ducking could be mounted by a troop of guards against an attorney who had had the nerve to serve upon one of them a writ for a debt.[39] An essayist might be burned in effigy for suggesting the naturalization of foreign Protestants.[40] Any unpopular figure might suffice. Radical preachers were a popular target; one was "rough musicked" at Towcester in 1767.[41] William Huntington, a Calvinist preacher, complained that, "I am the sport of fools, and the song of drunkards; and often go from the meeting to my house in a shower of stones, attended with a band of rough music" (Huntington 1795: 239). Contests of representation were everywhere. When Sir Charles Palliser left London for his countryseat he decided that it would be appropriate that a spontaneous demonstration of affection should greet his arrival. So he sent instructions (and money) in advance that the local church might ring its bells. The vicar, incensed that the peer did not attend church, instead informed the parishioners who promptly greeted the grandee with a monstrous cacophony.[42]

FINAL THOUGHTS

To sum up, when thinking broadly of justice, the good people of England and Wales were often, it seems, suffused with a kind of historical romanticism. Justice recognized historical entitlement far more than it suggested novel advancement. Justice lived in a mental past when kings were good, all men had their due and all wives were undoubtedly virtuous. Important changes in the history of ideas were signalled when justice began to shift to the aspirational from the archaeological.

In the meantime, communities were imbued with a sense of their right to do justice according to traditional forms. Those forms were often so intertwined with festivity that it is often difficult, and perhaps scarcely meaningful, to say whether festivity led to justice or justice to festivity. Both justice forms and festive forms though were sufficiently flexible to be appropriated for other purposes. As such they both took their place in the great convulsions occasioned by the transition to a more modern market economy and informed the micro-politics played out on the streets between contending interests. Eventually, a state was to emerge able to rationalize the legal processes, to project its power into communities and to take justice into its custody. In the meantime, however, there was nothing whimsical, trivial, or folksy about popular justice or rough music in the eighteenth century. As the wayward musicians understood very well, on the contrary, for the moment there was everything to play for.

CHAPTER TWO

Constitution

Handel's Solomon *and the Constitution at Covent Garden*

JOHN SNAPE

To Angela Kershaw.

Crown'd by the gen'ral Voice, at last you shew
The utmost Length that *Musick*'s Force can go:
What Pow'r on Earth, but Harmony like Thine,
Cou'd *Britain*'s jarring Sons e'er hope to join?

(Anon. 1724: 1)

INTRODUCTION

Theatrical performance, as much as self-conscious accounts of government and law, can facilitate an understanding of the constitution's cultural significance in eighteenth-century Britain.[1] In this context Handel's oratorio, *Solomon* HWV 67, premiered at Covent Garden Theatre, Westminster, on March 17, 1749 (Hurley 2009b), is richly significant. *Solomon*, writes Vickers, combines "lavish choral writing, masque-like elements, humanistic drama, a celebration of sexual love, a discussion of principles of correct kingship, and patriotic opulence" (Vickers 2007: 14). Quoting lines reproduced in the epigraph, Smith explains how contemporaries ascribed to the music of George Frideric Handel (1685–1759) the transcendent power of healing "the [British] nation of its disabling political divisions" (1995: 210). "The idea," writes Smith, "that a man of the present day, and not a philosopher or statesman but a composer, could actually make the state harmonious is very striking indeed" and "extraordinary testimony to Handel's public significance." "[T]he possibility," she adds, "that deliberate political allusions in ... [Handel's] librettos might ... be ... prescriptive and intended to prompt action" is particularly thought-provoking (1995: 210).

That *Solomon* might be a musical exhortation to political unity, through an idealized depiction of the constitution, requires a conception both of the oratorio and of what the eighteenth-century constitution was doing. *Solomon*, says Brewer, is "a paean to the Hanoverian regime" (1997: 373). This is maintainable, though not particularly suggestive. More stimulating is Smith's argument (1995: 310) that *Solomon* is one of Handel's oratorios drawing on "The Idea of a Patriot King," by Henry St John, Viscount Bolingbroke (1678–1751) (Bolingbroke [1749] 1997). Though written in 1738/1739, Bolingbroke's work was only "published for sale" in 1749, having circulated in a "clandestine edition" in the early 1740s (Gerrard 1994: 185). "Consciously modelled on Machiavelli's *The Prince*, ... [the "Patriot King"] favored a return to the purity of the original constitution ... achieved by a moral, patriotic prince," eradicating constitutional corruptions (Dickinson 1970: 260–261) and envisaging a "golden age." *Solomon*'s bi-partisan libretto "exalts peace and trade, proclaims national prosperity, shows Church and Crown endorsing each other's interests to the benefit of society, and ... depicts the monarch—no arbitrary, absolute ruler—dispensing true justice" (Smith 1995: 310). What the *constitution* did in eighteenth-century Britain involves distinguishing between two ideas. The modern one, not relevant here, articulated in Thomas Paine's 1791 "Rights of Man" (Paine [1791] 2008), envisages an exhaustive, constitutive document, created by "the people," before the erection of government, and ranking as "fundamental law" (Loughlin 2010: 278–279). "The ancient idea of the constitution," however, drew "on the metaphor of the body politic, was bound up with the health and strength of the nation, and ... evolved as the nation increased in vitality" (Loughlin 2010: 275). The Westminster magistrate Henry Fielding (1707–1754) considered that the constitution of the "Commonwealth," or "body politic," included both its laws and the "Customs, Manners, and Habits of the People" (Fielding [1750/1751] 1988: 123); Battestin and Battestin 1989). The ancient idea is the one adopted here. Reverence for the laws is a crucial part of each conception. In accepting, with reservations, Smith's identification of aspects of the libretto with Bolingbroke, this chapter explores *Solomon*'s potential constitutional significance, and, within that, the light that *Solomon* throws on law's cultural importance in mid-eighteenth-century Britain.

The chapter has six interlocking sections. The next one analyzes certain features of the constitution, and of the law within it, that become significant in *Solomon*. The second considers how both composer and poet were likely untypical adherents to that constitution. The third explains the constitutional significance of *Solomon*'s subject-matter, genre, and place of performance. The fourth explores the constitutional significance of *Solomon*'s architecture. The fifth examines how the characters in the oratorio embody constitutional values. The sixth discusses the centrality to those values of the idea of law. The conclusions draw these strands together and show how they inter-relate.

Handel's works must always be viewed skeptically. This chapter offers only one view. Hicks, for example, doubts that any convincing "parallels ... [between *Solomon* and] Hanoverian England" can be drawn, asserting instead that "it is demeaning to tie the work down to the period of its creation" (2007: 7). Hunter advises us to question everything we thought we knew about Handel (2015: 445). Nonetheless, relating *Solomon* to the eighteenth-century constitution does seem worthwhile. Handel and his poet flatter their audience's intelligence. They do not draw glib absolutist parallels. Like many eighteenth-century philosophers, they are circumspect. The fact that no contemporary interpreted *Solomon* for us (Smith 1995: 309) suggests that its message was clear.

THE EIGHTEENTH-CENTURY CONSTITUTION

While Britain's "balanced constitution" attracted eulogies, the real legacy of the 1688 Revolution was the close relationship between Crown and Parliament. In "A Dissertation upon Parties" (1733–1734), Bolingbroke described the constitution as "that assemblage of laws, institutions and customs, derived from certain fixed principles of reason, directed to certain fixed objects of public good, that compose the general system, according to which the community hath agreed to be governed" (Bolingbroke [1749] 1997: 88, quoted Loughlin 2010: 278). Baron de Montesquieu (1689–1755), a friend of Bolingbroke's, thought Britain's constitution unique. It was not monarchical, in the sense of having honor as its principle, nor did the nobility's seigniorial rights curb monarchical excess as in France (Montesquieu [1748/1750] 1949; Shackleton 1961; Rahe 2009). Instead, Britain was "a republic, disguised under the form of monarchy" (Montesquieu [1748/1750] 1949: 68; Shackleton 1961: 287; Rahe 2009: 55).[2] James Thomson (1700–1748), who popularized the expression "Britain's matchless constitution," eulogized, in "Liberty" (1736), the "mutual checking and supporting powers" of "Kings, Lords, and Commons" (Thomson 1736, quoted Loughlin 2013: 6). Nevertheless, as Shackleton says, "[i]n truth the vital characteristic of the British constitution … was the solidarity and not the separation of the legislative and the executive powers" (1961: 300). Philip Yorke, Earl of Hardwicke (1690–1764), the Lord Chancellor, disclosed the reality, in notes of an audience with George II (reigned 1727–1760), in January 1744:

> *King.* I have done all you ask'd of me. I have put all power into your hands and I suppose you will make the most of it.
>
> *Ch.* The disposition of places is not enough, if your Majesty takes pains to shew the world that you disapprove of your own work.
>
> *K. My work !* I was forc'd: I was threatened.
>
> *Ch.* I am sorry to hear your Majesty use those expressions. I know of no force: I know of no threats. No means were us'd but what has been us'd in all times, the humble advice of your servants, supported by such reasons as convinc'd them that the measure was necessary for your service. (Hardwicke [1744] 1952)

George is thus persuaded to accept his ministers' policies because they are in his interest (Miller 1983). This was the reality of the late 1740s. When Handel first arrived in Britain from Düsseldorf (aged twenty-five), in November 1710 (Burrows 2012), it was only three years since Anne had withheld the Royal Assent to a parliamentary Bill, for what turned out to be the last time (Williams 1960a: 30). Bolingbroke was, in late 1710, Tory Secretary of State. It was the Tories' Whig successors, notably Sir Robert Walpole (1676–1745), who accomplished the "solidarity" of legislative and executive (Shackleton 1961: 300). When Montesquieu published his views on the "separation of powers" in 1748 (Montesquieu [1748/1750] 1949: 151–162 (XI:6); Shackleton 1961: 298–301), which were different from Bolingbroke's "mixed constitution" (Shackleton), he was evidently writing about what was by then a rather old ideal.

A principal theme of the Revolution settlement was the protection of property rights, which Sir William Blackstone (1723–1780) later characterized as one of "[t]he three basic liberties protected by the constitution" (Loughlin 2013: 88, citing Blackstone [1765–9] 2016: I: 93–94). The 1689 Bill of Rights, by article 4, expressed the ideal by banning levies without parliamentary consent. In doing so, it actualized the aphorism of James Harrington (1611–1677), that "[t]he man that cannot live upon his own must be a servant; but he that can live upon his own may be a freeman" ([1700] 1992: 269). A people subject to non-parliamentary levies is not free because, then, property is unprotected. In 1741, David Hume accepted "that the opinion of right to property has a great influence" in determining "The First Principles of Government" ([1741] 1987: 32: 34; Harris 2015: 177). Rightly or wrongly, *we* tend to think of "property" as referring to a thing (land or chattels) and of proving title to it by reference to some document or (in the case of land) to a governmental record. In the eighteenth century, though, *property* signified *not* the thing itself but a person's legally-protected physical *control* over the thing (Blackstone [1765–1769] 2016: II.2; Gray and Gray 2009). Entitlement to exercise that control, proved by "the raw fact of physical possession ... and [,in the case of land, by] ... a succession of ... documentary transfer[s]," depended on having a better "title," or "entitlement," than "anyone else" (Gray and Gray 2011: 87–88). "Possession," with its natural law origins, was "nine points in the Law." Defined thus, property was pervasive. Here are some examples. In *Ashby v. White* (1701–1705), for example, the House of Lords reversed, to the Commons' fury, a decision of the King's Bench, that the latter was not competent to adjudge on a man's right to vote. The Lords[3] agreed with Lord Holt CJKB's dissenting judgment,[4] that the elector had such a property in his vote that it was justiciable in the King's Bench (Hoppit 2000). In Montesquieu's *Persian Letters* (1721), the Troglodytes exchange the state of nature for "liberty under positive laws" thereby instituting private property (Montesquieu [1721] 1993: 52–61; Hont 2006: 405). In *Entick v. Carrington* (1765), Lord Camden CJCP declared that, "[b]y the laws of England, every invasion of private property, be it ever so minute, is a trespass."[5] The libretti of Handel's English-language choral works are replete with eulogies to *liberty* (Smith 1995): "The Mountain Nymph, sweet *Liberty*" (*L'Allegro, Il Penseroso, ed Il Moderato* (Milton, Harris and Jennens 1740: 6)); "'Tis Liberty, dear Liberty alone," "Come, ever-smiling Liberty" (*Judas Macchabaeus* (Morell 1747: 5)); and, strikingly, "And Liberty, that Life of Life itself, / And Soul of Property ... " (*Alexander Balus* (Morell 1748: 11)). What these are exalting, though, is the right of *property*. For Handel, eager to make and retain a fortune in Britain, the national emphasis on property must have been enticing. By 1749, Montesquieu had written that Britain was the "[o]ne nation ... in the world that has for the direct end of its constitution political liberty" (Montesquieu [1748/1750] 1949: 151; Rahe 2009: 68, 137–138). Property and Anglican Protestantism, as the national religion (Smith 1995: 321), were directly associated. "One cannot overestimate," Ellen Harris writes, "the importance of the Protestant religion and in particular the Church of England to the history of this period" (Harris 2014: 266). In *Solomon*, property as possession, and its association with liberty, is clothed with significance.

The perception was that what characterized the British constitution were "known laws," and people's right to litigate. Though the law was often condemned (e.g., by Jonathan Swift) as a web to catch the poor, there was also an ideal of accessible justice (Hoppit 2000). Powell J and Lovell B had been reminded, in a Northampton assize sermon of 1708, that "the men of Wealth and Power have no Protection by Law against the just complaints of the Poor ... *the Law is open* ... and the Law considers not who is High, or who is Low, but who has Right" (Downes 1708: 11, part quoted Hoppit 2000: 460). However, by 1750, the common-law courts had become too expensive for poorer people to use (Lemmings 2011: 59, referring to Brooks 1998: 15), and even non-common-law jurisdictions were declining. The time-lapse since *Ashby v. White* highlighted the change: Matthew Ashby, the plaintiff, was "a poor cobbler in Aylesbury" (Hoppit

2000: 46). Lemmings quotes "a correspondent of the *London Magazine*, writing in 1740, ... [bemoaning] the inability of people with modest means to prosecute their rights in the courts" (2011: 72). He instances, too, the dramatic decline in the business of the King's Lynn Guildhall Court between 1700 and 1750, in which there had once been a good deal of "relatively poor" plaintiffs, "nearly half of them" appearing "as plaintiffs in their own right" (2011: 60). Some believed that this amounted to an undermining of the rule of law (Lemmings 2011: 59). In *Solomon*, this concern seems to be placed center stage.

HANDEL AND POET AS BRITISH SUBJECTS

Handel, naturalized as a British subject in 1727 (Burrows 2012: 157), seems to have had Whig sympathies. He "cast his vote for the sitting Whig, Lord Trentham,"[6] at the Westminster By-election of 1749 (Simon 1985: 178), eight months after *Solomon*'s first performance. Confident, imposing, Handel circumspectly avoids our gaze in a closely-contemporaneous portrait (Figure 2.1).[7] *Solomon*'s poet is unknown, though most believe its former attribution to the Reverend Thomas Morell (1703–1784) is wrong. Recently, Pink has argued plausibly that credit belongs to Moses Mendes (*c.* 1690–1758), "a wealthy City stockjobber from a well-to-do Portuguese-Sephardic Jewish family based in London" who, it would appear, "converted to Christianity" prior to being "awarded an Oxford MA on 19 June 1750" (Pink 2015: 214, 217). Mendes was evidently the anonymous author of several "entertainments" performed at Drury Lane. Of these, *The Chaplet* (1749), with a score by William Boyce (1711–1779), stands out (Pink 2015).

Only British subjects could lawfully hold an estate in land,[8] so naturalization raised the possibility that Handel might purchase a freehold. His naturalization Act's standard wording provided that Handel:

> be ... Enabled and adjudged able to all intents purposes and Constructions whatsoever ... to demand Challenge Ask Take retain have and enjoy all or any Manors Lands Tenements hereditaments Goods Chattels Debts Estates Trusts and all other privileges and Immunities Benefit and Advantage in Law or Equity belonging to the Leige people and Natural born Subjects of this Kingdom. (Simon 1985: 284; background in Deutsch 1955: 202–205)

Instead, Handel continued to hold, at £60 a year, a lease of 25 Brook Street, off Hanover Square, his address since its construction *circa* 1723 (Simon 1985: 176; Riding, Burrows and Hicks 2001: 23). Handel could vote in Westminster elections because of his naturalization and the particular borough franchise. Unlike in the shires (Langford 1989: 718), electors in Westminster (Middlesex) did not need to be 40-shilling freeholders. Instead, there was "scot and lot" (Sedgwick 1970: 121), whereby "the vote depended ... on the payment of the poor or church rate" (Porritt [1903] 1963: 30–33; Maitland 1908: 356; Holdsworth 1938: 560). What Handel evidently prized was his house's location and amenity. He wrote *Solomon* in the first-floor back-room ("the composition room") "between 5 May and 17 June 1748" (Hurley 2009b: 596). *Solomon*'s "Nightingale Chorus" ("May no rash Intruder disturb their soft Hours" (Anon. 1749: 8; Bärenreiter 2014: 113)), of which it is said that "no more perfect marriage of music and English words has ever been consecrated," was written "during the season of their song; ... [Handel] may even have heard them round the corner in Berkeley Square" (Dean 1959: 520, 526). Handel, not having "exclusive possession of the theatre," also rehearsed *Solomon* on March 4 and 14, 1749 (Burrows 2012: 395), in the first-floor dining room (Riding,

FIGURE 2.1 George Frideric Handel in 1749. Engraving by John Faber the Younger, after Thomas Hudson. Source: Victoria & Albert Museum.

Burrows and Hicks 2001). Unsurprisingly, eighteenth-century nuisance and property law developed, in part, to regulate neighborly relations in such as these Mayfair streets. "At times," reflects Riding, "Handel must have been a very noisy neighbour" (Riding, Burrows and Hicks 2001: 73).

The eighteenth century, as mentioned, much prized equal treatment under law. Sir John Hawkins (1719–1789), attorney-turned-music-historian, recalled that Handel "would frequently ... [remark] on the constitution of the English government; and he would often speak of ... [its toleration of his Lutheranism] as one of the great felicities of his life" (Hawkins [1776] 1963: 911; quoted Burrows 2012: 495). Handel was a Crown pensioner and though, like commercial people generally, he took his chance under the rule of law, the pension cushioned him from "expensive" failures as *Solomon* eventually proved (Dean 1959: 526; Vickers 2007: 14; Hunter 2015: 175–190). Were Mendes established as *Solomon*'s poet, it might mean that less specifically Christian, and more legal, factors are important to understand its context. Mendes held properties in London, Norfolk, and Surrey (Pink 2015). The years after 1746 witnessed fiery discussion of what, in 1753, became the Jewish Naturalisation Bill. For a wealthy British-born Jew, post-1688 conversion to Christianity, though prudent, e.g., to hold land with clear legal protection

(Henriques 1908: 191–195; Roth 1964) and to widen commercial opportunities (Perry 1962), was not imperative. Though outsiders, both Handel and Mendes actively chose the Hanoverian regime.

SOLOMON AND THE BRITISH CONSTITUTION

The choice of Solomon (see Sam. 2:16, 2.19; Kgs 1:1–11; Chron. 1:22, 1:28, 1.29; Chron. 2:1–9 (Smith 1995: 352) and Josephus (*Jewish Antiquities* 8.2–7)[9] (Smither 1977)) is significant. Its context was an "identification between contemporary Britain and ancient Israel in Handel's oratorios" (Hunter 2015: 47). Solomon was important to Freemasons (Pink 2015), a signification that will deepen with contextual understanding of Handel's works. Handel's audience would anyway have been familiar with Solomon, since all would have attended church or synagogue (the law still required weekly attendance at the parish church).[10] The significance of Solomon's name (Chron. 1:22) is a pun: he is "a man of ... peace (*shalom*)" (quoted Weitzman 2011: 8). That his importance endured for post-1688 Protestants is clarified by the poet's "use of ... the future perfect ... the rhetorical trick of designating the present marvellous action as the inspiring historical record of the future" (Smith 1995: 258):

> Swell, swell the full Chorus to Solomon's Praise,
> Record him, ye Bards, as the Pride of our Days;
> Flow sweetly the Numbers that dwell on his Name,
> And rouse the whole Nation in Songs to his Fame.

Important for liberty is the fact that Solomon is a *king*. "The English would be less free if there were no king in England," said Montesquieu (quoted Rahe 2009: 279). "Monarchy was neither secularized nor demystified by the Glorious Revolution nor by the 1702 Act of Settlement" (Gerrard 1994: 188). Anne had touched for scrofula ("the king's evil") as late as 1714 (Somerset 2012; Boswell [1791] 1980). Solomon's peace was secured by conciliation, not conquest. He was "quickly able to establish peace on all his borders ... through diplomacy—treaties, alliances and trade" (Weitzman 2011: 10–11). The Treaty of Aix-la-Chapelle, ending the War of Austrian Succession (Marshall 1974), "was being negotiated while Handel was writing *Solomon*" (Smith 1999: 9). How different such peaceful preoccupations were from those of the oratorios premiered in Handel's earlier seasons: *Judas Macchabaeus* (above) and *Joshua* (Anon. 1748a). Each of these consolidated state-building by celebrating the destruction of alien religious-political values.[11] *Solomon*'s more peaceful preoccupations were replicated in *Susanna* (Anon. 1748b), possibly also Mendes' work, and portraying a pastoral idyll disrupted by the lust, mendacity and murderous intent of two elderly judges, aroused by watching the beautiful Susanna bathe. "*Shalom* [*sc.* Solomon]," though, "does not merely convey the absence of war," Weitzman writes. "[I]t also conveys completion or wholeness ... which anticipates another aspect of his life, Solomon's role as a completer" of the temple David could not build because of his bloodstained hands (2011: 11). This wholeness suggests, too, abundant commerce, apposite in what Montesquieu called Britain's "commercial empire" (Spector 2012: 18). Coffee houses, arenas of constitutional debate (Cowan 2005), were an everyday indication of Britain's commercial and maritime might. The oratorio often reminds us that Solomon is the son of David, *not* David himself: the completer, *not* the founder (Smith 1995).

Solomon is an oratorio, not an opera, and was therefore performed without stage sets or character costumes. By the time of *Solomon*'s composition, Handel had not composed an *opera* since *Deidamia* in 1740 (Best 2009). Oratorio, as sacred church drama, originated in seventeenth-century Rome (Keates 2016), but Handel transformed it, in mid-eighteenth-century Britain, into sacred theatrical drama (Smither 1977). The process was problematic, some exception being taken to theatrical mounting of sacred works (Hogwood 2007). However, oratorios' significance transcended the religious, as implied by the following description:

> [A]ll of them were performed in the manner of a concert without scenery, costumes or stage action, although the soloists were presumably mindful of the dramatic nature of their contributions in most works. They were probably placed at the front of the platform, with the chorus and the orchestra positioned behind them. It seems that on some occasions the venue was specially decorated ... and it was reported that at the first performance of *Deborah* "The Pit and Orchestre were cover'd as at an Assembly, and the whole House illuminated in a new and most beautiful manner" (*Daily Advertiser*, 20 March 1733). (Landgraf and Vickers 2009: 456)

To those in boxes and stalls, this would have been a representation of co-operation among "the Quality" of Georgian state, church and society: male soloists in fine coats and wigs; female soloists in fashionable dresses and wigs; the Chapel Royal choristers in their surplices. The co-ordination of these with a large orchestra required Handel's wise management,[12] especially since "the soloists were [generally] situated as a group away from the remainder of the singers" and "the chorus ["may have" been placed] in two facing blocks" (Butt 2009: 146). *Solomon's* orchestration was utterly sumptuous. Handel "must have commanded a very large orchestra at this period ... Nothing, it is clear, was to be stinted for the golden age ... Apart from strings and continuo instruments, the orchestra includes flutes, oboes, bassoons, horns, trumpets, and drums" (Dean 1959: 525). Recordings of performances using eighteenth-century instruments, or accurate copies, illustrate the dramatic effect of all this. The use of a "serpent" (Simon 1985: 245) in Paul McCreesh's recording of *Solomon* is inspired (McCreesh 1999). This was a military instrument (McCreesh 1999) and the association of property, commerce and a militia was an eighteenth-century constitutional axiom (Smith 1995). The serpent's mellow bass in the march-like double-chorus, "From the Censer curling rise" (Bärenreiter 2014: 122), together with kettledrums and natural trumpets, suggests military might as the foundation of commercial prosperity. The dispositions of audience and musicians portrayed both order and a porosity between performers and audience. The reference above to an "Assembly" (of the Quality) underlines a constitutional significance. So too does the fact that there seems to be no published record of a riot at an oratorio.[13] Schmitt's characterization of a constitution, as a "unity" arising "out of 'a pre-established, unified will'" of the people, "that is, 'something existential', [that] establishes 'the unity in political and public law terms'" (1928: 65, quoted Loughlin 2010: 212) is entirely apposite here. Rather than *having* a constitution, the state of the United Kingdom of Great Britain *was* a "constitution, in other words, an actually present condition, a *status* of unity and order" (Schmitt 1928: 60, quoted Loughlin 2010: 212). The constitution, like the oratorio performance was, importantly, in Loughlin's words—"a scheme of intelligibility." The performance continued even "if the people singing or performing change[d] or if the place where they perform change[d]," since "unity and order" subsisted in the oratorio and its score," exactly "as the unity and order of the state resides in its constitution" (Schmitt 1928: 60, quoted Loughlin 2010: 213). A performance of *Solomon* was therefore more than an entertainment: it was an *enactment*, a manifestation, of the constitution. It was "'the concrete, collective condition of political unity and social order of a particular state [i.e., Georgian Britain]'" (Schmitt 1928: 60, quoted Loughlin 2010: 213).

Covent Garden Theatre[14] as the venue for *Solomon* was important too. Comparable chiefly with the Theatre Royal Drury Lane, Covent Garden was a "patent theatre," deriving its right "to present theatrical entertainments not from licences issued by the Lord Chamberlain or the local authority, but by direct grant from the Crown" (Sheppard 1970: 1, 71). Moreover, the Licensing Act 1737,[15] besides imposing stage censorship, had restricted theatrical performances to Covent Garden and Drury Lane as two of only three possible venues (Battestin 2008). The Theatre Royal Covent Garden was built on land the freeholder of which was the Duke of Bedford. In order to mount his oratorio season, Handel used to enter into some type of occupation agreement with John Rich (1692–1761), who held a lease of the theater from the Duke. In 1749, the theater was just over fifteen years old, it could hold an audience of around 1,400, and it evidently had a good acoustic (Landgraf and Vickers 2009). Yet its status as a theater royal did not necessarily imply frequent royal attendance. George II rarely attended theatrical performances after Queen Caroline's death in 1737 (Burrows 2012), so it is unlikely that he experienced *Solomon*. Frederick, Prince of Wales (1707–1751), possibly *did*, however (Taylor 1984; McGeary 2009). Frederick was identified with Bolingbroke's work (Gerrard 1994) and, though Handel's relationship with Frederick was scratchy (Simon 1985), as the heir apparent, many saw in him a gilded, unified, future for Britain. Frederick was also the intended dedicatee of Montesquieu's *The Spirit of the Laws* (Rahe 2009). If a performance of *Solomon* illustrated Bentley's definition of drama, i.e., "A impersonates B while C looks on" (Bentley (1975), quoted Carlson 2014: 2), what Frederick and the audience at Covent Garden saw, in 1749, was the British Constitution as it might yet be, with Frederick at the center.

Solomon's wordbook, for the audience to follow, had two further features. First, as frequently, the composer was given as "*Mr.* HANDEL" (italics added), denoting "property or professional standing" (Langford 1989: 65; Hunter 2015: 14, 175). Secondly, it was "Printed for J. and R. TONSON and S. DRAPER in the Strand," though the printer's name was absent. Jacob Tonson (1714?–1767) and Richard Tonson (1717–1772), booksellers sympathetic to Whiggism, employed their relative, Somerset Draper (bap. 1706–1756) "as ... their financial agent and negotiator of terms with authors" (Robarts 2009: 195, 644). Handel presumably chose them carefully and Draper would have negotiated with Handel in the composition room at Brook Street.[16] Tonsons and Draper were cleverly bi-partisan: though Whigs, they were intimate with the Tory Dr. Samuel Johnson (1709–1784) (Boswell [1791] 1980). Someone who wanted to experience *Solomon*, complete, in Handel's lifetime, could only have done so under Handel's direction, at Covent Garden, with non-factional, like-minded people.

CONSTITUTIONAL ARCHITECTURE IN *SOLOMON*

Part I, Scene 1, of *Solomon* opens with the king among his priests, including Zadok, and some of his people. It seems that they are in the temple courtyard at Jerusalem as the temple is being finished. Except that the temple is the place of judgment, Smith's suggestion (1995) that temple- and palace-building shows a responsible use of public funds, may perhaps be doubted, given what were regarded as legitimate public purposes for taxation in the eighteenth century (Snape 2017). Solomon's God-given wisdom (Swanston 1990) shapes a constitution. Because of the Revolution settlement "our [Protestant] Religion is incorporated into our civil Constitution, and become a legal Part of our Property," as a contemporary sermon had it (Rogers 1749, quoted Smith 1995: 321). In an accompanied recitative, Solomon, as "the instigator of temple worship" (Smith 1995: 90), ascribes order to God and invokes God's presence in the temple:

> Almighty Pow'r! who rul'st the Earth and Skies,
> And bad gay Order from Confusion rise;
> Thy finish'd Temple with thy Presence grace,
> And shed thy heav'nly Glories o'er the Place.

The "gay order" of creation is structured by laws, in Montesquieu's words, "laws as invariable as those of the fatality of the Atheists" (Montesquieu [1748/1750] 1949: 1). Caterina Galli (1719/24–1804), something of a specialist in male character roles, was the first to sing the part of Solomon. Perhaps there was a stir in the audience as, sumptuously attired, she rose in the flickering candlelight, to sing this air. Earlier in the scene, a chorus of priests has exhorted the people to begin praise to the Almighty in which, not only the Israelites, but also "distant Nations" will "[r]esound" their "Maker's Name ... / And glow with holy Flame." All peoples will discover their true nature as creatures of the Creator and of a divinely inspired ordering of each political society.

A king so blessed is blessed, too, in his erotic relations. In Scene 2, the company is joined by Solomon's Queen, Pharaoh's daughter. Solomon's Queen was originally sung by Giulia Frasi (fl. 1740–c. 1772), described as having a "sweet and clear voice" but criticized for being "cold and unimpassioned" (Burney, quoted Hurley 2009c: 244–245). This is at odds with the fact that, on the evidence of the score, she must have "excelled in expressive music" (Hurley 2001: 254).[17] In a biblical extrapolation, king and queen declare their love for each other in the presence of priests and people (Smith 1995). They are not physically present in a garden but, as Swanston suggests, in his theological study of Handel's oratorios,[18] to have an understanding of nature is to participate in the divine ordering of things (Swanston 1990). Apprehension of their place in creation is what gives human beings a sense of the natural law. That sense is best gained in the garden of the mind (Swanston 1990). In the second section of the subsequent Air, Solomon's Queen recalls her place in that order:

> But completely bless'd the Day,
> On my Bosom as he lay,
> When he call'd my Charms divine,
> Vowing to be only mine.

Solomon's natural order is *not* the Hobbesian state of nature: it is not the "war ... of every man, against every man" (Hobbes [1651] 1955: 82). It is instead an order of divinely inspired right reason, evoked in the music and imagery of the subsequent numbers. Eventually, the Nightingale Chorus ushers king and queen to their bed. For the Patriot King, how fleeting is its soft embrace (Smith 1995: 271).

With two choirs, Part II opens in blaze of drums and trumpets (Bärenreiter 2014), as a prelude to translating these natural understandings into a juridical context. The divine source of Solomon's wisdom is emphasized (Scene 1) and the chorus hail Solomon's concomitant happiness:

> FROM the Censer curling rise
> Grateful Incense to the Skies;
> Heaven blesses David's Throne,
> Happy, happy Solomon.

Live, live for ever, pious David's son;
Live, live for ever, mighty Solomon.

The audience's older nobility may have relished the echo, in the closing phrases, of the Coronation service in Westminster Abbey, on October 11, 1727.[19] Solomon, though, must sit in judgment. An Attendant (Part II, Scene 2) announces the petition of "two Women," one of whom is declaring "her Story to the Crowd," while the other carries a "new-born Infant." The attendant sings that they "beseech the King's Command / To enter here." "Admit them straight," replies the Patriot King, "for when we mount a Throne, / Our Hours are all the People's, not our own."

The women appear with the baby (Part II, Scene 3). The audience see the wordbook designate them as "1 Harlot" and "2 Harlot." The audience would not have been surprised by female litigants: only "married women were disqualified from suing at common law by the doctrine of coverture" (Lemmings 2011: 63), and even this was relaxed in non-common-law jurisdictions. Whether or not the harlots are "ladies of Solomon's court" (Burrows 2012: 496), they are certainly outcasts, "personifications of the threat that uncontrolled female sexuality represents" (Rooke 2012: 171). How Solomon "deals with them in their otherness … determines the picture of … [Solomon] as wise or foolish" (Rooke 2012: 171). The judgment scene might therefore be a comment on contemporary concerns about lack of access to justice by the poor. Their lack of representation is suggestive.

Poetry and music establish both the trepidation of the first harlot (Giulia Frasi) and the stridency and aggression of the second. The first harlot explains that they lived together and that each of them "bore a Son." However, the first harlot continues, the second's baby died. So, while the first harlot and her baby were fast asleep, the second stole the surviving baby from the first's arms, substituting her own "Lump of lifeless Clay." All of this would have been sung in the pure tones for which Frasi was famous (Hurley 2009c). In a trio (in F sharp minor),[20] the first harlot claims possession of the child (in "hesitant dotted rhythms"), interrupted by the second's accusations of falsehood (in "hammered-out even notes"), as Solomon muses that "Justice holds the lifted Scale" (in a "stately motion based, in a pun Handel must have enjoyed, on the step-wise motion of a musical scale") (Harris 2014: 222). The second harlot, admonishing Solomon to "be just, and fear the laws," cuts to the chase:

I cannot varnish o'er my Tongue,
And colour fair the Face of Wrong:
This Babe is mine, the Womb of Earth
Intomb'd, conceals her little birth.

The second harlot was sung by Sibilla Gronamann, "Handel's second soprano in 1748 and 1749," who had sung in *Alexander Balus* and *Susanna* (Hurley 2001: 265; Gilman 2014: 191–193). Gronamann was an experienced ballad-opera singer and it seems clear that her less refined soprano voice projected a charactherful contrast with that of Frasi's on that March evening in 1749 (Hurley 2001; Bärenreiter 2014). The earth, at once womb and tomb, suggests a Nature different from that which inspires natural law's "right reason."

What a difficult case this is. "[W]ith no witnesses and by implication no guarantee of honesty from the self-interested … [parties], it appears utterly intractable" (Rooke 2012: 173). Nonetheless, Solomon's judgment is swift: equal division of the baby by the "faulchion." The second harlot instantly (in F major)[21] hails Solomon's "Sentence" as "prudent and wise," the violins of the orchestra giving out "a quick turning figure ... that curls like a contemptuous sneer" (Harris 2014: 222). There is a moment of horror. Possibly, for some of the audience, Rubens' *The Judgement of Solomon* (*c.* 1617). (Figure 2.2) flashes across their mind.[22] F minor (Burrows 2012) signals the first harlot's distress (Bärenreiter 2014). "Can I see my infant gor'd," the first harlot chokes, the orchestra silent under these words, signifying "her apparent loss of all support" (Harris 2014: 222–224) and hence – possibly – the momentary suspension of all natural law. With "'ever more searing" silences from singer and orchestra, the first harlot "heartbreakingly resolves [see Harris 2014: 224)] (Handel writes 'risoluto' in the score)":

> Rather be my Hopes beguil'd [pause],
> Take him all [pause]—but spare my Child. (See Harris 2014)

So Solomon gives judgment for the first harlot, "in an *accompagnato* that modulates from B flat major to G sharp minor" (Burrows 2012: 428). In a duet, the first harlot praises the king and the king praises God (in E major),[23] again ascribing the penetrating insight of *Solomon*'s judgment to divine inspiration. A chorus of Israelites extols Solomon's wisdom in A major. Solomon has affirmed the importance of domestic stability of possession.

FIGURE 2.2 The Judgement of Solomon. Peter Paul Rubens, *c.* 1617. Source: National Gallery of Denmark.

> From the East unto the West,
> Who so wise as Solomon?
> Who like Israel's King is bless'd ?
> Who so worthy of a throne?

"Dramatically and musically, this is one of Handel's most colourful scenes, with a lively tonal progression" (Burrows 2012: 429). This musical evocation of Solomon's thwarting of the second harlot's bad faith extols exactly what Montesquieu approved in a speech of 1725 (Spector 2015). It also transforms the first harlot (Rooke 2012). Rooke points out that the first harlot is turned by the judgment away from self-interestedness (the definition of "harlotrous") to self-sacrifice and to concern "for nothing so much as the good of her child" (2012: 171). Thus transformed by good laws applied wisely, she is in a position to give thanks for the laws under which she and her baby live. It harks back to the Northampton Assize sermon. The subsequent reference to "armed Bands" might in turn be taken as an allusion to the advance of the Jacobite army in 1745 and the transformed first harlot's new support for the regime and for the militias (Smith 1995) that mustered to confront the Jacobites.

Part III begins with one of only two instrumental movements in *Solomon*, "the Arrival of the Queen of Sheba," whose "rhythmic vitality represents ... the general flurry of making ready" for the reception of Nicaule, Sheba's queen (Dean 1959: 523). Nicaule, while certainly impressed by the temple, is keen to hear and know Solomon's "heav'nly Strain." If Part II was about "stability of possession" in domestic law, then Part III is about the other aspect of "the laws of nations," the mutual duties and rights of princes. Stability of possession in the latter context involves promoting peace between princes. Accordingly, Solomon directs a courtly choral masque, evidently to demonstrate the harmonious accord between his people and their sovereign. Its effect upon Nicaule is to strengthen the natural, though fragile (Hume [1739–1740] 1978), bond of peace between her and Solomon. Nicaule's response raises the possibility of the two other "fundamental rules of justice" (Hume [1739–1740] 1978: 567) being observed: the observation of promises (through "alliances" and "leagues") (Hume [1739–1740] 567; Koskenniemi 2009: 27–28) and commerce through the consensual transfer of property (Hume [1739–1740] 1978). These two elements of the laws of nations are comprised in the coda to Bolingbroke, people being "busy to improve their private property and the public stock," and the ocean being covered by fleets "bringing home wealth by the returns of industry" (Bolingbroke [1749] 1997, quoted Smith 1995: 310). The consequent accumulation of gold, the mercantilist axiom of prosperity, consequent on Solomon's "jealousy of trade" (Hont 2010: 1), is expressed in Solomon's avowal that "Gold now is common on our happy Shore" (quoted Smith 1995: 311). British diplomats at Aix had tried, and failed, to negotiate a secure and comprehensive peace treaty and peaceful relations in India between the East India Company and its French counterpart (Marshall 1974). At the masque's conclusion, Nicaule (sung also by Frasi) pays Solomon tribute and bids him farewell in a richly harmonized air, "Will the Sun forget to streak?" designed "to give Frasi the sort of slow, solemn air at which she excelled" (Hurley 2001: 258). She is as likely to forget the splendor of Solomon's kingdom, or his wisdom, as the sun is to forget to rise each morning. The "Grand Chorus" that closes the oratorio proclaims, epigrammatically, that:

> The Name of the Wicked shall quickly be past;
> But the Fame of the Just shall eternally last.

So, in *Solomon*, law and justice figure at the center of a triptych emphasizing the origins of justice, its benefits at home and its emulation abroad. The constitution is constantly reaffirmed in successive wise governmental judgments. Smith suggests that political references in a Handel libretto *might* be intended to prompt the hearer to *action*. That such references are also "intended to affect attitudes" is a given (Smith 1995: 210). Not only does this discussion demonstrate the truth of Smith's arguments, it also underlines Harris' inferences about how Handel's friends clung on to hopes that litigation would ultimately vindicate the righteous. Harris shows how (Harris 2014), in March 1749, Mary Delany (one of Handel's longest-standing London friends) would have been preoccuppied by a suit in Chancery against her husband, the Rev. Patrick Delany, ultimately unresolved until 1758.[24]

EMBODIMENTS OF CONSTITUTIONAL VALUES

In eighteenth-century constitutional law, the Crown's prerogative included three key functions: as "a constituent part of the supreme legislative power," as the Crown-in-Parliament; as "the fountain of justice," being the "distributor" of judicial authority; and, "with regard to foreign concerns," as "the delegate or representative of his people" (Blackstone [1765–9] 2016 I: 169; 171; 163). A performance of *Solomon* evidently communicated the exemplary discharge of these functions by an ideal British monarch. Here, we consider how Handel and his poet communicated the *qualities* necessary in the individual discharging them. First, Handel specifically allocated the role of Solomon to a contralto.[25] Though, today, Solomon is often assigned to a male alto, Handel's choice suggests that Solomon transcends the sex of the individual singing the role. Emphasis is thereby placed, not on the physical being, but on their virtues. In the Apocrypha, wisdom is female (Wis. 8:2). Secondly, Solomon's virtues are portrayed through the responses of other characters to his royal actions. Solomon's qualities alone do not make the constitution but they enhance its effectiveness in a way that the failings of a lesser monarch would undermine it. The other, minor, characters cannot always fully grasp Solomon's qualities. Solomon's Queen perceives that he is blessed "with each Virtue." When Solomon's virtues are not before her eyes, she shuns the court "and loath[es] the Light." As "Pharaoh's daughter," she does not know of Solomon's God, nor does she specifically praise Solomon for his wisdom.

Thirdly, Solomon is not merely knowledgeable but *wise*. Though he realizes he has been blessed with knowledge, this would be as nothing, were it not for his wisdom. He understands what he must do with his knowledge. Even if Solomon could name "each Herb and Flow'r / That drinks the Morning Dew," his judgments would be the "idle Claim" of a "Pedant," because he would have lost "the Substance" (Swanston 1990: 127). Solomon is therefore "happy," not only in his subjective state of mind, but also in the Aristotelian sense of being superior, as partaking in the divine (Aristotle [*c*. 350 BC] 2004; McMahon 2006). Solomon's piety and wisdom together make him mighty:

Prais'd be the Lord, from him my Wisdom springs;
I bow in-raptur'd to the King of Kings …

Such wisdom should come to all God-fearing Anglican Protestant kings, and to those right-thinking people who support them in the constitution. At his Coronation, George II *first* took the coronation oath, as prescribed by the Coronation Oath Act 1688,[26] to uphold the laws, and was *then* presented with the Bible (Blackstone [1765–9] 2016: I;

Smith 1995).[27] As in politics, so in art. Solomon has the knowledge: divine inspiration will guide him in deploying it. Solomon does not initially know, any more than we do, who the real mother of the baby is. Recognizing this, he nevertheless knows what to do, because he has the ability "to trace with Art, / The secret Dictates of the human Heart." His initial decree, to cut the baby in two, becomes a means of *proof*. His ability to parse the human heart comes from his "sympathy" (e.g., (Hume [1739–1740] 1978: 317), the second harlot's inability from her lack of it.

> She who could bear the fierce Decree to hear,
> Nor send one sigh, nor shed one pious Tear,
> Must be a Stranger to a Mother's Name—
> Hence from my Sight, nor urge a further Claim

Whether this Solomon is an idealized portrait of George II or a depiction of an ideal of virtuous kingship, intended to move Frederick (as heir), and those who support him, is arguable. On the latter, the libretto does seem to owe something to Bolingbroke. On the former, however, not only was George II Handel's patron (Young 1950) and patron of the Foundling Hospital (Hogg 2009), in the chapel of which—incidentally—Handel directed excerpts from *Solomon* on May 27, 1749 (Dean 1959), George II was in a similar relation to George I, as the second of a new royal dynasty, as Solomon was to David. The view is taken here that, whether Solomon is George II or an idealized Frederick is a subsidiary question. The key point is that it is a depiction of the perfection of the British Crown and its prerogatives, as discharged by someone of high virtue.

In the eighteenth-century constitution, both the Archbishop of Canterbury and the Lord Chancellor were key officers of state, there being "no clear-cut distinction between churchmen and statesmen" (Jarrett 1965: 52). As the Hardwicke quotation shows, the Lord Chancellor had close access both to the king and also to other ministers. "Hardwicke's chancellorship," writes Underhill, "was probably decisive in establishing the convention that the Lord Chancellor should be a member of the Cabinet [council]" (1978: 150). The archbishop, at least early in the eighteenth century, "sat in the Cabinet Council and as late as 1713 a bishop was employed on a diplomatic mission, as one of the plenipotentiaries at the Peace of Utrecht" (Jarrett 1965: 52). Whether the prophet Nathan (not portrayed) was to be associated with the Chancellor, and Zadok (see Smith 1995) with the Archbishop or another senior Anglican cleric, is debatable. Zadok was originally sung by the popular ballad-opera tenor Thomas Lowe (*c*. 1719–1783), whom audiences recognized from *Alexander Balus* (Glowotz 2009) and from his first elderly judge in *Susanna* HWV 66, (Vickers 2009), so maybe some character traits lost to us were conveyed in 1749. Zadok's place in the drama may allude to the clerical origins of the Lord Chancellor's office (Underhill 1978). Such notions can be suggestive only. The Lord Chancellor and the Archbishop, whichever is associated with Zadok, had constitutional roles that required wisdom, that merged public and private, and that exhorted subjects' loyalty to sovereign and constitution. The Zadok of *Solomon* is the priest who, with Nathan, "anointed Solomon [king]" (Kings 1:39, adapted) in Handel's celebrated 1727 Coronation Anthem, *Zadok the Priest*, HWV 258.[28] In *Solomon*, Zadok appreciates that, with Solomon, it is not knowledge but wisdom that is important:

> Search round the World, there never yet was seen
> So wise a monarch, or so chaste a Queen.

The Archbishop had a role in relation to the royal household. Zadok, too, appreciates from familiarity the multiplicity of Solomon's virtues:

From Morn to Eve I cou'd inraptur'd sing
The various Virtues of our happy King;
In whom, with Wonder, we behold combin'd,
The Grace of Feature with the worth of Mind.

Bishops were expected to preach loyalty to the monarch. Hardwicke's friend, Thomas Herring (1693–1757), who became the Archbishop of Canterbury in 1747, had (in September 1745) "preached in York Minster a sermon couched in the strongest terms of loyalty and zeal" to, and for, the House of Hanover (Sykes 1934: 76). Looking at Solomon, sings Zadok, is like standing "[o]n Jordan's sedgy Side" and comparing the various trees growing there. In fancy, Zadok is standing with a country gentleman on an exotically-planted estate. Solomon is like "the tall palm that lifts the Head," its "tow'ring branches" being such that we are "scornful" of "each meaner Tree" (i.e., lesser men or pretenders to the throne). "Thus thou art first of mortal Kings, / And wisest of the Wise." So the archbishop (who has placed the crown on the king's head (Blackstone [1765–1769] 2016: I) preaches the king's superiority to other pretenders. He also extols, through the "future perfect," the importance of Solomon's example to future kings (Smith 1995: 258).

The subject's constitutional duty to respond in kind to such benefits is illustrated principally by the first harlot. She, less exaltedly, shares Zadok's earlier insight about the superiority of wisdom to mere knowledge. In the duet of Part II, Scene 2, after Solomon has awarded possession of the baby to her, the first harlot's line is: "Thrice bless'd be the King, for he's virtuous and wise." However, she is grateful to the *King* rather than to God. "Thy Thanks be return'd all to Heav'n," is Solomon's pious admonition. But this is not just piety: reminding the people of this, and their response, is the lynchpin of the strengthening political order over which Solomon presides. Accordingly, the first harlot's response to the king's injunction is to exclaim: "How happy are those who in God put their Trust!" What the first harlot has in common with the second is that their characters are revealed by their responses to authority and judgment (Rooke 2012).

The duties of individual subjects to the sovereign and to the constitution can be explored only lightly in *Solomon*. The second harlot and the Levite restrict kingly virtue to mere virtuosity or prudential calculation (Benner 2017). The second harlot, mistaking Solomon's evidential test for the determination of the case, hails the sentence as "prudent and wise." She thereby "shows herself to be heartless and calculating," contemptuous of the constitution, and of the king and the law within it, and never describing herself as a mother (Rooke 2012: 180). The Levite, too, attempting to invoke the "future perfect" (Smith 1995: 258), associates greatness with virtue alone: "'Tis Virtue only makes a Monarch great." True, in the Levite's mouth, "virtue" may refer to a combination of Aristotelian virtues. It may refer to Machiavellian *virtù*—that is, "virtuosity" (Crick 2003: 57–59)—and, if so, it shows that the Levite has only a reductive sense of what makes a virtuous king. The Levite was originally sung by the bass Henry Reinhold (*d.* 1751), familiar to Handel's audience as the "Philistine Giant," Harapha, in *Samson*, and the second elderly judge and Chelsias in *Susanna* (Clausen 2009; Hurley 2009a; Hurley 2009b). These are all character roles and, given that the foregoing quotation follows immediately on the recitative in which "Solomon describes ... how he was led by God to the throne along a route that involved killing three of his opponents, including his half-brother Adonijah" (Smith 1995: 307; Rooke 2012: 178). This sense of kingship's moral ambiguity, and the redemptive potential of divine deference, may have afforded some balm to those involved in suppressing the '45.

In 1785, the poet William Cowper (1731–1800) reservedly acknowledged Handel as "the more than Homer of our age" (Cowper [1785] 1967: 233, quoted in Hogwood 2007: 242). Cowper, the homeric scholar, was making no idle comparison, since a Handel oratorio's capacity to evoke human qualities, out of which a political order could be wrought, was often lauded by Handel's contemporaries, as the epigraph suggests. Homer, as McClelland explains, was concerned to say how people should behave, both to gods and other mortals. Pervaded with "a sense of order and symmetry," the "Homeric world ... was a world fit to live in," even before politics entered the world (1996: 4–8). There is a sense of this with Handel, of an experience both didactic and exhortatory. The theater was no state but it portrayed what the state might become. "That we are at this time in a state of emancipation from the bondage of laws imposed without authority," wrote Hawkins in 1776, not about the constitution but about music, "is owing to a new investigation of the principles of harmony" by Handel at Covent Garden ([1776] 1963: 902). We are reminded of this in the masque of Part III. The virtues of Solomon and of the constitution are such that the people will willingly act in concert with him as their Sovereign.

CENTRALITY OF LAW TO THE CONSTITUTION

Solomon evokes the benefits of the unity of king, lords, and commons, especially the augmentation of state sovereignty through the willing co-operation of sovereign and nation. This is not Montesquieu's analysis, as mentioned above. Rather, the masque in Part III, involving Solomon and the chorus, is a clear depiction of the "mixed constitution," of the power of the Crown-in-Parliament as the ultimate legislative authority. The Crown-in-Parliament is where, said Blackstone, "absolute despotic power, which must in all governments reside somewhere, is entrusted ... [and it] can, in short, do everything that is not naturally impossible" (Blackstone [1765–9] 2016: I: 107, quoted Loughlin 2013: 30). Henry VIII's words characterizing the Crown-in-Parliament, in 1542, that "we at no time stand so highly in our estate royal as in the time of parliament, wherein we as head, and you as members, are conjoined and knit together into one body politic" (quoted Graves 1985: 80) would have been well known to many of Handel's audience. The expression of the Crown-in-Parliament, in the eighteenth-century constitution, as today, is the operative wording of a statute. "Be it enacted," that wording runs, "by the King's most Excellent Majesty, by and with the Advice and Consent of the Lords Spiritual and Temporal, and Commons, in this present Parliament assembled, and by the Authority of the Same, That ..." The masque gives musical expression to the spirit of constitutional unity thereby implied.

In the masque, sovereignty is depicted by Solomon directing his people in a succession of choral tableaux. Within them, we have an image of the sovereign's capacity to legislate, to confront various contingencies through music's laws. Solomon bids "his musicians perform in turn a 'lulling' measure, a stirring battle-piece, a tale of 'hopeless love ... full of death and wild despair', and a song of calm weather after storm" (Dean 1959: 513). "Handel ... makes the conditions of oratorio performance a part of his dramatic presentation," writes Swanston. "We have been encouraged to accept the singer on the platform, in contemporary evening dress, as Solomon in his court, and now we are being encouraged to see Solomon as our contemporary" (1990: 130). The music shows that, what might otherwise be discordant, is instead harmonious, like the laws of nature. Britain's political oligarcy of the 1740s, the people to whom the message of the oratorio is directed, need to listen. They correspond to the prosperous elite who can afford to subscribe to a season of oratorios. The bi-partisan co-operation in Parliament of the MPs drawn from this elite is what the Crown desperately needs. Members' legislative duties increasingly keep them at Westminster and away from their country estates (Langford 1991). In 1743, the *Craftsman* recalls a time when MPs had been content with lodgings in the Strand or Covent Garden (Langford 1991). These times are gone, though, and now they hold leases or freeholds in Westminster (Langford 1991). On March 18, 1749, Hardwicke's daughter-in-law, Jemima, Marchioness Grey (1722–1797), writes to a friend that, "I was at the new Oratorio of Solomon last Night, which has some prodigiously fine things in it" (quoted Hunter 2015: 61). Jemima belongs by marriage to a family well acquainted with the work of Montesquieu, through the *Persian Letters* and early copies in French of *The Spirit of the Laws*. When Charles Yorke, Hardwicke's second son,[29] meets Montesquieu, in October 1749, Yorke evidently tells the latter that Hardwicke, the Lord Chancellor, has already approvingly read Montesquieu's book (Shackleton 1961). The landed families, of which the Yorkes are one, are all Protestants, because no Catholic or Jew can be an MP (Perry 1962; Langford 1991). Though Catholics in fact possess land, they do so without legal protection. Purported inheritances, purchases or other acquisitions of rights in land by "Persons professing the Popish Religion" are void.[30] Whether a Jew can validly hold such an estate is undecided too (Henriques 1908: 193–194; Roth 1964). Hunter has successfully discredited the notions that a primary appeal of Handel's oratorios lies with a "rising middle class" (2015: 17) or that Jewish people attend in numbers and has confirmed that there is as yet no evidence for Catholic attendance. Instead, Hunter's work has suggested that *Solomon* may direct a specific constitutional message to this very small, yet decisively important, constituent. In support, Hunter quotes a letter-writer from 1738 (Fielding, apparently) stating that "every Body knows that ... [Handel's] Entertainments [oratorios] are calculated for the Quality only, and that People of moderate Fortunes cannot pretend to them" (Hunter 2015: 18). What *Solomon* conveys to this small group is what was discussed above. The constitution is never finished but is always being reconfigured. From the foundation of the state onwards, all is impermanent, but if those in authority are wise and God-fearing, all will be well. The music of the masque, in Part III, binds Solomon's people together with him and with God. Linking *Solomon*'s masque with seventeenth-century masques of Henry Purcell (1659–1695), Dean detects "a peculiar irony that the Jewish scriptures should have provided the raw material for an art whose true kin is the Parthenon frieze and the drama of Aeschylus and Sophocles" (1959: 515). It is no accident that, in the masque, Solomon invokes, not *harmony* but music, i.e., *mousikē* (Murray and Wilson 2004). ("Musick, spread thy Voice around, / Sweetly flow the lulling Sound.") This was the constitution *enacted*.

If the masque in Part III evokes the might of the Crown-in-Parliament, then the judgment scene of Part II depicts the Crown as the "the fountain of justice and general conservator of the peace of the kingdom" (Blackstone [1765–9] 2016: I: 171). The placing of the judgment scene before the choral masque (Part III) emphasizes that divinely inspired natural laws both predate and survive the initiatives of the legislator. The formation of a state cannot ignore these natural laws because they are sacred and immutable. *Solomon* invites the hearer to recognize the constitution as embodying an idea of justice existing in a pre-political reality. All of the virtues cultivated in Solomon's mind have been carried forward and instantiated in the political order, an exalted version—perhaps—of Montesquieu's Troglodytes. Nature, recalled by Solomon and his Queen in Part I, denotes closeness to God and an understanding of one's true being. The institution of political society, spiritually done, not only respects that fact, but multiplies the bounties that nature provides and that scripture celebrates. The judgment scene, in which Solomon wisely applies known laws, vindicates this world-view. At least three objections have been made (Smith 1995) but, for various reasons, they can be refuted.

The first objection is that, in *Solomon*, the king personally sits in judgment. James I's claim to sit as a judge had been rejected in *Prohibitions del Roy*.[31] Not even James II had claimed this right, even though judging is a king's prerogative (Lemmings 2011: 56). However, the king was the fountain of justice, even under the Revolution settlement. In an idealized evocation of the constitution, a king might well sit in judgment. Judges in Westminster Hall sat under the royal arms. The report of *Ashby v. White*, for example, appears under the heading "Pleas before the Lord the King at Westminster." The 1749 audience believes the Bible's literal truth and, in there, Solomon is the judge (Kings 1:16–27).

The second objection is that Solomon "makes ... [the law] up" (Smith 1995: 326). "It would have been perfectly possible," says Smith, for the poet "to insert at least some reference by Solomon to the known (Mosaic) Law as guiding him in his judgement" (1995: 327). Smith refers to a sermon similar to the assize sermon cited earlier, disparaging arbitrariness, stressing the fear of God, and extolling known laws. This objection, too, can be met. Solomon's is not a judgment as to the *law* but as to the *facts*. It is not about what constitutes a mother but who the mother is. The law is surely clear: the harlot with the better title gains possession of the baby. The rejoinder might be that what Solomon is "making up" is procedural law or the law of evidence (how to find out who the true mother is). Recall, however, that the audience is being asked to assume that there is nothing to guide Solomon here as to *which* known *evidential* rule to apply (Elster 1989). Solomon must rely on his God-given wisdom. A "Solomonic judgment" is, by definition, on the limits of rationality (Elster 1989: 128–129).

A third objection is that Solomon's relationship to the law is ambiguous (Smith 1995). The "clamour" of the Harlots is "for disputed Right." Common law was silent in their case but natural law favored stability of control or possession. Common law gave a right of custody or control only to a married father, not a mother, in relation to legitimate children (Blackstone [1765–9] 2016: I). The common law certainly did not recognize the relationship of unmarried mother and child (Blackstone [1765–9] 2016: I). However, natural law would have required possession to be protected and restitution for the dispossessed (Hume [1739–1740] 1978). Applying natural law to the case of the first harlot and her baby restates their legal relationship in property law terms consonant with the golden age. Such "corrective" or "commutative" justice relies on a "norm of equality" requiring "every victim of wrongdoing," including harlots, "to be compensated equally, regardless of merit" (Aristotle [c. 350 BC] 2004: 121; Fleischacker 2004: 19). *If* the first harlot had dispossessed the second, *then* the second would have been entitled to possession. This, however, did not happen. The second harlot's claim therefore fails. The attendant, sword and baby in either hand, is commanded to return the latter to the first harlot. Such a property law restatement of the issue, which is how the judgment scene was understood,[32] means that Solomon's judgment affords justice even to a harlot. Someone whose societal status denotes self-interest nonetheless gets redress. The first harlot regains the baby, not because she is good, but because the baby is *hers*. There is no need for judicial discretion: simply the wise application of a just rule. The first harlot, outcast no more, becomes part of political society.

CONCLUSIONS

Solomon had three performances in 1749, being revived only once, mangled, in 1759 (Dean 1959). Maybe its vision of the golden age passed with Frederick's death in 1751. *Solomon* is remarkable because the constitutional virtues of Britain's limited monarchy are illustrated by a naturalized Saxon and (possibly) a Christianized Jew through the choice of a biblical archetype, depicted in a musical triptych and surrounded by characters throwing into relief some key constitutional concerns. Property, different attitudes to which composer and poet demonstrate, is illustrated by a sacred subject in a secular context, by the true award of the baby and by the stability of property in law. The importance of rule by law, not men, is placed at *Solomon*'s heart. The masque evokes the legislative might of the Crown-in-Parliament, the judgment scene the unifying power of the Crown as the fountain of justice. *Solomon* exhorted its first audience, as the descendants of the beneficiaries of the Revolution settlement, to support Frederick, the Hanoverian heir. *Solomon* was addressed to the judges in the audience as surely as Hardwicke's words were addressed to a grand jury: "the laws of *England* are adapted, the best of any in the World, to the Security of the Property, the Liberty, the lives of Men" and "the Guard of this Constitution, the Price of the Blood of your Ancestors" (quoted Lemmings 2011: 128). *Solomon* and Hardwicke's words are vivid illustrations of the values against which three centuries of faith and ideology have reacted: socialism; feminism; Irish nationalism; anti-colonialism; Europeanization; anti-racism; welfarism; Catholicism; communism, and so on. The artistic beauties of *Solomon* command everyone's attention. However, the constitutional values it propounds, and the reactions they have provoked, are why *Solomon*'s enactment of the eighteenth-century constitution claims a twenty-first-century lawyer's attention.

CHAPTER THREE

Codes

REBECCA PROBERT

Codes may operate at different levels, and in a way that may be complementary or conflicting. Legal codes—whether in the narrow sense of an articulated body of legal rules or the broader sense of the principles underpinning a particular area—may or may not be consistent with the cultural norms of society. This in turn will affect how the law operates in practice, although, given the strong cultural norm of compliance with the law, compliance with any given legal requirement should not automatically be seen as evidence of its congruity with broader cultural attitudes.

The regulation of marriage and its alternatives in the Age of Enlightenment provides a particularly suitable case study of the relationship between legal and social codes. How couples should marry was the subject of written legal rules throughout the period, although the source of these rules changed from the church to the state, and that change has been seen as a form of codification of marriage. The rewritten rules have been widely seen as in conflict with cultural norms (Lasch 1974; Gillis 1985; O'Donovan 1985; Parker 1990), but in fact a study of both social practice and cultural artifacts suggests otherwise (Probert 2009).

Other aspects of marriage—for example *when* one married—were also regulated by the law, at least in the sense that there was a recognized minimum age at which one could legally marry, and a rather higher minimum age at which one's choice of spouse could not be gainsaid. These minima were, however, supplemented by social expectations about when one should marry. By contrast, the question of whom one could marry was left almost entirely outside the law—with the very narrow exception of members of the Royal Family—and left to depend for the most part on powerful cultural norms.

Whether one married was also subject to regulation, in that those living together outside marriage might find themselves subject to both community disapproval and religious sanctions, although the falling away of the latter and the emergence of a new approach to disputes arising out of illicit sexual relationships reveals much about the changing culture of the time. Exit from marriage, by contrast, was heavily regulated in the sense of being highly restricted, but provided fertile ground for would-be codifiers such as Bentham to set out their vision of what a future legal code should look like.

This chapter will accordingly trace the different codes that applied to whether, whom, when, and how one married, before looking at the limited regulation of life after marriage.

WHETHER ONE MARRIED

While a significant proportion of the population remained single—whether on account of preference or the lack of a suitable partner—the cultural norm was for couples to marry. Alternatives were attended with obstacles and disadvantages, which could be legal, religious, and social.

The legal disadvantages, it should be admitted, were heavily influenced by gender. Women who had been promised financial recompense for entering into a relationship outside marriage might find difficulty in enforcing such promises through the courts if the agreement was deemed to be contrary to public policy. Exactly what was seen as contrary to public policy shifted over the period: the first half saw men being relieved from promises made to prostitutes, on the basis that they could be assumed to have been "imposed on" by such "designing women"; after the mid-eighteenth century, however, it was those promises that assumed the continuation of the immoral relationship that were liable to be struck down (Probert 2012).

Children born outside marriage would be illegitimate, with no possibility of legitimation by a subsequent marriage, and only entitled to such support as the poor law could compel. Some men did make explicit provision for the children that they had fathered, and if so the law would respect their wishes. But the law did not assume that this was what a man had intended, and so any gift to one's "children" as a group would normally be construed as excluding those born outside marriage.[1]

Religion also remained a powerful force, both psychologically and institutionally (Houlbrooke 1989; Jacob 1996; Spaeth 2000). On the one hand, as Amanda Vickery has pointed out, "only marriage promised true sexual fulfilment for Christians" (2009: 79). On the other, there was the deterrent of the potential prosecution for fornication and adultery within the church courts, the possibility of which continued in some places well into the second half of the eighteenth century (Hinton 1994; Probert 2012).

Among the elite, however, it has been suggested that the Christian ideal of chastity was in conflict with a new code of libertinage, the latter being a code that by its nature involved the flouting of other codes. James Grantham Turner has drawn attention to the way in which a section of the elite displayed their sense of privilege and entitlement by behaving as if they were above the normal rules of society. It was a code that had its own language: dueling became a matter of "honor" and fornication and adultery were elevated to "gallantry" (Stone 1990; Dabhoiwala 1996; Turner 2002: 224; Rubenhold 2009; Thomas 2009).

The middle classes took a rather different view. As Keith Thomas has observed, "there is little evidence to suggest that the Hanoverian middle classes took a more sympathetic view of masculine sexual misconduct than their predecessors had done" (2009: 169). Indeed, some have taken the view that a distinctive code emerged among them in order to differentiate themselves from the moral laxity of the aristocracy: Margaret Hunt has commented that the term "whoring" was used to refer to almost any extramarital sex and was seen as "a sort of magnet vice, one that led inexorably to gaming, criminality, extravagance, and nonpayment of debts" (1996: 68). Parallels were drawn between the emulation of those higher up the social scale and illicit sexuality, most graphically in Hogarth's *Harlot's Progress* (Figures 3.1 and 3.2).

The cultural codes that applied to women were also rather different from those that applied to men. Sexual freedom was always, of course, more risky for a woman than for a man because of the risk of pregnancy. Elite status did not protect them from criticism,

FIGURE 3.1 Harlot's Progress, plate II. William Hogarth, 1732. Source: Wellcome Collection.

with "women of fashion who intrigue" being placed at the top of the hierarchy of harlots in *A Congratulatory Epistle from a Reformed Rake* (1758). As Hallie Rubenhold has noted, eighteenth-century instructive literature "was unequivocal in its threat of a dark and dejected fate for those women who 'turned out of the right path'" (2009: 173). Novels, too, provided numerous warnings as to the danger of flirtations and affairs. In Eliza Haywood's novel *The History of Miss Betsy Thoughtless* (1751), Betsy's even more thoughtless school friend Miss Forward engages in clandestine meetings that result in her pregnancy; her lover refuses to marry her, her child dies, her father casts her off, and she becomes mistress to a merchant. Not contented with this,

> as few women who have once lost the sense of honour, ever recover it again, but, on the contrary, endeavour to lose all sense of shame also, devote themselves to vice, and act whatever interest or inclination prompts them to; Miss Forward could not content herself with the embraces nor allowances of her keeper, but received both the presents and the caresses of as many as she had charms to attract. ([1751] 1986: 197)

The downward spiral was a familiar story.

There was, in addition, a change in the way that women were seen: "over the course of the eighteenth century the female body began to be seen as naturally chaste, rather than predictably sinful" (Gowing 2014: 136). While Defoe's Moll Flanders and Roxana

FIGURE 3.2 Harlot's Progress, plate V. William Hogarth, 1732. Source: The Metropolitan Museum of Art, Gift of Sarah Lazarus, 1891. 91.1.132. Courtesy www.metmuseum.org.

jumped willingly into bed, later female characters were depicted as falling prey to the wiles of seducers. Ultimately, though, motivations were less important than actions. The fate of Julia Delmond in Elizabeth Hamilton's *Memoirs of Modern Philosophers* (1800) was painted in even darker colors than that of her earlier eighteenth-century counterparts: persuaded by the philosophical arguments of Vallaton to elope, she is subsequently abandoned by him, pregnant, and despite the care of her forgiving friends, dies. She begs them to tell her mother "that I did not fall a prey to depraved inclination; that my judgment was perverted by argument, not seduced by flattery; and that when I yielded to the specious reasonings of my betrayer, I thought I was setting an example of high-souled virtue, which soared above the vulgar prejudices of the world" ([1800] 1992: Vol. 3, 300).

As a result, while no doubt many Georgian men had sexual relationships outside marriage, and some maintained mistresses both before and after marriage, these relationships were usually on a commercial footing. Some began as housekeepers or servants and the nature of the relationship changed over time (Rubenhold 2009; Vickery 2009). Others advertised themselves as desirous of putting themselves under the protection "of any person of rank and fortune" (Beauman 2011: 62) and could drive hard bargains about the terms of any such arrangement. Margaret Hunt (1996) has suggested that the figure of the prostitute exemplified both illicit sex and excessive expenditure, and it is true that novels abounded in warnings about the lack of frugality to be expected of mistresses. As Mr. Goodman expatiates in *The History of Miss Betsy Thoughtless*, while it was

> in the interest of a wife to be frugal of her husband's substance, because she must be a sharer in those misfortunes which the want of economy creates ... it is in the interest of a mistress to sell her favours as dear as she can, and to make the best provision she can for herself, because her subsistence is precarious, and depends wholly on the will of his who supports her. ([1751] 1986: 306)

In a similar vein, in Samuel Richardson's *Clarissa* (1747–1748), Belford muses on the problems of keeping a mistress, whose lack of security and separate interests encourage them either to lay money by for themselves or squander it.

And even those who did engage in longer-term relationships outside marriage might still pay some attention to social codes by respecting the need to be circumspect, depending on the context (Trudgill 1976). The Earl of Sandwich seems to have been more open about his longstanding relationship with Martha Ray when in London than in the presence of local gentry at his country house (Brewer 2004). A common theme in many relationships of this kind was the social gulf between the man and the woman: even where the man was free to marry (and often he was not), the woman he was living with was not someone he would have married. Prominent examples include the thirty-year relationship between Lord Thurlow, Lord Chancellor from 1778, and Polly Humphries, the daughter of the keeper of Nando's coffee house at Temple Bar; Edward Walpole MP's four children by a milliner's apprentice; and Erasmus Darwin's relationship with his children's governess (Uglow 2003; Gatrell 2006; Clarke 2009). In other words, these were men who in flouting one cultural norm as to whether one should marry were indicating their adherence to another: the very clear norms about *whom* one should marry.

WHOM ONE MARRIED

While it would be going too far to claim that marriage in the Age of Enlightenment was a union of equals, ideas of equality certainly played a role in shaping cultural norms about whom one should marry—and not marry. John Armstrong's *The Oeconomy of Love* (1736) expressed a typical Enlightenment view in not only extolling the pleasures of sex but also reassuring his readers that "What Nature bids / Is good, is wise, and faultless we obey" ([1736] 1739: 19); just as typical, however, was his advice on dealing with the potential consequences. If the woman was "well-form'd / Virtuous, and equal for thy lawful Bed" (25), he should marry her; if, by contrast, "abject birth, dishonourable, and mind / Incultivate or vicious, to that Height / Forbid her Hopes to climb" (25–26), provision should simply be made to secure her from penury. Such norms held good across the social spectrum: in Elizabeth Inchbald's *A Simple Story* (1791), Lord Margrave reconsiders his proposal of marriage to Matilda when he hears that she has been cast off by her father, since in his view she is no longer entitled to the same level of recognition. The same view, albeit expressed from a different standpoint, is evident in Henry Fielding's *Tom Jones* (1749) in the rebuke leveled at Molly Seagrim by her mother—who, although she herself gave birth a week after her wedding, clearly differentiates her conduct from that of her daughter's on account of the unlikelihood of a marriage resulting in the latter's case: "you must have to be doing with a gentleman, you nasty slut; you will have a bastard, hussy" ([1749] 1996: 158).

Given these strong cultural codes, unequal matches were unsurprisingly rare. For every real-life Pamela, there were many more maid-servants seduced (or raped) and discarded. The few memorable exceptions of elite men marrying outside their social sphere were mostly "the product of the impetuosity of youth, the complaisance of age or the delay of faculties" and "certainly do not mean that there was not a very powerful prejudice against marrying outside one's order" (Cannon 1984: 77). As the clergyman Henry Stebbing wrote when considering proposed reforms to the law of marriage, "the world *naturally* runs this way without the help of laws. The lower classes of men have it not in their *power* to marry above their rank, or very rarely. The rich and great have as rarely so little *pride* as to permit them to marry below theirs" (1754: 48).

So money played an important role as a marker of equality as well as a prerequisite for the marriage taking place. The challenges of marrying without money were dolefully set out by Ann Lovely in Susanna Centlivre's *A Bold Stroke for a Wife* (1718): "Love makes but a slovenly figure in that house where poverty keeps the door" ([1718] 1969: 8). In Tobias Smollett's last novel, *The Expedition of Humphry Clinker* (1771), Lydia Melford dutifully submits to her family's decision that the actor with whom she has fallen in love is not a suitable match for her; her reward for such submission is the happy discovery that "instead of debasing her sentiments and views to a wretched stroller, she had really captivated the heart of a gentleman, her equal in rank and superior in fortune" ([1771] 1995: 313). The marriage can therefore take place, since it unites affection with suitability. Indeed, most of Smollett's heroes and anti-heroes are just as concerned with money as with sex (which is saying something). A lack of concern about money on the part of a prospective spouse may in itself be a cause of concern: in *The Adventures of Roderick Random* (1748), Narcissa's failure to inquire into the state of Roderick's finances makes him begin to worry about the state of hers. And some suitors explain bluntly that whatever their feelings, they are unable to marry a woman without money: in Haywood's *The History of Miss Betsy Thoughtless*, Sir Bazil Loveit responds to the news that the father of his beloved is refusing to pay a portion on her marriage with the admission that while he would "gladly accept my charming girl on the conditions the old miser offers" he is "so unhappily circumstanced as to be under a necessity of having ready-money with a wife" ([1751] 1986: 328). Over sixty years later, Jane Austen has Colonel Fitzwilliam somewhat plaintively tell Elizabeth Bennett in *Pride and Prejudice* (1813) that the younger sons of an earl "cannot marry where they like ... Our habits of life make us too dependent, and there are not many in my rank of life who can afford to marry without some attention to money" ([1813] 2006: 179). Only the most naïve and romantic—such as Marianne Dashwood in *Sense and Sensibility* (1811)—ignored this reality. The more sensible Fanny in Charlotte Smith's *Desmond* (1792) is all too well aware of the financial intentions of the "insignificant butterflies" who "flutter about" her in public and rates their attentions accordingly: "there is not one of them who has the least notion of marrying a young woman without a fortune" ([1792] 2001: 218).

Yet as such portrayals suggest, there was an important difference between being practical and being mercenary. Marriage for money alone attracted social disapproval, with Hogarth's moralizing *Rake's Progress* and *Marriage a la fode* warning of the potential consequences, and the proponents of reform to the laws of marriage condemning the "infamous sharpers" and fortune-hunters who might otherwise prey on the young and impressionable.[2] The importance of combining *both* financial suitability and affection was neatly articulated by Eliza Barter, the heroine of John Shebbeare's novel *The Marriage Act* (1754), when she declared that she would never "marry for Love, to lie upon straw;

or marry for Title, without that Passion to improve it" (149). Companionate marriage was the Enlightenment ideal. Indeed, Douglas Hay and Nicholas Rogers link its rise directly to changing cultural norms, suggesting that "[w]ith the decline of patriarchalism as a political force after 1688 and the steady infusion of Enlightenment ideas, couples demanded greater emotional compatibility within marriage and cherished domesticity as an ideal that was fundamental to social order" (1997: 40).

The case law of the period also reflects this expectation that suitable matches would be supported by affection. This is particularly evident in the body of cases dealing with the validity and fulfillment of conditions making third-party consent to the marriage a prerequisite for the payment of a legacy or other promised sum of money. Judges did not approve of trustees who promoted and then vetoed particular marriages. In one case, the then Lord Chancellor Lord Hardwicke—a man not generally known for his championing of young lovers—held that the marriage should be regarded as having been celebrated with the necessary consent: the match was "proper," and "the withdrawing consent, after such encouragement … a delusion on the young folks" since it was "not to be imagined, after they had fixed their affection by such encouragement, they will be very easily induced to alter it."[3] In another, it was similarly noted that it "would be a most cruel thing to suffer young persons to contract and entertain affection, and then *ad libitum* withdraw the consent."[4] Still, if the circumstances so required, prudence had to prevail, and consent could be withdrawn: as a later Lord Chancellor noted,

> it would be very dangerous, as a general principle … to hold that, if at a particular time a person *in loco parentis*, as guardian, upon a conscientious sense of duty thinks himself required to give consent, and previously to the marriage is duly informed of circumstances, that ought to have operated at first to make him withhold his consent, if he has once given it, he shall not afterwards alter his mind.[5]

Suitability of course involved considering a wider range of factors than just money. The view was that similarity in age, rank, condition and education was important to secure the success of the marriage. This too was evident in the approach taken by the courts. The consent of the Court of Chancery was required for the marriage of any of its infant wards of court, and it was a contempt of court to marry a ward without such consent. In deciding whether approval should be given to any particular marriage, the court acted as it thought a prudent parent would do, with the suitor's family, fortune, and age all being taken into account.[6] If there was even a suspicion that a ward might be married "unequally," preventative action could be taken to break off the match.[7]

The suitability of a particular marriage was also taken into account by the court when assessing whether the validity of a particular marriage should be upheld. While differences in age and status did not justify the marriage being set aside, they did lead the union to be regarded with disfavor and made the courts more receptive to legal challenges. In one case the secret marriage of a teenage boy with his grandmother's maid was struck down on the basis that the banns had not been properly called. Such differences were, of course, a matter of degree: in *Sullivan v. Sullivan*[8] the judge did acknowledge that the differences between the parties might pose a risk to the success of the marriage, "for … it is not to be denied that two persons coming together with very different educations and systems of manners and habits are not likely to have that correspondence and harmony of mind, without which the comfort of a married life cannot exist."[9] Nonetheless he concluded, in a flight of romantic rhetoric, that "the passion which leads to marriage is apt to overleap these distinctions, and that marriage levels them all, both in legal and moral consideration."[10]

The contrast between the temperate affection noted by the mid-eighteenth-century judges and the acknowledgment of the influence of passion in this later case is a telling one. Over the period there was a growing emphasis on the importance of romantic love as a basis for marriage, rather than a passion that might destabilize it. Joanne Bailey has commented on the "increasing idealization of love between spouses," noting that there was a greater stress on emotional intimacy from the mid-eighteenth century (Bailey 2010).

Such emotional intimacy required similarity of tastes as well as status, as reflected in Susan Ferrier's *Marriage* (1818): the heroine Mary has been taught "that there was a love which even the wisest and most virtuous need not blush to entertain— the love of a virtuous object, founded upon esteem, and heightened by similarity of tastes, and sympathy of feelings, into a pure and devoted attachment" ([1818] 1997: 321). The increasing importance attached to similarity of tastes and views, and the inspiration of Rousseau's *Emile* raised the possibility of trying to create the perfect spouse. Fortunately most of these attempts were confined to the pages of fiction, but Thomas Day's combination of personal wealth, social radicalism, freedom from external regulation, and total selfishness, enabled him to put theory into practice. Taking two young girls from the Foundling Hospital, under the pretense that they would be serving an apprenticeship to a married friend, he subjected them to a series of mental and physical tests in order to determine which was more suitable to be his wife. One was quickly deemed unsuitable and was sent off to become a milliner's apprentice; he eventually proposed marriage to the other but subsequently (and happily for her, one feels) changed his mind following some minor infraction of the rules that he had laid down for her. Her story nonetheless provided fodder for novelists, including Maria Edgeworth, whose father Richard had actually married two of the women to whom Day had once proposed marriage (Moore 2013). Edgeworth's novel *Belinda* (1801) includes a depiction of Clarence Hervey's "romantic project of educating a wife for himself" ([1801] 1994: 362), a project he abandons when he realizes that his choice cannot be an intellectual companion for him.

There was, however, perhaps an element of wish fulfillment in this and other novels by female writers in foregrounding such companionship. In *Emma* (1815), it is the education, accomplishments, and good sense of Miss Taylor and Jane Fairfax that make them attractive consorts for Mr. Weston and his son Frank Churchill respectively, while Mr. Knightley contradicts Emma when she claims that Harriet Smith's beauty will ensure she can marry whomsoever she pleases, arguing that "Men of sense, whatever you may chuse to say, do not want silly wives" ([1815] 1985: 63). Yet it should not be forgotten that only a few years earlier Mary Wollstonecraft had had to take issue with Rousseau's ideas of female education, and that the female characters depicted by male novelists continued to be remarkable more for their beauty than for their intelligence.

Of course, this discussion of the type of spouse who was deemed suitable by the codes of the day raises a further question as to who *decided* on suitability. Here the law had more of a role to play. Parents had the power to give or refuse consent to the marriages of their minor children. Before 1754 a marriage without such consent could still be valid, if clandestine; after that date, however, marriages by license were void if either spouse was under twenty-one and the relevant person had not consented. Given the increased importance of precisely whose consent was needed, the statute also codified the requirements of the canon law into a clear list.

At the same time, there was clear disapproval of those who sought to force their sons or (more usually) daughters into uncongenial marriages. Clarissa Harlowe, under pressure from her family to marry the man they have chosen for her, argues forcefully that marriage is too serious a matter to be entered into without fully approving of the other party and points out that a marriage cannot take place without her "consent of heart, and assent of voice," which she is determined not to give (Richardson [1747–48] 1985: 322). In *Tom Jones*, Squire Western's response to the news that his daughter Sophia has fallen in love is meant to be seen as characteristically intemperate: "in love, without acquainting me! I'll disinherit her, I'll turn her out of doors, stark naked, without a farthing"; Squire Allworthy, by contrast, "would on no account be accessory to forcing a young lady into a marriage contrary to her own will" (Fielding [1749] 1996: 238, 302).

Writers warned that unhappiness would result from arranged marriages. In *The Present State of Matrimony: Or, The Real Causes of Conjugal Infidelity and Unhappy Marriages* (1739), "Philogamus" identified one of the principal causes of unhappiness in marriage as being "that preposterous, unequal, and sometimes unnatural way of matching our young people, very often without taking the least Care in examining and comparing the different Ages, Tempers, and Constitutions, of the Parties" (29). Yet his was not a plea for marriages based on love alone, his solution being that parents should allow the parties time to get to know one another before the marriage.

By the time of Susan Ferrier's *Marriage* (1818) the father who orders his daughter to marry can be ridiculed—and safely ignored: Lady Juliana's father states that she "shall marry for the purpose for which matrimony was ordained among people of birth—that is, for the aggrandisement of her family, the extending of their political influence—for becoming, in short, the depository of their mutual interest" ([1818] 1997: 2) but she elopes with the man she loves instead. Admittedly, the fact that this match does not prove successful leads her to harp on "the never fading joys that attend on wealth and titles," but her belief that in so doing "she was acting the part of a most wise and tender parent" (186) is satirized in turn.

Again, it is in legal texts that we find the expression of the ideal, rather than the depiction of the undesirable. Blackstone emphasized that the power to consent to a child's marriage should be exercised as a responsibility rather than a right: in his view, it was

> another means, which the law has put into the parent's hands, in order the better to discharge his duty; first, of protecting his children from the snares of artful and designing persons; and next, of settling them properly in life, by preventing the ill consequences of too early and precipitate marriages. ([1765–69] 2016: 440–441)

This provides a useful link to the next issue of when it *was* deemed appropriate to marry.

WHEN ONE MARRIED

The clear cultural norms as to when one should marry can be seen in the relatively late age at first marriage. While the mean age at first marriage fell noticeably over the course of the period covered by this book—from almost twenty-eight years for men and twenty-seven for women in the last quarter of the seventeenth century to twenty-five-and-a-half years for men and under twenty-four for women in the first quarter of the nineteenth (Wrigley 1981)—even the later figures were significantly higher than the legal minimum of twelve for girls and fourteen for boys, and higher even than the minimum age at which it was possible to marry without parental consent.

The poor, of course, were counseled to delay their marriage in order to ensure that they had sufficient resources to set up home together. Fielding's humble but honorable Joseph Andrews delays his marriage to his beloved Fanny Goodwill following the intervention of Parson Adams, who had "persuaded them to wait till a few years' service and thrift had a little improved their experience, and enabled them to live comfortably together" ([1742] 2003: 86). The clergyman-poet George Crabbe had similar advice for his parishioners and readers in *The Parish Register* (1807):

> DISPOSED to wed, e'en while you hasten, stay;
> There's great advantage in a small delay:
> Thus Ovid sang, and much the wise approve
> This prudent maxim of the priest of Love;
> If poor, delay for future want prepares,
> And eases humble life of half its cares;

In extolling the prudence of one pair, Reuben and Rachel, who laid by some savings from their work and gradually put together the necessities for their household, he painted a perhaps not entirely alluring picture of their eventual wedding, her hands "[e]mbrown'd by Winter's ice and Summer's sun" and his hair touched by gray, and both having lost "life's bloomy flush" ([1807] 1988).

Implicit in this were the advantages that might accrue from the death of a parent or other relative as opposed to the disadvantages that would all too often result from a precipitate birth. On the one hand, death might mean an inheritance of money or property enabling the couple setting up home (Davies 1909); on the other, the absence of reliable contraception meant that the number of children was best limited by delaying both marriage and sexual intercourse. Hera Cook, for example, notes the role played by "individual caution backed up by community sanctions" in delaying marriage until the couple "had sufficient savings and income to support a new separate household containing a wife and children"; and that "[m]ost unmarried women would not have sexual intercourse except with a partner who had agreed to marriage, and the man would not make this offer until he could afford to do so" (2004: 17).

Those for whom resources were not an issue were encouraged to delay marrying for a rather different reason. To quote Crabbe once more:

> If rich, delay shall brace the thoughtful mind,
> T'endure the ills that e'en the happiest find:
> Delay shall knowledge yield on either part,
> And show the value of the vanquish'd heart.

The importance of taking time to become acquainted with one's spouse before committing to marriage was a key theme in the debates over the Clandestine Marriages Act in 1753. The Earl of Hillsborough endorsed the importance of a month's preparation for marriage on the basis that such a delay could be no hardship where the union was based on a solid foundation; the love that he acknowledged to be a "proper ingredient" in the formation of such a union "ought to be a sedate and fixed love, and not a sudden flash of passion which dazzles the understanding, but is in a moment extinguished."[11]

The same idea was reflected in a number of novels towards the end of the period. Fanny Burney's *Camilla* (1796), Maria Edgeworth's *Belinda* (1801) and Jane Austen's *Pride and Prejudice* (1813) all featured hasty marriages founded on either simple attraction or financial calculation and contrasted such unions with those entered into on the basis of reason, after trial and experience of each other. Camilla's sister Eugenia, for example, eventually marries the man she loves after he realizes her sterling character "and reason and experience endeared his ultimate choice"; by contrast, his sister, who marries for money, is described as "romantic without consciousness" and nearly ruins herself; while the teenage Miss Dennel marries in the hope of independence, but her choice is not based on character, disposition, sympathy or respect and proves an unhappy one (Burney [1796] 1972: 912, 488). Similarly, in *Pride and Prejudice* the marriage of Darcy and Elizabeth—founded on mutual respect that has to be earned on both sides—is contrasted with the purely strategic one of Charlotte Lucas to the silly Mr. Collins and the impulsive match between Lydia and Wickham. Elizabeth's own initial attraction to Wickham also has parallels with the "flawed first attachments" in *Belinda*; in the latter, however, it is time and Belinda's exemplary reading of moral philosophy that shapes her "increasing reliance on her own reasoned opinions" (Edgeworth [1801] 1994: x) and guides her choice of husband.

HOW ONE MARRIED

The formal requirements as to *how* one entered into a valid and binding marriage were to be found in legal codes. In the first part of the period these were expressed through the canons of the Church of England, and in the second by legislation passed in 1753 placing these requirements on a statutory basis. From 1754, non-compliance with the key requirements of the statute rendered a marriage void; prior to that date, however, all that was strictly necessary was for the ceremony to have been conducted by an Anglican clergyman, with marriages that did not observe the canonical formalities being designated as "clandestine" but nonetheless valid (Probert 2009). But the fact that one *could* marry in a certain way did not mean that one *should*: while the literature of the time reflected what was necessary for a legal marriage, it also expressed a clear set of norms as to what was regarded as a proper marriage. At the same time, the passage of the 1753 Act illustrates both the power and the limits of the state: at one level it represented an extension of the power of the state over the regulation of everyday life, but the workability of the new legislative provisions still assumed the power of the established church (O'Connell 2011).

So Defoe's Moll Flanders, for example, makes at least a show of protest at the idea of marrying in an inn "and at Night too" (1722: 190), while in William Congreve's play *The Way of the World* (1700) the numerous marriages at St Pancras and St James Duke's Place clearly take place within canonical hours. The cautious heroine of Richardson's *Pamela* checks that the chapel where her wedding to Mr. B__ is to take place has been properly consecrated, while in Fielding's *Joseph Andrews* Parson Adams is shocked at the suggestion that he conduct a marriage without banns or license. While the early eighteenth century saw clandestine marriages of all kinds being conducted, it is instructive to note Lovelace's difficulty in procuring a license for his intended marriage to Clarissa—since, as he commented "the lady is of rank and fortune, and … there is no consent of father or *next friend*"; clearly not all officials were willing to take applicants' oaths at face value (Richardson [1747–48] 1985: 703). Even pornographic texts displayed awareness of the legal requirements: in *A New Description of Merryland* (1741), it was noted that the "Lease for Life" "'tho not perhaps the *best* Tenure, is the *most encouraged by Law*," while the procedure of giving notice, obtaining a license and marrying before an officiant were described in full, albeit in an extended agricultural metaphor (Mudge 2004: 281). Squire Western might fulminate in *Tom Jones* that formalities are "all stuff and nonsense" (Fielding [1749] 1996: 300), but he is clearly in the minority.

Characters throughout literature display a keen awareness of the distinction between being contracted to marry and actually being married. In Congreve's *The Way of the World*, for example, Lady Wishfort declares "I'll be married tomorrow, I'll be contracted tonight" ([1700] 1967: Act 3 Scene 1). Haywood's Betsy Thoughtless is similarly asked whether she is "married, or contracted" ([1751] 1986: 277). For a marriage, it is clear that a clergyman is necessary: in John Gay's *The Beggar's Opera* (1728), Macheath tells Lucy Lockit that "if we can find the Ordinary"—i.e., the chaplain—"I shall have no Scruples of making you my Wife" ([1728] 1986: 84); when they fail to do so, the wedding has to be deferred to a later opportunity. Smollett's Peregrine Pickle is even more desperate to wed his hard-won Emilia as soon as possible, but obtains a license and secures the offices of a clergyman in order to do so. The necessity of the person conducting the ceremony being ordained is driven home in Richardson's *Pamela*: Mr. B__ originally planned to have someone impersonate a clergyman, aware that this would not constitute a marriage, but eventually, swayed by Pamela's virtue, ensures that their marriage is conducted by a properly ordained clergyman.

While the necessity of an ordained Anglican clergyman being present is clear, the *sufficiency* of their presence, without more, is also evident. In Smollett's *The Adventures of Peregrine Pickle* the marriage of the hero's aunt Grizzle is originally intended to take place in church, despite the fact that the groom "had never been at church since he first settled in that parish" ([1751] 1964: 37), but an unexpected delay, and a desire for some privacy, leads to the parson being prevailed upon to perform the ceremony in the garrison. In *Clarissa*, meanwhile, the awareness that a clergyman can marry a couple in any place, without banns or license, is a cause of concern both to those who fear the heroine will be forced into a marriage that is distasteful to her and those who fear the binding nature of the union. Thus Clarissa's correspondent Anna Howe takes fright when she hears the proposal that her friend is to travel to her uncle's and counsels her against it: "You must, if possible, avoid being carried to that uncle's. The man, the parson, the chapel, your brother and sister present!—they'll certainly marry you to Solmes" (Richardson [1747 8] 1985: 239). Her admirer Lovelace, meanwhile, musing on her charms, declares that "had a parson been there, I had certainly been a gone man" (492), and when he is assuring Clarissa of the sincerity of his promises, he vows that "this moment I will send for a minister to put an end to all your doubts and fears" (914).

Indeed, clandestine marriages abounded in novels during the early part of the eighteenth century. A skeptical reader might suspect that they were more abundant in literature than in life, but since it was estimated that by the 1740s around half of all marriages in London were conducted by Fleet parsons, marrying couples in taverns or private houses without banns or license, the reverse might actually be true (Brown 1981; Outhwaite 1995). While the presence of an ordained Anglican clergyman ensured that the marriage would be legally recognized (assuming no other impediment), the seedy reputation of the Fleet was reflected in the fact that in the novels of the period a clandestine marriage is usually the choice of a minor or disreputable character rather than the hero or heroine (Figure 3.3).

Even the heedless heroine of *The History of Betsy Thoughtless* has certain qualms as to the advisability of entering into a marriage clandestinely. When her suitor, the so-called Sir Frederick Fineer, proposes a secret marriage, she is concerned that there may be some

FIGURE 3.3 Fleet marriage. Robert Chambers' *Book of Days*, 1864, from an earlier engraving by J. June, 1747. Source: wikimedia.

impediment to their union that he has not disclosed; his subsequently pretending to be on his deathbed almost results in her consenting to their marriage but luckily she refuses in time. The heroine of Frances Sheridan's novel *The Memoirs of Miss Sidney Biddulph* (1769)—set fifty years prior to its publication date—is less cautious, and the novel illustrates the problems that could arise if appropriate formalities were not observed. At the heart of the novel is the attraction between the eponymous heroine and the somewhat ambiguous hero Falkland. Sidney is in love with Falkland, and he with her, but she refuses to marry him when she learns that he has had a child by another woman, Miss Burchell. In fact, she insists that he should marry Miss Burchell. The marriage between Falkland and Miss Burchell is conducted privately, before a clergyman "on whose discretion he could rely" ([1769] 1999: 323). Falkland then arrives at Sidney's house to tell her that he has shot his wife and her paramour upon discovering them in adultery together. He is in a somewhat emotional state and Sidney eventually agrees to marry him. The marriage takes place scarcely more than thirty-six hours after Falkland's arrival, in a private house, before two witnesses. After the wedding has taken place the characters learn from a messenger that Falkland's wife survived the shot and that the marriage is therefore bigamous and void. The episode also serves to illustrate the ambiguities of Sidney's own character: she is rather too ready to be convinced of convenient truths.

By contrast, marriage in church is used by novelists as a marker of good character. Thus Joseph Andrews and Fanny are united in marriage in the church of the parish where Joseph has his settlement, the banns having been duly published; Tom Jones—after his sexual adventures—weds Sophia Western in the chapel at Doctors Commons; and in *Ferdinand Count Fathom* the saintly Renaldo and Monimia marry in church before a priest, having obtained a license. Marriage in church is also part of a belated attempt at respectability for Defoe's Roxana when she decides to retire from her career as a prostitute.

From 1754 on, of course, marriage in church was an essential requirement for those marrying in England and Wales unless the parties were marrying by special license. The parties need not be regular churchgoers to regard this as the proper place to wed: the "collier's wedding" depicted by Edward Chicken takes place before a crowd, some of whom were "never twice in Church before" (1764: 19).

Novelists had perforce to send characters further afield if they wished to escape this requirement, and the elopement became a standard plot device. In *The Expedition of Humphry Clinker* (1771) a couple are observed "bound to Edinburgh ... in quest of a clergyman to unite them in marriage, without the formalities required by the law of England" ([1771] 1995: 197), although the bride-to-be changes her mind and elopes

FIGURE 3.4 The Elopement. Thomas Rowlandson, 1792. Source: Yale Center for British Art, Paul Mellon Collection.

with someone else to Coldstream "where there was a parson who dealt in this branch of commerce" (199). For some, the idea of the elopement had a romantic allure: in Richard Brinsley Sheridan's 1775 play *The Rivals*, Lydia Languish is severely disappointed to find that instead of the becoming disguise, rope-ladder, moonlit flit to the border and Scotch parson she is to "go simpering up to the altar" (Act 5, Scene 1). But Sheridan makes it clear that she is a very silly girl and her hopes "the errors of an ill-directed imagination" ([1775] 1906: Act 5, Scene 3). By the end of the period Gretna had rather lost this romantic cachet and was becoming too common: the possibility of eloping there is swiftly dismissed in Ferrier's *Marriage* (1818) on the basis that it has "become too vulgar an exploit. I read of a hatter's apprentice having carried off a grocer's heiress t'other day" ([1818] 1997: 488) (Figure 3.4).

Would-be codifers such as Bentham may have favored the introduction of secular marriage (Sokol 2011), along with contractarians such as Locke (Witte 1997), but there is little evidence that this resonated with cultural understandings of marriage in this period.

LIFE AFTER MARRIAGE

Once the knot was tied, the law had relatively little to say about how husband and wife should conduct their married life. No formal code laid down obligations of fidelity or support: instead, then as now, what the law regarded as essential to marriage had to be inferred from the factors that would justify its termination.

As Elizabeth Foyster and James Marten have noted, "[a]ny increased enlightenment emphasis on the value of companionate marriage did not imply equal relations between men and women" (2010: 11). Nowhere is this more evident than in the fact that a full divorce with the right to remarry was available throughout the period on the basis of a wife's adultery—albeit only by private act of Parliament—while a husband's adultery only justified a separation. Only in the nineteenth century was a parliamentary divorce finally granted to a wife.

This double standard did, however, reflect the cultural code that a husband's adultery was simply less serious and less blameworthy than that of a wife. Male fidelity was not necessarily expected. In Eliza Haywood's novel *The History of Jemmy and Jenny Jessamy* (1753) "the author permits her heroine only the mild stipulation that 'when we marry you will either have no amours, or be more cautious in concealing them;—and in return, I promise never to examine into your conduct'" (Sobba Green 1991: 31). Admittedly, this did not go unquestioned: Haywood's feistier heroine Betsy Thoughtless leaves her adulterous husband on the basis that he has broken all of his matrimonial duties. And even depictions of wifely tolerance of blatant adultery are a little more subversive than they at first seem. In Charlotte Smith's *Desmond*, Geraldine's unworthy husband Verney consorts with prostitutes, drinks and gambles: she refuses even to complain in letters to her sister Fanny, pleading "Do not, my love, teach me to yield too easily to a sensibility of evils, which, since they are without remedy, it is better to bear with equality of mind, and with resignation of heart" ([1792] 2001: Vol. 2, 79). That both she and Betsy are rescued from their unfortunate marriages by the convenient deaths of their husbands might be seen as merely facilitating the development of the plot, but it also sent a message that the conduct of these husbands was to be condemned.

Admittedly, female infidelity almost invariably resulted in disgrace and divorce in the literature of the time. Novels held out little hope of an unfaithful wife making a happy second marriage with her lover. The worldly Adelaide in Susan Ferrier's *Marriage* makes a strategic match to a duke, despite being in love with another man; she then elopes with the latter and is divorced as a result. In addition, in the action for criminal conversation that her husband brings against her lover, the damages awarded are so high as to require the latter to be "for ever an alien to his country" ([1818] 1997: 433); although they do marry, she finds that he is indifferent to her and that she is "friendless in a foreign land" (451). Other divorced wives do not even have the consolation of an unhappy second marriage. In Austen's *Sense and Sensibility* (1811) we learn of Colonel Brandon's first love, Eliza, who was unhappily married; "fell" and was divorced: he muses that "I could not trace her beyond her first seducer, and there was every reason to fear that she had removed from him only to sink deeper in a life of sin" ([1811] 1994: 200). Maria Rushworth's fate in *Mansfield Park* (1814) is little better: she elopes with Henry Crawford, hoping that they will marry after her husband has divorced her; when she realizes that this hope is in vain, "the disappointment and wretchedness arising from the conviction rendered her temper so bad, and her feelings for him so like hatred" that they are for a short while "each other's punishment" and then separate ([1814] 1966: 431). She might not have ended up on the streets, but the close of the novel sees her sharing a home with her aunt, Mrs. Norris, which some may regard as punishment enough.

But would a formal code of marriage have given women any more power? Any such code would, of course, have reflected the assumptions and mores of the day. Jeremy Bentham's draft marriage code would have allowed both husbands and wives to obtain a divorce on the basis of the other's adultery, but even he did not advocate absolute parity. For one thing, a single act of adultery by a wife would be sufficient for a divorce, but a wife would have to show repeated acts of adultery by her husband. In addition, his list of the circumstances that would extenuate a spouse's adultery and lead to them being privately admonished rather than publicly divorced was also slightly different for husbands and wives: both, he thought, should be able to claim "lack of intention, ignorance of the law, innocence of intention, intoxication ... and compulsion," a list that Sokol has described as puzzling and readers might feel provides rather too many flimsy excuses; wives could also rely on a formal separation order, desertion, or their husband's adultery, or "deference to authority," while husbands could cite provocation or a wife's refusal or reluctance to engage in conjugal relations. The latter could be on account of the wife's infirmity or even her absence (which one might think would be a *necessary* condition for adultery, but not a sufficient one). Similarly, while Bentham's suggestion that a model marriage code should be drawn up and distributed to all newlyweds might seem to be ahead of its time, his proposed terms were most definitely rooted in the age. Wives, for example, were expected to sign up to their subordination to husbandly authority (Sokol 2011: 41).

The literature of the time indicates a rather more nuanced view of when obedience was appropriate. Advice literature counseled women to take care in choosing a husband, in order to ensure that they would be willing to obey him. And some clearly felt that a husband might by his conduct forfeit any right he would otherwise have to obedience: to quote Betsy Thoughtless once more: "When a husband ... is ignorant of the regard he ought to have for his wife, or forgets to put it in practice, he can expect neither affection nor obedience, unless the woman he has married happens to be an idiot" (Haywood [1751] 1986: 473).

CONCLUSION

Overall, it would seem, legal codes were seen as having an important role to play in supporting cultural ones. While particular laws might be identified as problematic, the absence of law was not advanced as an option. In Elizabeth Hamilton's 1800 anti-Jacobin novel, *Memoirs of Modern Philosophers*, the titular philosophers revel in an account of life among the "Hottentots," with the tellingly named Mr. Glib praising the "whole nation of philosophers, all as wise as ourselves! ... All alike! All equal! No laws! No government! No coercion! ... Take a wife today: leave her again tomorrow!" ([1800] 1992: Vol. 1, 321). His character stands as a warning both against abandoning all laws and taking travelers' tales too literally: he subsequently leaves his wife and children, and his claim to be acting on principle—on account of the immoral tendency of matrimony—does not obscure the fact that his children end up in the workhouse. It is left to the virtuous Harriet to explain why some external constraints are valuable:

> Alas! my dear, we need not look into the page of history, we need not examine into the conduct of the world at large, but just only take an impartial view of what passes in our own breasts, to be convinced of the necessity of a higher standard of excellence than can be found in human nature. (Vol. 2, 49)

CHAPTER FOUR

Agreements

TIMOTHY J. DODSWORTH

To understand the cultural history of legal agreements in the period of the Enlightenment, it is essential to broaden our gaze beyond the formal rules of contract and consider how agreements of all kinds were entered into and by whom, the role of trust on the one hand and legal advice and enforcement mechanisms on the other, the perceived effect of entering into an agreement on those concerned, and how the very concept of an agreement was at the root of political theory in this period. With such general considerations in mind, we begin with a specific case.

In 1706 the former apprentice John Sheffield was involved in a legal wrangle before the Court of Exchequer. At the age of twenty-one he had been sent out to Maryland by his master Thomas Starke, a London merchant involved in tobacco import (Price 1987). Under the terms of their agreement all profits—and all losses—were to be shared, in what was known as a joint venture. John, however, seems to have encountered some difficulties and upon his return owed Thomas Starke money. Nonetheless, he returned to Maryland and sent across several consignments of tobacco, for which Thomas should have reimbursed him. However, Thomas Starke then died, leaving his affairs in the hands of his wife. She alleged that money was owed by John Sheffield, while John Sheffield alleged that money was owed to him. Unravelling the documents, as the court then had to do, reveals the large level of trust that had underpinned the agreements between the two men and equally a distrust of the courts.

This simple case provides telling details about commercial culture at the time, and illustrates how the formal legal structures were in many ways peripheral to everyday practice. While there were statutes governing apprenticeship, and clear legal principles on the making of contracts, what was important in the case of Thomas Starke and John Sheffield was the basic agreement that they would vouch for each other and compare their ledgers periodically to work out which one of them owed the other. Very little of this was in writing, and even that which was recorded indicated that much was to be worked out at a later date. Their agreement was therefore based on trust in each other, the written contract being mere evidence of a certain state of affairs at a given moment in time which even the court would only take as the starting point for an investigation.

This had implications for the way in which business was conducted. The interconnection of business people meant that only in very few cases would merchants take their disagreements to court. They would much rather have their disagreement arbitrated by other, respected merchants. Indeed, in *Sheffield v. Starke* there were no fewer than four attempts to arbitrate. The reason that the case came to court at all was the inexperience of the widowed Mrs. Starke. As an outsider, perhaps feeling at a disadvantage, it is understandable that she would see the courts as the place to have the rights of the matter determined. For commercial men, by contrast, the ongoing relationship would have been more important.

THE MAKING OF AGREEMENTS

Communication was one of the central developments in the enlightenment period, both nationally and internationally. The process of enlightenment, the trend towards the use of reason which should be open to all, was dependent on the communication of ideas and opinions. Cross-cultural contacts and international links grew increasingly common, not only for the upper classes who had the leisure to write and travel but also for the clerks of the East India Company, sailors and missionaries who criss-crossed the globe in the course of their day-to-day business and in so doing contributed to the flow of ideas.[1] After the establishment of the official General Post Office in 1660, it became possible to speak almost of an information overload. Newspapers, short letters (billets), pamphlets, cartoons, and even paintings acting as social commentaries all emerged in an unprecedented volume, and were circulated more widely than ever before (Figure 4.1).

Dan Edelstein and his colleagues at Stanford University have made this information explosion visually clear by mapping out the social networks of the time.[2] Some 15,000 letters were sent across the network of Europe between 1700 and 1720 alone. This traffic of correspondence represents a vast exchange of knowledge and ideas.[3] The philosopher John Locke alone wrote 3,000 letters to people from all walks of life and influence within England and further afield, intending to collect together and connect individual

FIGURE 4.1 A country Post Office. Edward Villiers Rippingille, 1837. Source: © The Postal Museum 2018.

intellectual thoughts, drawing them out of their vacuum into a more public forum. Edelstein depicts the main routes that the letters took as bolts of light shooting across Europe. It is a suitable image, for by the middle of the eighteenth century the exchange of letters and ideas respectful of other languages and cultures was regarded as a distinct intellectual strand within the enlightenment movement in general.

Such exchanges also fostered a whole range of agreements. Scholars would often write on behalf of friends and colleagues asking for publishing agreements, accommodation, the loan of books, and even research positions. Hungry for news, academics both created the demand and supplied the means for the publication of journals, books, and pamphlets. Agreements between individual members of the community abounded, since the recommendation of a friend or colleague amounted to acceptance within the prestigious circle. Positions at the academies which were springing up all over Europe by the second half of the eighteenth century were often funded through agreements stemming from "Republic of Letters" contacts.

Molding and developing the humanitarian basis of enlightenment thinking was not confined to the brainstorming, discussions, and lectures taking place in European academies. Rolf Engelsing argues that beside the other revolutions which grew in the enlightenment era, a "reading revolution" took place towards the end of the eighteenth century (Engelsing 1974). Far more printed material was available to be read. Books were increasingly read only once, and silently, as compared to the previous norm of only the Bible and possibly Bunyan's *The Pilgrim's Progress* being repeatedly read aloud. Lending libraries, albeit operating with subscription fees which excluded even many middle-class readers, began opening their doors during the eighteenth century. New forms of reading matter were available to them, the novels of writers such as Defoe, Swift, Richardson, and Fielding forming a new and significant literary genre. The number of newspapers that were published and read also increased significantly: in 1690 fewer than a million newspapers were printed each year but within a century this had increased to around 14 million.[4] This increase did not preclude older ways of transmitting information, since newspapers would be read aloud so that even the illiterate would be able to keep up with the news (Barker 2000). The fact that the newspapers would include law reports naturally meant that the law itself was spread more broadly and that there was a more general understanding of how agreements needed to be made in order to have legal effect.[5]

Discussions, arguments and agreements also formed the staple business of the many coffee houses that sprang up across the period. Coffee houses as such were not a new idea in the enlightenment period. The idea of drinking coffee (or Caffey) had come to England at the beginning of the seventeenth century, although the taste had apparently required some getting used to. What was new, towards the end of the seventeenth century, was the specialization and the function of the coffee house. Before the coffee house had become popular business was conducted mainly at the place of exchange, or later in the taverns and inns (Clayton 2003). However, due to the rather heavy drinking in taverns it was generally accepted that it was no place for reaching agreements. The coffee houses brought a sober environment for business to be conducted and agreements to be discussed, away from those that would "drink away their Brains, and piss away their estates" (14). Taverns remained a good place to recruit workers (Clayton 2003), but business deals were generally struck in coffee houses.

Coffee houses would offer the latest books and newspapers or journals to their customers for the price of a cup of coffee (Outram 2013). Since the price of coffee was generally the same regardless of the coffee house one frequented, some owners diversified into other activities to increase their profit margins. Some offered additional specialities with the coffee, for example adding liquor or in the more up-market establishments, sugar. On the other hand with business generally conducted in the coffee houses they became a marketplace in themselves. The owner of a coffee house would receive mail, sell tickets, sell supposed medicine, etc. In fact in some coffee houses, patrons would be able to send their letters overseas by leaving some money and the envelope in a bag next to the door. The money was a "tip" for the master of the ship that would carry the letter. Differences in approach and clientele were self-reinforcing: coffee houses began to specialize and there was a general understanding that upon entering a particular coffee house one would provide information that was relevant to that particular type of clientele. This meant in turn that different coffee houses would attract different kinds of people and that the type of businesses one intended to pursue would lead to certain coffee houses (Clayton 2003).

As a result, coffee houses provided the ideal ground for discussion of a multitude of topics. This could lead to many disagreements but it could also bring parties together. On one level this led naturally to the making of new agreements, but the nature of the forum also encouraged new ways of making agreements. From these, new forms of contracts and even new industries arose.

These trends can be illustrated by a close reading of two contrasting pictures. The first picture is the "Scene in a London Coffee House" (*c.* 1695)[6] (Figure 4.2) which shows what seems to be a typical picture of a coffee house at the end of the seventeenth century. The warm colors show an inviting environment where there are discussions, paintings, and a seemingly sophisticated exchange of ideas. It is clear that the environment is strictly

FIGURE 4.2 Scene in a London Coffee House. Anonymous, *c.* 1690–1700. Source: The British Museum.

for men, with the only woman left out of the conversation on the far left, her role simply to serve the coffee. The men's attire differs quite significantly: the man second from the right is wearing a pink coat and a powdered wig whereas the man on the far right is wearing plain black clothing. This illustrates the fact that in coffee houses the men, although not from the same social standing, could meet as equals.

In terms of agreements, there is a significant amount of paper to be seen which the men are pondering. This captures the increased use of written documents for large commercial transactions that occurred at this time. While this was in part due to new formal requirements imposed by the law, it also reflected a change in who was entering into such contracts. As circles of acquaintances and contacts widened, contracts were entered into between individuals who did not necessarily know each other well. Rather than arrangements with known individuals based on trust, formal written contracts supplied the means of recording the agreement and enforcing the respective rights of the parties in case of later *dis*agreement.

Other coffee houses developed from social spaces into commercial fora. Chief among these was Lloyd's Coffee House, which opened in 1688. Originally located in Tower Street, close to the Pool of London and within the City of London, it became quickly accepted that upon entering one would be questioned as to news and one could pick up the current shipping news. This access to information opened the doors to new markets and before long insurance deals were being brokered in the Lloyd's coffee house. As a result, the maritime insurance market Lloyd's of London was born.

The very fact of such insurance deals was in itself the product of increased awareness of risk. As it was depicted in around 1798, Lloyd's was a place for gathering information (Figure 4.3) assessing the risks, informal negotiation and entering into formal written agreements. The concept of insurance contracts developed during the enlightenment period and reflected contemporary concerns (Ellis 2004). There was both a greater variety of such contracts and greater sophistication in their drafting. For example, it was not only property that could be insured (something that had become particularly popular since the Great Fire of London in 1666) but also business ventures. This gave rise to complicated underwritings for overseas business ventures. The term "underwriting" in fact explains the intricate nature of the insurance deals. Individuals were able to sign (also termed "scratching the slip") their names at the bottom of the shipping documents (hence "under" writing) which meant that they were willing to take the risk of the vessel not returning safely or the business venture going sour. The insurance brokers would be the ones holding the documents and their task was to ensure that the parties signing the documents had the means to fulfill their obligations in the event of a venture failure. If the ship returned safely or the business venture was successful the party who had taken the risk, the underwriter, would be paid a premium.

In the image of the Lloyd's coffee house several characters are intently reading the latest maritime news (assessing the risk in light of weather and other events) or possibly checking the terms of existing agreements. The two sharp-featured men in the forefront of the picture are probably the risk-averse insurance brokers whose main job was to negotiate the agreement and ensure that the underwriters would have sufficient financial funds to meet any potential liability. One of them is listening to another man whose triangle hat and weathered facial features identify him as a seafaring man, probably the captain of a ship, although whether he is negotiating terms for a future agreement or expostulating against the harshness of an existing one is difficult to discern. On the right-

FIGURE 4.3 Lloyd's Coffee House, London. William Holland, 1798. Source: Bettmann / Getty Images.

hand side another negotiation seems to be going on between two men, with a lawyer sitting behind them, patiently waiting to commit the agreement to writing.

The contrast to the "Scene in a London Coffee House" is striking. Dark colors dominate and it seems unlikely that those depicted in the later scene would have been welcome in the earlier one, particularly some of the shadier characters. There was a distinction between coffee houses for business—such as Lloyd's—and those for open discussion (Clayton 2003). Only a handful of characters in the later scene are actually drinking coffee, and in place of the artwork decorating the walls of the coffee house there is a large clock signifying the importance of time in the transactions.

There were other ways in which the very existence of these institutions both depended on and fostered changes in the ways agreements were made. The very availability of the coffee depended on a change away from small local dealers that knew each other to long chains of contracts where neither end of the chain had ever heard of the other. Previously prices, demand, and information about the buyer or seller were restricted to the individual marketplace or at most within a radius of twelve to fifteen miles around that marketplace (Muldrew 1998). By 1787, whole new geographical areas could now be accessed through the founding of postal systems throughout Europe and the British Empire creating opportunities for agreements to be negotiated outside the previous limitations of parochial boundaries.

This kind of development generated a need to make plans for when one of the links in the chain broke. It also depended on the availability of credit. Changing ideas about the legitimacy of credit and debt meant that individuals in the commercial world were able to issue and endorse letters of credit everywhere (Broadberry and O'Rourke 2010). Private individuals could now mortgage their land or their assets in return for cash (Broadberry and O'Rourke 2010). Access to credit had of course to be supported by a mechanism that would allow the enforcement of contracts in cases where a debt was not paid. This is what set Britain apart from most of Europe, in that the court system[7] was mainly (with some exceptions) centralized and systematized (Broadberry and O'Rourke 2010). The binding nature of an agreement of debt was therefore backed by the state which in turn provided confidence in the markets.

Nor was the role of the state limited to enforcing agreements between individuals and companies. The protection of commerce was one of the main aims of the state and policies were put in place to restrict anyone except the state's own companies from trading with colonies and importing.[8] Such was the case with the phenomenally successful East India Company. The secret of its success lay in the agreements the Company had with the Crown where protection was granted for the trade monopoly of the Company. These kind of agreements were only reached by paying large sums of money, disguised as loans, to the Crown in order to maintain the profitable monopoly (Hunter [1900] 1912).

Until 1668 the relationship between the Company and the Crown had been kept a secret. It was the case of *Skinner v. The East India Company* that brought it to public attention. Skinner had had his ships confiscated by the Company and the case became public knowledge. The House of Lords held that the Company was in the wrong and awarded Skinner damages, overriding the Charter. Eventually, however, the case was resolved in favor of the Company (Lawson 1993). The political struggle aside (Pike 1894), it seems that the Company's power reached far beyond the court's decision. It almost seems as if the agreement between the Company and the Crown had been elevated to a constitutional character that had now been broadcast across the country for all to see. The influence of this agreement cannot be underestimated: it restated the political powers of the times but also affirmed the powers of the Company and the hunger for further trade and exploration. The Company's well-known, aggressive political approach to "agreements" abroad reflected the regime of the time all in order to secure the wealth of the Crown.

The breakdown of political support, together with the resolution removing the monopoly rights of the Company in January 1694, caused the eventual decline of its power (Lawson 1993). This was not only of significance to the Company in terms of its agreement with the Crown, but it was also a shift in the parameters of the agreement between Parliament and the Crown. The signal that was sent was that trading privileges were now a matter for Parliament. The change in the political landscape and the new-found threat of rival companies[9] meant that the policies of the East India Company had to change. The strong interventionist nature of the Company in international politics was accordingly replaced by a non-interventionist approach. Undoubtedly the political landscape played a significant role in the change in approach but the agreement (or breakdown of that agreement) influenced the Company culture and international politics. The agreement itself influenced national politics in that it allowed the Jacobean fear of monopolies to re-appear and change the distribution of power.

At the same time there seems also to have been a discussion on the value of trade and exchange itself. On September 25, 1713 *The Tatler* wrote of the disparity between imports and export and the need for the equivalence in exchange. The idea that there might be more money leaving the country than entering it (although it was cheaper to import) was seen as signifying that countries the writer considered to be equal were not being treated equally and the conclusion was that there was a need to intervene in the free trade to ensure "fair" agreements were reached. In this case the countries under discussion were England and France; tellingly, a very different approach was adopted when the trading partner was outside Europe. In 1778 the directors of the East India Company installed a painting in their London Headquarters titled "The East Offering her Riches to Britannia" (Figure 4.4). Britannia is positioned higher than any of the others in the image. A woman, representing India, kneels and offers Britannia her pearls. Britannia seems to be disdainfully picking a specific pearl necklace—the choice is hers. A further woman is offering her a Ming vase, representative of China. A long line of laborers has formed bringing bales of cloth. Below Britannia the British lion looks dangerously at the woman with the pearls. Yet further below Old Father Thames is looking the other way. The ships of the Company appear in the center of the image, though in the background. The image represents the new-found confidence of the Company (particularly in light of the fact that China was in no way subservient at that point in time). However, the image also reveals more about the bargain that has been struck. The culture of wealth that the trade had brought to London was generally welcomed (though in the picture the city looks away, almost in shame, not wanting to know where the wealth has originated). The protection of the lion indicates the imbalance of power in this relationship.

FIGURE 4.4 The East Offering its Riches to Britannia. Spiridione Roma, 1778. Source: © British Library Board. All Rights Reserved / Bridgeman Images.

The East India Company provided a glimpse of how large-scale agreements must have been viewed by the public and the influence these agreements must have had. We will continue with this theme in the next part of the chapter when we take a look at the kind of agreements the East India Company made and how these were culturally displayed.

DIFFERENT TYPES OF AGREEMENTS

Employment Contracts

The East India Company also had profound and practical effects on the making of agreements, in particular the nature and terms of employment contracts. The Company was faced with the unusual difficulty that those it employed to carry out its business were not under its direct control. The directors sat in London and most of its employees—or, as they were termed, servants—were abroad. To address this, the Company drafted lengthy agreements that set standards on legal holidays and created a system of retaining control of its servants abroad (Furber 1976; Lawson 1993).

Typically servants would begin their service at the age of seventeen, and the lengthy contract would include a covenant of indenture. It would also include a bond signed by two sureties on the employee's behalf (Hejeebu 2005). This was a form of security that bound two other parties to the agreement. These other two parties would be putting their livelihood at risk and thereby providing significant security to the employer. The contract also explained all the duties that the servant owed to the Company. For this purpose the Company made use of standard form contracts which were to become popular during the industrial revolution.[10] The servant would be sent abroad and would act as an agent for the Company. Rather than attempting to control all the actions of their servants, however, the Company allowed them to undertake their own trade, personal development and the use of company warehouses (Pappenheim 1918). The contract displayed interesting traits that may be found in modern contracts, with clearly defined parameters for promotion and allowances for personal initiative. Should the servant be found importing products back to England, however, the Company would be able to levy a 200 percent fine of the value of the product (Hejeebu 2005).

While such agreements exhibited certain exploitative elements that would later come to be challenged by legislation, they also laid the foundation for a new culture of employment contracts. The state of general employment contracts can be illustrated by returning to a familiar area of business—the coffee houses. As with most industries of that time, coffee house owners would offer apprenticeships to young men. The idea would usually be to gain experience. Usually, and this is evidenced by the apprentices in the East India Company or generally with merchants, the apprentices would go on to work in the industry of the master. However, the merchant handbook advises apprentices that it would not be a good idea to follow their masters into the coffee house business but to seek employment elsewhere (Clayton 2003). It seems therefore that the main reason for having an apprentice in a coffee shop was cheap labor and possibly the opportunity for apprentices to make contacts. This in turn created its own problems. Satires of the time often depict the exploitation of the coffee boys who were expected to run errands, deliver letters and of course serve the customers in the coffee houses. At the same time the apprentice is often depicted as stealing from the master in order to make ends meet in light of the minimum pay (or in the case of "Punch Spiller" sipping the coffee of patrons as he brought them their drink, then claiming he had spilled it on the way). It seems therefore that the agreement was based on the opportunity to learn, in the case of coffee houses, broadly how to do business and to build a network within the master's business. The cost was of course very little pay from the master. In some cases apprentices would go on to build a good reputation in a particular industry which meant that they could (and would) open their own coffee houses (Clayton 2003).

However, the personal manner in which business was conducted changed from being the only way to conduct business with the rise of joint stock companies and the possibility of purchasing shares.

Companies

A different kind of agreement was that which linked those investing in new commercial ventures. The agreement between Sheffield and Starke with which this chapter opened took the form of a joint venture whereby losses and profits were shared. This was a more cautious approach to overseas ventures than that taken by many merchants, the usual approach being for the merchant to provide all the venture capital and hold all the risk with the partner that was sent abroad earing a commission.

Not all individuals were so cautious. Joint stock companies might at first sight have seemed like a way of spreading the risk of investment. Rather than one individual providing all of the capital for a particular venture, the joint stock company enabled a number of individuals to invest their money and reap the financial rewards proportionate to the amount of stock they owned. That, at least, was the theory. In practice many invested in ventures that were highly dubious and unlikely to yield a profit. One such endeavor was the idea of creating a harbor in Harburgh, Germany. The project failed before construction could ever start. Nor was the risk limited to losing the money invested. One of the main difficulties with these agreements for shares in joint stock companies was that the capital invested by the public was not the limit of the liability. The investor would become a member of the company and if the company went into liquidation the creditors of the company would call on the members for the rest of the capital.

Many of the joint stock companies that had been floated were doomed to fail from the beginning but there seemed to be general consensus that these business ventures could simply not fail. The Financial Crisis in 1696–1697, however, saw the collapse of many joint stock companies with the consequence that many individuals' life savings vanished in a very short period of time. The state decided to intervene and restrict (or essentially banish) the incorporation of joint stock companies. This culminated in the Bubble Act which came into force in June of 1720. It meant that permission had to be granted by Parliament for the flotation of new concerns (Cummings 1987).

The threat of the time seemed to be the unregulated speculation in dubious adventures which seemed to be doomed from the outset. The new legislation, however, did little to curb the public appetite for such speculation which in turn meant that new ways were found, based on dubious agreements, to fulfill these perceived needs.

The precarious nature of these ventures was depicted in George Cruikshank's etching "A Scene in the Farce of lofty Projects as performed with great success for the Benefit & amusement of John Bull" (1825). The sky is littered with different kinds of balloons but it is the advertisements that cover the buildings beneath that thrust the message home. The building on the left reads "General Balloon Office" and the shop is called "Rack & Ruin." The building to the right of that is called "Office of the honourable company of moon Rakers capital 999.999.999." Most of the houses have to be supported by large wooden planks. Their dilapidated state, combined with the flimsy balloons, predicts the inevitable demise of the ventures. Bringing together these elements makes it clear to the viewer that there is no hope for these schemes. Yet the people in the picture seem to be going about their business as usual, reflecting the fact that despite the bubble bursting the general public was happy to invest in these companies which often had little chance of ever being successful. The likely cause of the rush to invest is the image of the joint stock company from the days of the East India Company where the monopoly granted by the Crown secured a guaranteed return manifesting a public image of the joint stock companies as a whole being a solid investment.

Despite the image depicting people falling from their balloons on the right and left of the picture it is unlikely that this was a comment on the morality of the stock market, but rather spelling out the loss to these unsuspecting victims. The agreement to buy shares in this sort of company would have been seen as wholly legitimate (although the sellers of the shares would have been considered rogues). By contrast, there were some agreements which from their content were seen as morally repugnant.

Agreements, the Devil, and Morality

One of the most significant changes from the seventeenth to the eighteenth century was the rise of reason. The view that everything could and should be explained rationally meant that there was little room for witchcraft as an explanation of unfortunate events. While there were still some isolated cases—in 1712 Jane Wenham was sentenced to death for conversing with the devil in the shape of a cat—the witch hunt was more or less over. At the same time a change in religious attitudes meant that the devil had moved from punisher to pervasive tempter (Davies 2007). Previously someone would be possessed with the devil, against their will, taken over by satanic powers. In the Enlightenment, by contrast, the devil offered temptations to individuals to do his bidding. Succumbing to such temptations might indicate that the mind of the individual was weak but at least they had done so by their own free will.

There does seem to have been a distinction though between how the devil would appear particularly when it came to men and women. A chapbook from Plymouth tells the story of a daughter who had been sent to her room due to her disobedience. She sulks in her room and the devil appears and takes her by the hand:

> He said, fair creature, why do you lament?
> Why is your heart thus fill'd with discontent?
> She said my parents cruel are to me,
> And keep me here to starve in misery.
> He said then if you will be rul'd by me,
> Revenged of them thou shall quickly be

The devil by taking her hand and enquiring into her misery builds a relationship and then tempts the girl with the desired result. For women the devil would be the tempter but men would make a pact with the devil following on from the Faustian pact. In January 1698/9 a man by the name of Presser was convicted because they had found a paper in his pocket by which he had sold himself to the devil.[11] The chapbooks of the time—cheap, small paper-covered booklets—enjoyed similar stories. A man named John Wats was persuaded by the devil with a great bag of gold and much more for twelve years, after his father had refused to give him more funds, if he signed the pact. John signed the agreement in his own blood. The element of blood seems to signify the importance of the agreement and in a way the fact that it was irrevocable, though there was no real need since the religious teaching of the eighteenth century implied agreement to a pact with the devil where a sin was committed. In all cases the irrevocable nature of the agreement with the devil was clear. In the chapbook *A Timely Warning, to All Rash and Disobedient Children*[12] Thomas Williams had promised himself to the devil for twelve years. Now that his time had expired (and it seems he regretted his decision), sitting in the midst of several divines whom his parents had invited to pray with him', "the devil, in dreadful storm of rain, thunder, lightning, and hail, fetched him away, dashing out his brains against the walls of the room."

The display of the agreement with the devil, though different between men and women, was in all cases, whether implicit or explicit, in effect irrevocable and the end result, the fetching by the devil, was always an inevitability. The fact that the devil was now entering into agreements tells us something about the emerging idea of the rational self; the fact that these agreements were irrevocable tells us something about the way in which contracts were seen. As a party to a contract, the devil was able to enforce its terms in the same way as any other contracting party would be able to do.

Marriage Contracts

A degree of ambiguity about the values that should underpin agreements was also to be seen in a very different type of agreement, the marriage contract. Although the idea of marriage based on love rather than a politically or financially sensible arrangement was not new, it was by no means accepted as the ideal. Particularly within the middle and upper classes, the idea that parents should play a key role in arranging suitable marriages still held sway. It was, however, attracting an increasing amount of criticism.

Hogarth in his series "Marriage à la mode," painted between 1743 and 1745 (Figure 4.5), heavily criticized the idea of marriage as a bargain regardless of the compatibility of the two persons being united. The set of six paintings documented a marriage settlement through the increasingly depraved consequences leading to the premature death of both parties. The picture entitled *"The Marriage Contract"* provides an excellent critique of society at the time. It depicts Lord Squanderfield on the right pointing to his family tree, his side of the agreement. On the other side of the table the merchant, father of the bride-to-be, is reading over the contract. The money on the table gives an indication of the large sum that the parties are contracting for and it is indeed likely that Lord Squanderfield requires the money to build the elaborate building visible through the window. The lawyer is positioned between the merchant and the lord attempting to hand over a contractual document that (or so it would seem) the lord is rejecting.

There are several elements of this image that reveal Hogarth's view of contracts in general and marriage contracts in particular. The agreement is revealed as a bundle of information, its length denoting its importance, and the presence of the lawyer its complexity. The attitudes of the merchant and the lord differ significantly: the merchant is reading the contract intently while the lord seems not to regard any perusal as necessary. This difference represents the clash of the two worlds that under normal circumstances would not be doing business: for the merchant the written agreement is an essential element of business but for the aristocrat a man's word was supposed to be enough. Finally, the division of the picture between the making of the agreement in the center and the couple on the left nicely illustrates how love (or what should be love) has been

FIGURE 4.5 Marriage à la mode, plate I, The Marriage Settlement. William Hogarth, 1743. Source: Imagno / Getty Images.

sidelined from the agreement-making process. The children that are to be married have no say in the agreement that is being struck, and indeed nothing to say to each other.

Twenty years after Hogarth's critical series of pictures, Greuze produced his depiction of a rural marriage contract in France (Figure 4.6). In contrast to Hogarth's scenes of disaster, Greuze, influenced by Rousseau, presents us with a homely view of a happy union. In line with Enlightenment thinking, the focus here has shifted from the court and upper classes, to idealizing wholesome country life and family values. In contrast to Hogarth's picture, here the couple take center stage, a little bashfully perhaps, but with their affection for each other palpable in their clasped hands. Indeed, there are hints in the picture that the couple may have let their passions run away with them: the broom at the forefront of the image may indicate that the couple may have "jumped the broom" in other words had to get married quickly. The crib, just behind the broom, may provide another hint as to why this marriage had to happen so quickly. This may also explain the slightly ambiguous expressions on the faces of the surrounding family. But whatever their views of the union, the structure of the picture indicates that the family is no longer central to the making of the marriage. In a similar vein, the document that is presumably recording the marriage agreement does not take center stage as it does in Hogarth's picture, but appears to one side.

What is also telling is the different reactions to the two pictures. Greuze's picture was a very popular success at the Salon of 1765, while Hogarth had difficulty selling his works

FIGURE 4.6 The Marriage Contract. Jean-Baptiste Greuze, 1761. Source: DEA / G. DAGLI ORTI / Getty Images.

at the time (Bomford and Roy 1982: 46). The implication is that Greuze was depicting what people wanted to believe, while Hogarth was identifying an uncomfortable truth about what was happening in practice. Wealthy patrons who had arranged suitable marriages for their daughters were unlikely to want to contemplate the possibility of the marital unhappiness, infidelity, and death so graphically portrayed by Hogarth.

The misuse of the marriage contract was depicted rather differently in John Gay's *The Beggar's Opera*. The highwayman Macheath had promised the jailer's daughter Lucy Lockit, that they would get married, despite his already being secretly married to Polly Peachum. In custody he speaks to himself:

> "To what a woful Plight have I brought myself! ... I am in the Custody of her Father, and to be sure, if he knows of the matter, I shall have a fine time on't betwixt this and my Execution.—But I promis'd the Wench Marriage—What signifies a Promise to a Woman? Does not Man in Marriage itself promise a hundred things that he never means to perform? Do all we can, Women will believe us; for they look upon a Promise as an Excuse for following their own Inclinations.—But here comes Lucy, and I cannot get from her". (Gay [1728] 1986: 39)

The differentiation then to Macheath is between a man's understanding of a promise and a woman's. Although he did make the promise he feels he should not be held to his word. It is merely a promise that was made without significance, not an agreement that needs to be honored.

BONDS OF SOCIETY

The making of agreements between two parties was clearly influenced by external factors such as what was required for legal recognition and the changing expectations of what a contract should contain. At the same time the constitutional crisis and "enlightened thinking" also had an impact on contract law as a discipline. It must therefore be considered what influenced academic writers of that time and what influence they had on shaping contract law. What changes did the courts make to contract law in order to fulfill public expectations and in how far did they represent enlightened values?

Under James II the idea of secure property rights had regularly been dispensed with and as a result the security in agreements between individuals was under constant threat from the monarchy. The revolution in 1688, and the consequent passage of the Bill of Rights in 1689, put an end to this anxiety. The monarchy was now limited (one could say by an "agreement" between the sovereign and Parliament) and a regime was introduced whereby the binding nature of property rights was to become a reality. Commerce could accordingly flourish under the new-found security and promise of "justice." The separation of powers and the freedom of the courts from outside interference not only gave the term justice a new meaning but also had an impact upon the freedom of individuals to enter into contracts. The removal therefore of power from the Crown on the one hand, and on the other the enhanced power of the courts to administer justice, together fostered economic stability and the cultural acceptance of the binding nature of the law and therefore the binding nature of agreements that were entered into.[13]

The enlightenment period was also a time where academics began to ponder the theoretical foundations of agreements. Transactions in the sixteenth century, dominated by face-to-face meetings in the marketplace, were usually concluded by the giving of a symbolic penny to seal the deal. From this gesture arose the doctrine of "consideration" (Ibbetson 1982: 153–154), where something of value had to pass from the person to whom the promise was made to the person making the promise in order for there to be a binding contract. The foundational threat behind non-payment was the fact that the penny (or higher amount) had been paid as "God's penny," reflecting the dominant framework of Christian belief underpinning all promises (Muldrew 1998: 106). This religious motive was also evident in the legal concept of "the agreement." If a contract had been made under oath then it was a valid agreement on the basis that it was a promise to God.

From the middle of the seventeenth century the concept of consideration was developed still further by the courts and the academics. With this progress also came a shift in the response to breaches of contract, from punishing the wrongdoer to compensating the disappointed party for the loss of the bargain. Academics, particularly those based on the Continent, began debating the theoretical foundations of contract law in the middle of the eighteenth century and the development of law of mistake—a concept whereby one party is mistaken as to something relating to the contract and is aiming to get out of the contract on the basis of that mistake—shows a shift from the Roman categorization, to a fault-based theory, to finally Savigny's will theory. With Savigny's will theory, the doctrine of mistake, at least on the Continent, was underpinned by the notion of whether or not the mistaken party "willed freely" to enter into the contract. If they did not have the requisite will, they should be released from their obligations. The concept resonated with the foundational ideas of the enlightenment period of the free, enlightened individual entering agreements as a result of their own free choice.

The notion of the binding force of contract was also expanded beyond the realm of private law. The idea of a social contract—the theory that individuals' moral and political obligations are dependent upon an agreement between them and society—goes back to classical times but was adopted and developed in the enlightenment period. In *Leviathan* (1651) Thomas Hobbes outlined his basis for a social contract starting from the principle that life in a natural state is "solitary, poor, nasty, brutish and short," and driven by self-interest. To avoid this inherently anarchic state, he argued, individuals agree with one another to relinquish some of their rights, creating a state which passes laws to regulate social interaction, becoming a near-absolute authority. Citizens would, however, be released from these assumed obligations when a government was too weak to defend them.

In contrast, John Locke, writing sometime before 1689, believed that individuals in a natural state would be morally bound by natural law not to harm each other but would still need a government to act as a neutral judge to defend them ([1689] 1980: sections 13–14). In this way any government derived its powers from the governed. In turn, he viewed the agreement as broken when a government failed to secure the natural rights of its citizens.

A different approach again was taken by Rousseau, writing in 1762. He viewed the social agreement from a collectivist standpoint. If an individual lapsed back into his inherent egoism, society (by applying the law) would be expressing the will of the collective society. Since the governing laws had been made by society they acted as a civilizing influence which guided and helped to form the character of individual members of society. Again, the agreement between governing and governed could be broken if the "general will" of society was not satisfied.

Rousseau's friend, and critic of the social contract theory, David Hume had pointed out in 1742 that the concept of the social contract was a fiction, whether based on the divine right of kings or on the idea of government by consent of the people. Preferring the latter, he still proposed that pragmatically this had not actually occurred. This referred back to his argument in his 1739 treatise on human nature that international agreements between states, having been formed on the same basis of general natural law as the social contract, must be subject to the same rules.

Hume found his pragmatist conception of experience in the benefits produced by international law which both justified the existence of international agreements and supplied grounds for compliance and enforcement.

> The advantages, therefore, of peace, commerce and mutual succour, make us extend to different kingdoms the same notions of justice, which take place among individuals. (Hume 1739–40: 190)

However, although both nations must receive benefits, including future advantages, he suggested that in practice the sheer necessity of agreement is not so essential to existence between states as is it between individuals, therefore "we must necessarily give a greater indulgence to a prince or a minister, who deceives another; than to a private gentleman, who breaks his word of honour" (192). This, in his views, made international agreements by their nature weak.

As eighteenth-century jurisprudence understood the law of nations it was as a technique for producing agreements based on advantages and disadvantages, usually relating to security and/or wealth. In France, Mably wrote extensively on the nature and content of international agreements, insisting in his collection of and commentary on treaties since Westphalia that negotiation rules were a basis for a consistent foreign policy which was to achieve in treaties the real interests of a nation bearing in mind its position in Europe (Koskenniemi 2009). In pre-revolutionary France there was simply no coherent international law tradition, rather a collection of constantly negotiated and renegotiated treaties based on the politics of the day and negotiated by state officials hostile to lawyers and the idea of consistent principles of international law.

Similarly, Rousseau attacked the prevailing methods of diplomacy, alliances and treaties as being too dependent on the capriciousness of sovereigns:

> As for what is commonly called international law, however, its laws lack any sanction, they are unquestionably mere illusions, even feebler than the laws of nature. The latter at least speak in the heart of individual men whereas the decisions of international law, having no other guarantee than their usefulness to the power who submits to them, are only respected in so far as interest accords with them. ([1754] 1984: 423–424)

While Rousseau regarded treaties as having no practical significance, Hume interpreted the necessity of them according to the advantages produced. The focus in international thinking in Europe during the eighteenth century was clearly on maintaining the balance of power which derived reality largely from economics.

In Germany, Moser (1752) compiled treaties, amounting to ten volumes, with a view to identifying the practice of international agreements. He found that the basis for past agreements was the concept that European states were free and equal, not bound by any general international law, but that reflected in their treaties was the desire to maintain the balance of power with occasional checks for tendencies towards universal monarchy.

Moser was an academic outsider at the time and although his work was constantly in use he received much criticism. Georg Friedrich Martens, who later compiled the largest repository of treaties and international agreements, criticized him for the way in which he separated at the basis international law and the natural rights of the social contract. Martens found no positive European constitution behind treaties but insisted that the basis be recognized as the natural law of the social contract which sovereigns seek to follow in their international agreements (Koskenniemi 2009). Germans may well have considered that natural law inherently possessed a higher metaphysical rank than their positive law concepts but ultimately it came to be understood that the role of the sovereign was to enter into international agreements in order to promote the good of their people. In the event of conflict in which the duty of a people stands opposed to its right of self-preservation then the latter must prevail.

The German philosopher Gottfried Achenwall contributed to this debate when in 1756 he published his comparative study of the constitutions of major European states. This truly reflected Enlightenment principles in suggesting that each part of a state and states internationally should operate in harmony with each other to produce agreements and treaties based on social contract principles (Achenwall 1752). Statecraft and diplomacy should ensure that treaties are generally adhered to, he argued, not out of moral considerations but out of self-interest.

And so the European stage was set for Adam Smith to deliver his famous discourse on the *Wealth of Nations* in 1776 in which he built on his friend Hume's views on self-interest. This was the answer to the central problem of the lofty nature of natural law theories which until now had depended on the altruism of otherwise self-centered individuals. Appeals to self-interest were, he contended, the way to achieve one's ends: after all, it was not from "the benevolence of the butcher, the brewer or the baker that we expect our dinner, but from their regard to their own self-interest. We address ourselves not to their humanity, but their self-love in his favor, and show them that it is for their own advantage to do for him what he requires of them" ([1776] 1976: Book I, chapter 2, 16).

This shift in focus caused by the discovery of the natural laws of economics meant that through regarding the national economy as a whole, happiness could be achieved without state involvement at an international level, through protective tariffs and mercantile intervention on a political level. Greatly facilitated by the increase in geographical scope, reliability, and competence of the postal system and other social media, fellow Scots David Hume and Adam Smith were able to deepen their friendship and thereby their discussions.

One of the major advances of the Enlightenment was the reformed approach to international treaties. During this time the sacred concept of the balance of power began to be considered in terms of relative nation wealth. The management of wealth on an international plane could no longer be via regulations if the social contract based on natural law was to be upheld as an underlying principle of the era.

One of the most famous chapters of Smith's work embodies and expands this message:

Every individual is continually exerting himself to find out the most advantageous employment for whatever capital he can command. It is his own advantage, indeed, and not that of society, which he has in view. But the study of his own advantage naturally, or rather necessarily, leads him to prefer that employment which is most advantageous to society. ([1776] 1976: Book IV, chapter 2, 419)

This argument is perfectly in line with natural jurisprudence as Smith goes on to explain the logic that if we can buy cheaper from abroad than by making at home the answer lies not in an agreement regulating imports but in the investment of the difference gained in buying from abroad into a more profitable venture. The basis is the ego of the individual and the end result is individual and ultimately national happiness in line with the aims of enlightenment theory. The emphasis moves away from politics in the negotiation of agreements and treaties to economics.

CONCLUSION

Agreements in the Enlightenment period appear in a variety of forms. In some cases, as the foundation of new orders such as the joint stock companies, they are disguised behind the theme of "trading in shares." They are used as international devices to legitimize the suppression of foreign trading nations but they are in the same context the tool by which employees, through enticing and threatening, are kept in check. New forms of cross-cultural agreements, facilitated through coffee houses, meant that the administration of contract changed and still changes with the altering culture.

Writers such as Rousseau allowed the agreement to be elevated from agreements between individuals (or companies) to a political level where the question of "breaching" the promise is based on political, contextual changes but the basis remains the enlightened, self-interested individual's will.

The contrast between bare promises, e.g., Macheath's promise to marry, and conclusive agreements is supported by the cultural belief in the binding nature of the contract. Whether it is the pact with the devil from which there is no release even with the assistance of the church or it is the marriage contract which an outsider cannot penetrate (either because the couple and their agreement are supported by society or due to the agreement being supported by love), the agreement is both a beginning and a conclusive ending.

CHAPTER FIVE

Arguments

Reputation and Character in Eighteenth-Century Trials

DANA RABIN

Cultural historians of law assert that rather than a closed and segregated system of rules and penalties composed and imposed, the law is a product of daily life, formed by its cultural context even as it forms its cultural context. In order to demonstrate the co-constituted nature of law and culture, I take my readers away from the verdict and into the trial and its context, focusing on the arguments made in eighteenth-century English criminal trials. Such arguments are far more revealing of eighteenth-century culture than the bare fact of the verdict and sentence. As Cynthia Herrup has argued, "a verdict is the clearest point of a trial's history, but the weakest focus for an historian. It is a filter built from artificial materials and one that obscures as much as it clarifies, reinforcing rather than upsetting the notion of a trial as a story with an objective ending."[1] Herrup asserts that a focus on the verdict "sets the law above rather than within society."[2] This chapter, by contrast, brings readers into a conversation in legal and cultural studies that understands law as a reflection of wider culture. The conversation begins with a case.

In February, 1733 twenty-three-year-old Sarah Malcolm was indicted for the murders of Ann Price, Elizabeth Harrison, and Lydia Duncomb, accused of stabbing and strangling them while they slept. She was also indicted for the theft of a silver tankard, some linen, and a large sum of money. The gruesome murders took place in the Inner Temple in London. Malcolm admitted to the thefts, but she went to her death denying any involvement with the murders. She told the magistrate, Sir Richard Brocas, that the murder resulted when one of the servants awoke in the midst of the crime. Facing the death penalty, Malcolm took the stand in her own defense, pleading not guilty at London's Old Bailey on February 23. She argued that the blood found at the murder scene was not that of the victims but instead her own menstrual blood. After her conviction, she continued to argue for her life, denying the murder and presenting herself as a devout Roman Catholic. The shocking events and revelations were covered extensively in the newspapers, and Malcolm was tried in the court of public opinion as well as at London's central criminal court. William Hogarth visited Malcolm in the condemned cell at Newgate prison two days before her execution and later used the sketches he made there to paint her portrait. (Figure 5.1) During the visit, he is alleged to have said "I can see by this woman's features that she is capable of any wickedness."[3]

FIGURE 5.1 Portrait of Sarah Malcolm. William Hogarth, *c.* 1733. Source: National Gallery of Scotland.

Malcolm's scandalous case provides evidence about the prominent place of character and reputation in the arguments advanced in the eighteenth-century courtroom. Given her admission of guilt regarding the theft, the money found hidden in her hair, and her bloody shift, prosecutors confirmed her dangerous, threatening, and irrevocably criminal character while Malcolm went to great lengths to try to save her life by admitting to criminality but insisting on her redeemable character.

References to her character and reputation recurred throughout the trial as the prosecution explained "how well practiced she was in wickedness." Although Malcolm's employer, John Carrol, told the court that "she was recommended to me as an honest woman by a gentleman in the Temple," the moment he heard about the murders, he dismissed Malcolm, saying "No Body that was acquainted with Mrs. Duncomb shall be here, till the Murderer is found out." As if confirming her impugned character, Malcolm admitted that she had pawned some of Carrol's waistcoats and identified bloody linen found under Carrol's bed as hers. The servant women who found the bodies testified that Malcolm joined their efforts to break into the locked room where the bodies were found. Ann Love implied that Malcolm had a devious character when she told the court that Malcolm "pretended she came to enquire of the old Maid's health." Love reported that Malcolm had lived with Dunscomb and that Malcolm had visited her "under pretence of looking for the key of her master's chamber." Roger Johnson, a prisoner at Newgate, testified that he "had some knowledge of her, because she us'd to come thither to see one [Alexander] Johnson, an Irishman, who was convicted of stealing a Scotchman's Pack." Johnson went on to say that after her visit, Malcolm "went into the tap-house among the felons, and talk'd very freely with them."[4] Malcolm's acquaintance with a fellow Irishman and convicted criminal and her familiarity with Newgate placed her firmly in an underworld and made her guilt more believable.

Unable to counter the prosecution's arguments, Malcolm's last strategy was to imply that she could be redeemed and that if granted her life, she would comport herself with righteousness and rectitude. She acknowledged her "vicious inclinations" and presented herself as "a condemn'd woman" who warranted "an ignominious Death which my crimes deserve." She promised to "suffer willingly" and "thanked God that he has granted me time to repent."[5]

THE CRIMINAL TRIAL, ITS SETTING AND DYNAMICS

Cases like Malcolm's were famous criminal cases that caught the attention of the public and spurred rumors and discussions; others were the mundane fodder of the Old Bailey, which met eight times a year to hear serious cases, most of them felonies, punishable by death. The criminal legal system was a sorting process. During the seventeenth and eighteenth centuries strict laws, harsh punishments, and flexible enforcement characterized the English criminal process. In the eighteenth century England's "bloody code," which grew to prescribe the death penalty for over two hundred offenses (from arson, murder, and riot to smuggling and poaching), served as the backdrop for every serious felony. As Douglas Hay has argued, the ruling class who created and enforced the law "maintained their rule and moulded social consciousness" with "their discretionary use of the law."[6] These harsh criminal statutes created a judicial system in which mitigation was essential and could be applied at any time, from the discovery of the crime up to the moment of execution. The lack of an organized police force meant that most defendants had been caught red-handed by their victims or witnesses; trials often focused on the degree of an offender's accountability rather than strict questions of guilt or innocence.

During the eighteenth century changes in trial procedure and the explosion of print culture affected the dynamics of the trial, the presentation of evidence, and the trial's possible outcome. The introduction of defense counsel and the growing number and circulation of newspapers, pamphlets, and broadsides changed the trial's configuration and provided more opportunities to expound on arguments about motive and intent to shape the long, subtle process of selection in which jurors and judges, prosecutors and witnesses decided which accused offenders would be punished and how severely.[7] Meanwhile print culture expanded the audience of those readers and publishers who participated in the process of assessing the defendant's character and reputation.

Since the title of this volume invokes the Enlightenment as its temporal and cultural setting and context, the reader might be wondering what difference "Rights Talk" and the ideas expressed by Thomas Paine in *The Rights of Man* (1791–1792) made in the courtroom.[8] In fact the values of liberty and equality that resounded in the press, in popular pamphlets, and in legal commentary in the second half of the eighteenth century made very little difference in English courtrooms. Instead arguments in the eighteenth-century courtroom continued to pivot on character and reputation. These age-old signifiers remained the means by which communities arbitrated those groups and individuals who would or could be reintegrated and those who would not.[9] As the need for mitigation increased in the eighteenth century, extenuating circumstances, gender and age, community and religion became a part of the assessment of character and reputation, critically important to the criminal legal process. Although the global expansion of the British Empire coincided with a new local emphasis on rule of law and equality before the law, persistent questions of race, gender, status, nation, and boundary called attention to the contradictions embodied in enlightenment thought and its proclaimed universal values.[10]

In *De Republica Anglorum* (1583) the sixteenth-century political theorist Thomas Smith had portrayed the trial as an "altercation" between the two sides until the judge "hath heard them say inough."[11] François de la Rochefoucauld's 1784 account of a defendant's testimony was that:

> The accused is able to speak as much as he wishes and to defend himself as best he can; the judge never interrupts him. I actually saw, in one case, the prisoner interrupt the judge three times, and all three times the judge stopped to let him explain himself.[12]

When the prosecution completed its presentation, the accused responded to the charges against him or her with the support of witnesses, who until 1702 gave unsworn testimony. The accused faced intense pressure to construct a convincing defense with very little time to prepare and absolutely no knowledge of the evidence that would be brought against him or her in this intimidating and unfamiliar setting. Until the 1730s defendants could not call on legal representation. A prisoner's unmediated, unsworn response to the charges was considered the strongest defense. In this format, dubbed by John Langbein the "accused speaks" trial, the proceedings generally lasted between twenty and thirty minutes and compelled the accused to "serve as an informational resource at trial."[13]

To compensate for any disparity in power and knowledge between the prosecution and the defense, the judge was supposed to act as the prisoner's advocate. In complicated cases he could also assign counsel to the accused for advice in matters of law.[14] The judge might intervene to question the victim, the accused, and any other witnesses, interjecting comments and thinly veiled opinions. The judge directed every aspect of the trial: he controlled the flow of evidence, advised the jurors on how to weigh it, pointed out its strengths and weaknesses, and shaped the way the jury interpreted it.[15] The conversational nature of the trial and the exchange of questions and observations between the judge and jury gave the judge an informed sense of the jury's opinion of the evidence.[16] While some judges dispensed with summation or any detailed instructions to the jury, others charged the jury very specifically. Echoing Thomas Smith, in 1784 François de la Rochefoucauld (1765–1848) described the end of a trial at the Suffolk assizes:

When the judge finds that the evidence is sufficient, or that he has extracted everything that the witnesses and the accused can say, he rises and reads aloud to the petty jurymen his notes on the trial, expounds the law, indicates the most serious points, and gives the reasons for his opinion.[17]

The eighteenth-century trial, arbitrated mostly by middling men and local elites untrained in the law must have weighted heavily the opinion of the paid, professional, and learned judge.[18]

POPULAR PERCEPTIONS

People also read about criminal trials in the press. The late seventeenth and early eighteenth century saw rising literacy rates, the emergence of print culture, and a fascination with criminal biographies that led to an explosion in the number and kinds of stories about a range of criminals and their transgressions. The lapse in the Licensing Act in 1695 allowed for the development of an independent press.[19] The fascination with crime and the profits promised by its retelling created an industry of popular literature that included chapbooks, broadsides, ballads, newspapers and pamphlets that promised "true stories" about highway robbers, petty thieves, infanticides, and murderers.[20] Most prominent among this genre, the *Old Bailey Sessions Papers* (hereafter *OBSP*) began in the 1670s and featured published accounts of the work of the Old Bailey. A shorthand reporter recorded the trials which were published with ever-increasing detail at the end of each session. Produced as both entertainment and news, the reports gave sensational trials the best coverage, but for ordinary cases they accurately recorded the basic facts of the crime, the indictment, and the verdict, later including the opening statement by the attorney general as well as the judge's comments and questions. The courtroom drama featuring the words of prosecutors, jurors, judges, and defendants were recorded, published, read, and circulated more broadly than ever before. Other pamphlet accounts of crime, written by anonymous authors or sometimes attributed to the Ordinary (chaplain) of Newgate gaol who took advantage of his proximity to the prisoners in order to record, publish, and sell their stories, claimed to tell the prisoner's side of the story recounting the lives of condemned prisoners, detailing the prisoners' last days, and often including their confessions and repentance. Some pamphlets claimed to be autobiographies written by prisoners awaiting their death or reconstructed crimes that had been described in newspaper accounts or in the *OBSP*. They also drew on published trial transcripts, scaffold speeches, and confessions. Although not every detail they relate can be substantiated, the events they recount have been found generally consistent with information in indictments and other legal records, often providing insight into aspects of the legal process otherwise obscured.[21] These inexpensive printed sources, produced in response to the detection, prosecution, and punishment of crime, and consumed by a large and varied audience of readers and listeners, shaped and reflected popular conceptions of the law in the eighteenth century as well as ideas about reputation and character that played such an important role in the arguments made in court.[22]

As the press gathered its information about crime to satisfy the ravenous public appetite for these stories, they certainly had an impact on legal authorities and their knowledge of crimes and ongoing investigations. News about crimes and suspects circulated quickly, and "circuits of systemic newsgathering" developed.[23] Just as legal authorities staged the information they had before trial releasing it to the public in order to strengthen their case, so too the news had an impact on the trial shaping representations of suspects and their crimes. These evolving and vying representations were critical to the way the defendant's character and reputation would be assessed in the trial itself. While historians used to believe that these tabloid-like publications would be bought and read only by those of the lowest status, research documents the attraction of many of the middling sorts to these lurid details. They too consumed these pamphlet accounts. It is this segment of the population from which jurors were drawn.

EXPLANATIONS AND EXCUSES

Jurors used their discretionary powers to mitigate the harshness of the law and to apply it with selective rigor or leniency.[24] Property offenses constituted the majority of the felony cases that filled the court's calendar: the theft of goods valued at a shilling or more was grand larceny and a capital felony, while thefts under a shilling were petty larceny and non-capital.[25] Through "pious perjury" juries often undervalued the goods stolen and reduced the crime from a capital to a non-capital offense.[26] In addition to the undervaluation of goods, jurors could bring in a "partial verdict" that acquitted the prisoner of the indicted offense but convicted him of a less serious one. Jurors often reached such partial verdicts in cases of violent physical assault such as murder. By reducing a charge of homicide to manslaughter, juries avoided the imposition of the death penalty.[27] Jurors mitigated on the basis of an assessment of a myriad characteristics specific to each defendant such as age, sex, rank, standing in the community, good neighborliness, and respectability. Among these mitigating factors, the nature of the offense and its place within the context of the prisoner's life played an especially important role in the jurors' decisions about the excusable nature of the crime.[28] Strangers, those new to a community or migrating through it, were accused of crimes at a much higher rate and had a much more difficult case to make for mitigation and reintegration because they often had no one to vouch for them.[29]

One explanation for crime, insanity, had long served as its excuse.[30] Some defendants, in their attempts to seek mitigation for their crimes, elaborated and amplified a "language of the mind" stretching the insanity defense to include various mental states that ranged from delirium to confusion. Defendants represented themselves to the authorities as less than fully accountable for their behavior, admitting they had committed crimes but denying responsibility for their actions. These defendants spoke about mental distress, drunkenness, the pain of childbirth, and financial hardship as forces that overcame them and caused them to commit a variety of crimes from sedition to murder.[31]

During their brief deliberations jurors negotiated between their status as property-owning leaders of the community who found natural affinity with the political elite, the protectors of property who legislated the "bloody code," and their membership in their local community with its particular notions of acceptable or forgivable behavior. Jurors applied a flexible standard of proof which allowed them to assess the defendant's crime in the context of his or her general character.[32] They might raise the standard of proof to justify an acquittal on the grounds of insufficient evidence instead of on merciful grounds alone. Under the guise of the standard of proof, jurors could balance competing ideas about the enforcement of the law, the death penalty, and the specific character of each defendant.[33]

Langbein asserts that the "lawyerization" of the trial, the introduction of prosecutors and the increasing presence of defense counsel, silenced the accused.[34] Nevertheless, the emphasis on character and reputation persisted and if anything became more prominent.

In response to the intimidating and public setting, defendants developed many ways of talking about their crimes, often admitting their guilt while providing a wide range of explanations and excuses for their criminal behavior that they hoped would result in the jury's sympathy and secure a mitigated sentence. Whether influenced by the jury's new practice of sitting together in the courtroom, or the attention and success of the crime pamphlet, the coaching of counsel present at the magistrate's initial investigation of the crime or later at the trial, or the fear or prospect of transportation to the colonies or the death penalty, the accused and others who participated in legal dramas knew that they had only a brief court appearance at which to influence the trial's outcome and look ahead to the post-trial pardon process. In this setting it is not difficult to imagine that witnesses and defendants harnessed the tradition of the "accused speaks" trial, peppering their testimony with dramatic language to try to catch the attention of their listeners: the judge and jury, as well as the wider audience who read about or observed the drama and spectacle of the trial.

The pomp and circumstance that surrounded the trial were believed to be fundamental to the maintenance of the legitimacy of the law, especially the criminal justice system. Felony trials, whether held at London's Old Bailey or twice annually in provincial towns on the assize circuit, were a deliberately formal, intimidating, and effective display of the majesty, authority, and power of the governing classes. They were important events on the social calendars of provincial elites who met the judges at the county's border and processed with them into town. The coverage of trials in the press and the regular publication and increasingly comprehensive coverage of the *OBSP* ensured the circulation of cultural values about what made an upstanding character that might earn redemption and what kind of behaviors made reintegration impossible.

Contemporary literature, especially the novel, reflected a similar concern with questions of character echoing the kinds of excuses and explanations heard in court.[35] This is especially apparent in the novels of Daniel Defoe, which focused on the relationship between character, morality, and circumstance with a "casuistical emphasis on intention and qualifying circumstance."[36] In *Moll Flanders* (1722) Defoe discussed the distress of poverty and the emotional turmoil thought to result from indigence or even the threat of poverty.[37] When justifying her descent into a life a crime, Moll explained self-servingly that "vice came in always at the door of necessity, not at the door of inclination."[38] Although Defoe cast doubt on Moll's true intentions, he also described the apprehension of poverty which "doubled the misery" she felt and had an almost physical effect on her: she remarked that "the terror of approaching poverty lay hard upon my spirits."[39] The relationship between poverty and insanity haunted Moll. She described her state of mind as she contemplated her impending penury:

> I sat and cried and tormented my self night and day, wringing my hands and sometimes raving like a distracted woman; and indeed I have often wondered it had not affected my reason, for I had the vapours to such a degree that my understanding was sometimes quite lost in fancies and imaginations.[40]

She prayed "Give me not poverty, lest I steal."[41]

Moll recounted the stress and anxiety borne of poverty: "a time of distress is a time of dreadful temptation, and all the strength to resist is taken away; poverty presses, the soul is made desperate by distress, and what can be done?"[42] As she committed her first crime, she explained:

I am very sure I had no manner of design in my head, when I went out, I neither knew or considered where to go, or on what business, but as the devil carried me out and laid his bait for me, so he brought me to be sure to the place, for I knew not whither I was going or what I did.[43]

Moll refused intentionality and responsibility for the crimes she committed in a state of "distress." She disowned any malevolent intent and pointed to the devil as the perpetrator. She described herself as a passive victim, her mind distracted and her body at the mercy of outside forces beyond her control. Defoe's narrative alerted the reader of his skepticism about Moll's true motivation, even as he expressed sympathy for the plight of the poor.

Defendants and witnesses on their behalf defined criminal intent as an issue of character in which the offender tried to convince that jury that he or she was an upstanding member of the community and that the crime had been an isolated incident, an aberration of character. Defendants contended that a generally good reputation and a usually sober character served as proof that the offender lacked evil design and provided collateral against future mischief.[44] When John Moer was tried for horse theft in January 1716, the author of the *OBSP* summarized the verdict by saying "the prisoner, it seems, was a very honest man, a trooper (cavalryman), and being in drink thought what he did was a very harmless frolick."[45] In 1742 when Richard Harwood tried to break into William Roberts' house by climbing up a scaffold and into a window in the middle of the night, William Roberts dismissed the incident as "a drunken fit," and testified that he "has been with the said Harwood several times since and sold him upon credit a piece of Russia drab for a frock which he would not have done if he had thought the said Harwood had any ill design at the time of the attempt."[46] These neighbors seemed to have tolerated certain misbehavior that they considered harmless, and unpremeditated, measuring the damage of a given crime by assessing the nature of the offender's intent based on a broader knowledge and opinion of his or her personality and character.

In some cases of theft, the crime was presented as the result of necessity and the accused argued that he (usually it was a man) had to resort to crime in order to fulfill a role as provider—for self or for family—that he or she, had no other choice, and that even though the law had been broken, the crime was a part of an honorable character. When Richard Sweetman assaulted Mary Whitmarsh with the intent to steal her money in 1750, he told the court "I had a pistol in my hand, and was going to make away with myself, being in extremity and want, having a wife in a starving condition."[47] Valentine Dudden told the court that he stole two saws in 1772 because "I was really in want, and had been ill a great while; I did it through necessity; I am a carpenter."[48] Such arguments asked the justices, jurors, and judges to separate the individual's generally innocent character from the specific criminal act. Echoing Defoe's novel, the language in which defendants protested that they "lacked felonious intent" for crimes committed "from mere necessity" emphasized an understanding that poverty caused despair and impulsive, sometimes criminal behavior, a response to a specific set of extenuating circumstances. This testimony contained the claim that but for their penury, their moral instincts were good and their behavior within the law. In this context character shaped representations of intent.

No offense illustrates the localized relationship between intent, responsibility, and character better than deaths that resulted from fights that broke out in taverns or alehouses. In July 1721 Richard Grantham killed Norton Fitzgerald in a "sudden heat of passion." Witnesses represented this passion as both temporary and unusual. They described the two men as "intimate friends" and "a great many gentlemen" testified to the prisoner's "quiet and peaceable behavior."⁴⁹ Similarly in a case from the following year, several of Sergeant John Garton's fellow officers "gave the prisoner the character of being very humane, hardly ever known to be in a passion, and abuse men; but was remarkable for his lenity and even temper."⁵⁰ Testimony of deep friendship void of conflict between the killer and his victim accompanied descriptions of their comradery and the defendant's expression of deep regret and sorrow. In the depositions about Latus Ricarby's assault of Edward Purchas in 1758, the victim told the Justice of the Peace from his sickbed "that he does not believe the said wound was given through any quarrel, malice, or evil intent whatsoever."⁵¹ Purchas was convinced that Ricarby stabbed him with no evil intent because the accused was a friend who was drunk.

Just as a placid and calm temperament might exonerate or mitigate, a defendant's reputation for unprovoked violence, uncontrolled emotional outbursts, and indifference to the consequences of his or her actions bolstered an argument for harsher punishment or prolonged imprisonment. This negative testimony usually accompanied a recommendation for the continued detention of the accused. Two constables sent to arrest John Plaxton in 1729 described him as "so dangerous and desperate a man that he cares not what he does."⁵² In 1737, prominent members of the Ripley community filed an affidavit calling Robert Stephenson "very profane swearing drunken quarrelsome and dangerous" and urging his imprisonment. The petitioners cited Stephenson's "threatening words, barbarous and cruel treatment" of his neighbors, and unprovoked violent behavior in the past and expressed their fear of physical harm in the future.⁵³

Where did defendants like Sarah Malcolm and those less known offenders quoted above learn what kinds of arguments were effective in court? Bernard Mandeville took up this question in his *Enquiry into the Causes of Frequent Executions at Tyburn* (1725). He blamed jury discretion and frequent mitigation for the large number of repeat offenders who increased legal literacy by teaching the techniques of excuse to those arrested and awaiting trial. He warned against housing them together in Newgate where he opined that "nothing but the utmost Corruption can be expected from a Company of forty or fifty People in a Prison, who, everyone of them, singly consider'd were all the worst of Thousands before they met."⁵⁴ Beyond the "Encouragement to Vice" and the "Licentiousness" that would result from the proximity of the sexes, he cautioned that "Their most serious hours they spend in mock Tryals, and instructing one another in cross Questions, to confound Witnesses; and all the Stratagems and Evasions that can be of Service, to elude the Charge that shall be made against them."⁵⁵

Whether they learned to argue for mitigation from others with knowledge of the courtroom or from novels, pamphlets, images, and newspapers read, seen, or heard aloud in the taverns, coffeehouses, or drawing rooms of their masters and mistresses, these arguments appealing to the defendant's character and reputation as grounds for acquittal or a mitigated sentence often seem to have worked.⁵⁶ Peter King has demonstrated a consistent pattern of verdicts between 1740 and 1820 in which at least a third and sometimes nearly half the accused in Essex and elsewhere were discharged either by the grand jury or the petty jury and 10 percent of cases ended with a partial verdict.⁵⁷ After the pronouncement of the verdicts, jurors often explained their decisions either voluntarily or at the behest of the judge.⁵⁸

Although jurors left no notes about how they reached their decisions and why, we do have some insight about the grounds judges used to pardon convicted felons, and we can extrapolate from those to suggest what factors affected juror deliberation. William Blackstone (1723–1780) explained that a judge might reprieve a prisoner if he is not satisfied with the verdict, or the evidence is suspicious, or the indictment is insufficient, or he is doubtful whether the offense be within clergy, or sometimes if it be a small felony, or any favourable circumstances appear in the criminal's character, in order to give room to apply to the crown for either an absolute or a conditional pardon.[59]

Judges often cited extenuating circumstances to justify pardons; these mitigating factors could pertain to the crime (i.e., that the offense was unattended by violence, that the prisoner had not used a weapon, that the defendant was unarmed, that he returned the stolen object to its owner) or to the criminal (i.e., the prisoner's age, virtuous character, or good reputation). Families of convicted prisoners appealed to these same personal characteristics when they wrote letters seeking pardons for their loved ones.

EMOTIONS AND SENSIBILITIES

Much of the testimony made in these arguments for mitigation appealed to the emotions of those listening. Ideas about the expression of emotion in the eighteenth century, especially the emotive lives of elite men, were significantly shaped by the emergence of the language and culture of sensibility.[60] By the mid-eighteenth century "sensibility," which had referred to physical sensitivities, came to mean an emotional and moral faculty: it denoted a special and admirable susceptibility to one's own feelings and the feelings of others. As Adela Pinch has remarked, this period was marked by a "fascination with trying to account for where feelings come from and what they are."[61] Sentiment and sensibility and the relationship between emotion and morality preoccupied the literature of sensibility at its most influential and widespread from the 1740s to the 1770s.[62] Although novels are the best-known expression of the culture of sensibility, philosophical essays, newspapers, sermons, and crime pamphlets also shared these preoccupations. Scholars have concluded that "the era of sensibility defined relations between middle class British men and women and their social others: Indians, slaves, the poor, and the mad."[63] These relations were modeled in the literature of sensibility built upon the assumption that life and literature were directly linked. In its capacity to teach fiction or narrative "showed people how to behave, how to express themselves in friendship and how to respond decently to life's experiences."[64]

But emotion could work in several different directions in the courtroom. As Chief Justice of the King's Bench from 1754 to 1756, Sir Dudley Ryder (1691–1756) presided at criminal trials at the Old Bailey; he also served on the Home Circuit during the summers of 1754 and 1755. On Friday August 9, 1754 at Chelmsford in Essex, Ryder heard the case of Frances Cheek, accused of murdering her six-month old child. A neighbor found Cheek "kneeling over the body of [her] child, cut plainly with a chicken hook lying by bloody." When asked why she did it, Cheek "said nothing but that she should be hanged and knew nothing of the matter." A clergyman who saw her after the crime testified that "she was then distracted." In his notes on the case Ryder concluded that "she was two days after clearly not out of her senses, nor now at her trial nor during the intermediate time, nor any evidence given of her having been disordered before, but one witness said she was a hasty passionate woman." When he charged the jury, Ryder told them "they must consider whether she did the fact, and if so whether she was out of her senses when she did the fact, immaterial whether she was so afterwards when she reflected what she had done."[65]

A disagreement between the judge and the jury ensued. The jury "first said they were satisfied she killed the child but doubted her sanity" which would suggest an acquittal. Despite his own admission that Cheek "looked wild and disturbed" at her trial, Ryder "explained again to them the nature of the case rather against the prisoner" and sent them back to deliberate further. Ryder seemed concerned to distinguish between Cheek's distraught emotional performance at the trial and her emotional state when she killed the child. An hour and a half later (a lengthy deliberation by eighteenth-century standards) the jury brought in a conviction. Ryder noted that he "told them I was very well satisfied" and pronounced a death sentence to be followed by dissection—the ultimate punishment.[66] The conviction rate for infanticide had dropped by the second decade of the eighteenth century, so this 1754 conviction stands out as unusual.[67]

The separation of justice and sensibility did not, however, lead Ryder to repress his emotions or to portray himself as an unfeeling man, insensitive to the emotional testimony he heard. Quite the contrary: when he handed down Cheek's death sentence, Ryder reported that "I made a very proper speech *extempore* and pronounced it with dignity." In his diary, he described his feelings as he condemned Frances Cheek: "I was so affected that the tears were gushing out several times against my will." Self-conscious about the public nature of his emotional outburst, Ryder noted that "it was discerned by all the company—which was large—and a lady gave me her handkerchief dipped in lavender water to help me."[68]

By leaving his show of emotion until the pronouncement of the death sentence, Ryder achieved what he deemed an appropriate balance of emotion and justice. He enforced justice by insisting on a conviction and displayed sensibility when reading the death sentence. In his speech Ryder attempted to reclaim his authority and the authority of middle-class masculinity in a culture of sensibility. When he rejected acquittal and directed the jury to convict Francis Cheek, he asserted his authority over the trial. Gesturing to the middle-class jurors he reconstituted the trial as the setting for the traditional masculine values of reason, self-control, and stoicism while rejecting the efficacy of emotional arguments. Ryder's tears at the sentencing may have signaled some compassion that he deemed appropriate only at the post-trial phase of the criminal legal process. The male judges concerned to perform their heightened emotions inhabited a position of power that enabled them to do so while still upholding notions of an objective justice that considered only arguments relating to "the nature of the case rather against the prisoner," specifically their character and reputation.

Martin Madan (1726–1790) commented on the negative effect that appeals to sensibility had on jurors and their consideration of the facts of the case. He complained about judicial officials who "preferring their own feelings as men, to the duty which they owe the public as magistrates ... have been making so wanton and indiscriminate an use, or rather abuse, of certain discretionary powers with which they are invested."[69] Madan admonished juries who "frequently acquit the prisoner, against all fact and truth," giving "a verdict *according* to their *feelings*, but *against* their *oath*." He provided indirect evidence about the place of character and reputation when he counseled jurors that their verdict ought to reflect an evaluation of the facts of the crime alone. Madan listed liquor, youth, good character, and the influence of others as circumstances that struck "the minds of the jury" when they gave "verdicts diametrically opposite to the evidence which has been delivered."[70]

But not all commentators eschewed sensibility or its effects on the way jurors might hear arguments made in the courtroom. Manassaw Dawes (*d.* 1829) commented in

1782 that "criminals do not offend so much from choice as from misery and want of sentiment."[71] According to Dawes those with "vulgar minds ... are the least sensible of social right and wrong, have no sentiment, no taste, and are incapable of knowing their own good, or the good of others."[72] In order to understand the full dimensions of crime, Dawes embraced the affinity of sensibility and justice. In the courtroom

> men of sense will compassionate all human and social offenders, lament their offences, and sigh over the unhappy cause of them;—they will look upon the wretched prisoner ... and grieve over his condition.[73]

Dawes did not deny or discourage the effects of compassion on a jury. Instead he saw it as the beginning of a process of dispensing mercy.

> They will not be contented that he has offended, but they will examine why; and tracing the cause, be disposed to forgive an effect, which it was impossible to avoid; and thus feeling the force and power of the mind, they will sparingly punish the man.[74]

EMPIRE AND THE OTHER

These discussions of character and reputation reflect old means of deciding the parameters of community and defining insiders and outsiders. As the Empire expanded in the middle of the eighteenth century encompassing ever-greater cultural, religious, ethnic, and racial variation, legal authorities and subjects struggled over the legal status and treatment of Jews, gypsies, Africans, Scots, Irish, Catholics, and non-conforming Protestants, all of whom came to represent—at home in England—the consequences of British imperial expansion. Legal arguments framed as they were around individual character also negotiated the fine line between white, Anglican English men and women and the many groups of "internal others" who called London home but were not considered "true born Englishmen." British claims about equality before the law drew internal others into the legal and legislative system as they sought legal mechanisms for defining, defending, and differentiating their status and identity. In contrast to the professed discourse of rule of law and equality before the law, the English legal process maintained and sustained distinctions of race, ethnicity, gender, and class before the law folding them into older assessments of character and reputation.

Stories about criminal women attracted a tremendous amount of attention in the sixteenth and seventeenth centuries.[75] With the expansion of print culture in the eighteenth century these trial accounts, biographies, and images contributed to fears and anxieties about single women who were often portrayed as dangerous and threatening. Amy Masciola argues that among independent women, those who lived in groups and formed their own households, completely separated from men, were most troubling.[76] Although all women were considered suspicious and open to deviant influences, single women were portrayed as particularly uncontained, dangerous sexual predators in the seventeenth century and these images grew in the eighteenth century to include all women who were believed to lack emotional control and the ability to restrain their feelings or their behavior.[77] Related to and perhaps a catalyzing force in these negative representations of single women was the demographic fact that the number of single women increased in the late seventeenth century to an estimated 15 percent of the population which led to the emergence of the "old maid" as a social problem and a cultural trope associated with degeneration.[78]

The demand for domestic servants in the eighteenth century drew many young single men and women to London in the eighteenth century with a full 25 percent of the nation's residents spending at least part of their lives (mostly in their youth, employed as servants) in the city's environs. Women outnumbered men.[79] Domestic servants made up at least 10 percent of London's population: their independence and the autonomy they gained because demand outstripped supply and their proximity to middling families caused tension and conflict between servants and their masters and mistresses. The result was a growing suspicion of and disdain for female servants who were suspected of stealing material objects they cleaned, seducing the masters of the house, corrupting their young female charges, and generally upending the social order.[80]

The growth of Britain's empire over the course of the eighteenth century saw a change in the depictions of the individual and collective female body. When compared with non-English women, English women were considered civilized, domestic, and sexually contained. White women from warmer climates and women of color were represented as prone to excessive carnal desires and unrestrained sexual behavior. Felicity Nussbaum argues for the mutually constitutive character of these sexual profiles in which the colonized English woman's civility and virtue relied on the invention of the excesses of the "other" woman.[81]

When accused of crimes, single women, England's first internal outsiders, faced questions about their sexuality and their bodies. The alleged kidnapping and assault of Elizabeth Canning in January 1753 featured four single women, Elizabeth Canning, Mary Squires, Susannah Wells, and Virtue Hall. The explicit disputes about these women concerned their whereabouts, their physical integrity, and their moral character. At the Old Bailey trial of Mary Squires and Susannah Wells, Squires was accused of assaulting Elizabeth Canning, "putting her in corporal fear and danger of her life" and stealing "one pair of stays, value 10s the property of the said Elizabeth."[82] Wells was tried as her accomplice. The trial narrative prominently featured Mary Squires, a gypsy. Layered onto the arguments about single women, stereotypes about gypsies played a central role in the recitation of the crime and its subsidiary details. These descriptions corroborated unflattering, threatening expectations of this ethnic group: an association with criminality, an itinerant lifestyle, a livelihood in sales, distinctive dress, a familiarity with magic, and promiscuous sexuality.[83]

According to her trial testimony, when Elizabeth entered the house, she saw "the gypsey woman Squires" who "took me by the hand, asked me if I chose to go their way, saying if I did, I should have fine cloaths." Canning refused and in response Mary Squires took a knife out of the dresser drawer and "cut the lace off my stays, and took them from me." Canning told the court that she thought "she [Squires] was going to cut my throat, when I saw her take the knife." Squires then gave Canning "a slap on the face," pushed her upstairs into a hay loft, and said that "if ever she heard me stir or move, or any such thing, she'd cut my throat."[84]

Mary Squires spoke up several times during the recitation of the evidence against her to deny any knowledge of Canning and to declare "I am as innocent as the child unborn." Perhaps strategically, she did not speak in her own defense. Instead, several witnesses appeared on her behalf. Their testimony referred to and at times emphasized the negative characteristics associated with the group labeled the gypsies. John Giben said he had known Squires for three years and provided her an alibi. He testified that between the first and the ninth of January 1753 Squires and her children had stayed in his inn, the Old-Ship, in Abbotsbury, six miles from Dorchester and about 130 miles southwest of London.

William Clark corroborated this account saying that he had seen Squires at Giben's inn when he went to "have a pot of liquor" on New Year's Day. Clark explained that the last time he saw Squires was on January 10, 1753: "I met with them on the road, we went some way together, we parted at Crudeway-foot, four miles from Abbotsbury and three from Dorchester." Thomas Grevil testified that he had seen Squires and her children in Coombe (near Salisbury) on January 14 adding that they "stopped there but one night." All three men cited the itinerant nature of Squires' lifestyle to support their contention that she had not been in London on the night of Elizabeth Canning's abduction.[85]

The testimony of her alibi witnesses connected the constant travel associated with Squires and with gypsies to their engagement in commerce. When asked how long he had known the defendant, Clark told the court that he had seen Squires and her son and daughter "three years ago come March, at Abbotsbury, they came with handkerchiefs, lawns, and muslins to sell." Giben said the same adding that Squires and her children "offered them to sell to me, and others, my wife bought two cheque aprons."[86] Again Clark and Giben fulfilled expectations of Squires as an itinerant salesperson. This image of gypsies as rootless, shifty vagrants, engaged in some sort of commerce, often associated with smuggling, was reinforced when Clark added that he "saw them going about the town in the time, to sell things."[87] While this testimony supported the innocence of Squires and her children, it was still nonetheless built on negative stereotypes that reinforced Squires and her children as outsiders.

Several witnesses were asked about the clothes worn by Squires and her children. Canning described Squires "sitting in her gown with a handkerchief about her head." Asked what the children were wearing, Clark said that "the son [was] in a blue coat and a red waistcoat and had a great coat with him" while the daughter was "in a camblet gown." These questions point to images of gypsies dressed in colorful garb, characterized by one author as "od and phantasticke," and intersected with the specifics of this case: Squires' commerce in "handkerchiefs, lawns, and muslins," her supposed promise to Canning that in return for a life of prostitution, she "should have fine clothes," and the allegation that she cut and stole Canning's stays. Taken individually these details lacked any inherent criminality; considered together they worked as a condemnation of women's vanity, attributing to gypsies in particular a proclivity for drawing attention to themselves as potent sexual beings, managing their sexual image and destiny. Whether this was the intention of these witnesses or not, these references associated Squires in the minds of jurors and readers alike with depictions of gypsy women said to be trained for sensuality and lacking in shame.

In their rebuttal of Squires' alibi, the prosecution skillfully inserted a reference to magic, the black arts, and the supernatural so often associated with gypsies. John Inister said that he had spotted Squires "several times every day up and down before she was taken." He implied that he had seen her in Enfield when she claimed to be in Dorchester, and he added that "she walked into people's houses pretending to tell fortunes. She told mine once."[88] Squires was found guilty and sentenced to death and Wells to six months in jail. But contradictory evidence presented at the trial raised doubts about the facts of the case. An investigation by Sir Crisp Gascoyne (1700–1761), Lord Mayor of London, resulted in Virtue Hall recanting her testimony, and on May 21, 1753 Squires was granted a full pardon. Elizabeth Canning was brought to trial for perjury in April 1754; she was found guilty and transported to the American colonies.

Allan Ramsay (1713–1784) noted in his pamphlet written in June 1753 after Squires' pardon that he could not help being surprised to find upon what slight grounds [Fielding] and many other sensible men, had founded their belief in her [Canning's] veracity; and that they should be satisfied with evidence that seems to be in no manner adequate to the nature of the facts meant to be proved by it.[89]

Given Ramsay's observation, and our examination of the trial, I want to suggest that Mary Squires' otherness and foreignness were absolutely necessary in order to make Canning's story at all believable. Squires' conviction reflected a belief that gypsies were inherently dishonest, promiscuous, cunning criminals. Ramsay said as much when he explained that Canning's accomplices remained silent for "their own preservation" or because "their friendship for her makes them prefer her safety and character to the life of an old gipsey."[90] Ramsay seems to be looking for an explanation for the failure of the English legal system which in the absence of a paid police force depended so heavily on information provided by members of the community. Ramsay attributed the inaction of those who may have known something about the incident to their perception that their responsibility to testify was nullified by the gypsy's status as an aged outsider who did not belong to the local or national community.

The visual representations from the Canning case vividly map the categories of difference onto the bodies of the women involved. A picture (Figure 5.2), widely circulated and often reproduced, shows the two protagonists, Canning and Squires, side by side; the sharp distinction between them leaves no question as to what the viewer is to think about their respective innocence and guilt. Canning stares at the viewer with a modest but forthright look that captures the incapacity for deceit, the "Goodness, as well as Childishness and Simplicity of her Character" that Henry Fielding attributed to her when he said she was "a child in years and yet more so in understanding."[91] Her face,

FIGURE 5.2 Elizabeth Canning and Mary Squires. Anonymous, *c.* 1753–1760. Source: © The Trustees of the British Museum.

framed by a bonnet, is completely unobstructed. Although she wears a cape, it is drawn aside to reveal a tightly laced bodice that seems to encase her honor and her virtue. In contrast, Squires looks away from the viewer, her hat and closed cloak suggesting an effort to conceal and obfuscate. The image of Canning is bright, her skin excessively white in comparison to the darkness that enshrouds the portrait of Squires (Figure 5.3). The young woman epitomizes passivity and docility while the old woman embodies an active agent of threat and deceit.

With its exaggerated images of Mary Squires as a gypsy the case foregrounded long-held anxieties about vagrancy and concerns about insiders and outsiders as it revealed

FIGURE 5.3 Mary Squires. Thomas Worlidge, etched from a drawing by Richard Edgcumbe, *c.* 1753. Source: Courtesy of The Lewis Walpole Library, Yale University.

the reality of geographic mobility that shattered early modern notions of continuity, place, and community, considered the most trustworthy means of measuring character and credibility.[92] Depicted as a crone, a witch, and "the sovereign of the Lapland race," the prints present Mary Squires as a deceitful interloper, performer of black magic, unwelcome and constantly on the move. John Hill described Squires' face: "like that of no human Creature. The lower Part of it affected most remarkably by the Evil: the under Lip of an enormous Thickness; and the nose such as never before stood in a mortal Countenance."[93] Squires, the "gipsy," described by Fielding as possessing "scarce even the Appearance of Humanity,"[94] was portrayed as lacking all morality, credibility, or assimilability. The references to the gypsy as non-human, the "worst face of an uncivilized and unacceptable society," echo the descriptions of Malcolm's monstrosity.[95] In making an emotional appeal to judges and jurors defendants relied on finding some commonality between the two groups, a difficult or impossible task when the accused was dehumanized as a threatening foreigner and an outsider who did not belong.[96]

CONCLUSION

At the end of the eighteenth century, Edmund Burke pronounced in *Reflections on the Revolution in France* (1790) that the preservation of "good order is the foundation of all good things ... The people, without being servile, must be tractable and obedient. The magistrate must have his reverence, the laws their authority."[97] For Burke the growing discourse of equality and inalienable rights threatened every aspect of life especially the military while law upheld hierarchy, inheritance, and an aristocratic order.[98] In response Thomas Paine spoke of the "equal rights of man" and "the unity of man; by which I mean, that men are all of one degree, and consequently that all men are born equal, and with equal natural right."[99] These arguments generally stayed in the political realm, relating to nations, sovereignty, and the place of the people in the making of laws.

Few criminal trials in eighteenth-century Britain took up these lofty and abstract themes. Instead they often turned on evidence about character and reputation. Although as this chapter has argued the outcome was far from assured, as long as offenders caught in the criminal act made up the majority of those who came to trial, the prosecution had only to present evidence about the whereabouts of the prisoner and details of the crime he or she was caught perpetrating. Most of those accused or witnesses on their behalf responded that although they may have indulged in criminal behavior, their generally law-abiding behavior and their "sober reputation" served as grounds for a mitigated sentence that should spare their lives. In the latter half of the eighteenth century as the Empire expanded criminal cases arbitrated the struggle between white, Anglican English men and women and the many who called London home but were not considered English. Arguments about character applied negatively or positively to groups of England's "internal outsiders" creating and maintaining differences through hierarchies of race, ethnicity, religion, gender, and sexuality.

CHAPTER SIX

Property and Possession

JULIA RUDOLPH

After some Pause, it came my Turn to speak; Well, *says I*, 'tis very hard a Gentleman with such a Fortune as this, shou'd come over to *England*, and marry a Wife with *Nothing*; it shall never, *says I*, be said, but what I have, I'll bring into the Publick Stock; so I began to produce.

First, I pulled out the Mortgage which the good Sir *Robert* had procur'd for me, the annual Rent 700*l. per Annum*; the principal Money 14000*l.*

Secondly, I pull'd out another Mortgage upon Land, procur'd by the same faithful Friend, which at three times had advanc'd 12000*l.*

Thirdly, I pull'd him out a Parcel of little Securities, procur'd by several Hands, by Fee-Farm Rents, and such Petty Mortgages as those Times afforded, amounting to 10800*l.* principal Money, and paying six hundred and thirty six Pounds a-Year; so that in the while, there was two thousand fifty Pounds a-Year, Ready-Money, constantly coming in.

–Daniel Defoe, The Fortunate Mistress: Or, A History of the Life
and Vast Variety of Fortunes of ... Roxana ([1724] 2009: 266)

Roxana's breathless recital of her productive investments comes late in Defoe's novel, signaling not only the wise management of her ill-gotten gains but also the importance of property and possession in eighteenth-century culture. This depiction of financial-legal documents being "pull'd out" and proliferating—imagined records of lease and release, perhaps exhibiting the weighty significance of folded parchment along with the more ephemeral, smaller parcel of notes and rents—conveys both the sense of excitement and the potential for dangerous excess in a changing eighteenth-century economy.

The scene is also testimony to the prevalence of mortgages in the eighteenth century, their significant role in a changing law of property, and their central but controversial place in a newly expanding commercial system. The mortgage, and its depiction by novelists, playwrights, poets, and artists, thus provides an excellent case study of ideas about property and possession in eighteenth-century law and culture.

Since mortgages were an important feature of the expansion of a credit economy in late seventeenth and eighteenth-century Britain, they became one focus for wider societal debates about the nature of credit, the problem of debt, the value of land and other kinds of assets. Scenes of struggle over mortgage agreements, in works like Eliza Haywood's short fiction *The City Jilt* (1726) and William Taverner's play *The Artful Husband* (1717) for example, offered pointed contributions to these debates. These texts articulated varied positions in a long-running controversial literature regarding new wealth and social mobility. Here the values of new monied merchants, stockbrokers and "cits" (a contemptuous term used for townsmen and tradesmen) were pitted against the power of aristocratic landed interests. The kind of property one owned, and how it was possessed, were seen as determinants of identity and status.

Similarly, Daniel Defoe employed the image of mortgage as investment both in the scene described above, and in an earlier scene detailing Roxana's education in mortgage practice, in order to further his strong promotion of merchant values. Defoe depicted the famous banker, broker and investment advisor, Sir Robert Clayton (Figure 6.1), explaining to his client,

FIGURE 6.1 Sir Robert Clayton. Lorenzo a Castro, *c.* 1664–1700. Source: 0829/Sir Robert Clayton by Lorenzo de Castro. © The Governor and Company of the Bank of England.

That an Estate is a Pond; but that a Trade was Spring; that if the first is once mortgag'd, it seldom gets clear, but embarrass'd the Person for ever; but the Merchant had his Estate continually flowing; and upon this he nam'd me Merchants who liv'd in more real Splendor, and spent more Money than most of the Noblemen in *England* cou'd singly expend, and that they still grew immensely rich. (Defoe [1724] 2009: 189)

As this chapter will demonstrate, Defoe and others developed this critique of landed wealth by tying it to a critique of male power, property law, and inheritance practices. The expansion of long-term mortgage was, in fact, one feature of the development of the strict settlement, a way to structure inheritance so that an "entailed" estate would pass to named male heirs; this entail put obstacles in the way of any sale or alienation of the family property. Associated methods in estate planning aimed at preserving and sharing out family wealth, from the mid-seventeenth century on. By contrast with our contemporary use of mortgage as a means for individuals *without* estates to purchase property, in the eighteenth century mortgage was widely used by *propertied* Englishmen as a way to raise money. This use of mortgage signaled these Englishmen's attitudes towards property, underscoring their claims to long possession and their sense of entitlement to land. They typically mortgaged property as a means to provide portions, or funds, for daughters and younger sons, and viewed the mortgage as one part of a comprehensive plan to maintain a family estate (Clay 1981; Quinlan and Neal 1994; Shackleford 1994). This recourse to mortgage was actively encouraged by eighteenth-century attorneys and solicitors who helped to increase the number and kinds of mortgages available. Moreover, propertied Englishmen and Englishwomen entered into mortgage agreements as creditors as well as borrowers, and as Defoe's novel shows, men like Clayton helped to facilitate these investments. (Figure 6.2).

Making secured loans to landowners who wished to improve their land, as well as those who were in straitened circumstances, was regarded as sound strategy in an era of increasing investment opportunities. Prominent judges, local JPs and wealthy widows were among those who made such loans, and they played an essential role in the formation of local, as well as broadly British, credit networks (Duman 1982; Hoppit 1987; Laurence 2008).[1]

Because of this widespread use, multiple areas of mortgage law—as well as aspects of marriage and inheritance law—became implicated in the broader debate over socio-economic change. Mortgages featured in a developing critique of old landed power, but critics also expressed deep unease about the corrupting effects of new wealth, and worried that participation in the new financial sector could lead to ruin. Men "bred in the City," a character in Taverner's companion play to *The Artful Husband, The Artful Wife* (1718), pointedly comments,

> never keep their Words, and that's the only gentile Quality they have, but are guided by Interest: Profit's their Idol and Credit a staulking Horse, which they sell or barter when they can get by it. They set up, and then break for Profit; they give Notes, and never pay 'em for Profit; dissemble, cant, seem religious, deceive and all for Profit's sake. (1718: 26)

Here the profit-seeking financier was as suspect as the gentleman especially because his attitudes had the potential to undermine the trust at the heart of credit and community. It was also feared that the nation itself was in danger because of government reliance on credit financing by "the City," and the new growth of the public debt. Defoe's notorious image of

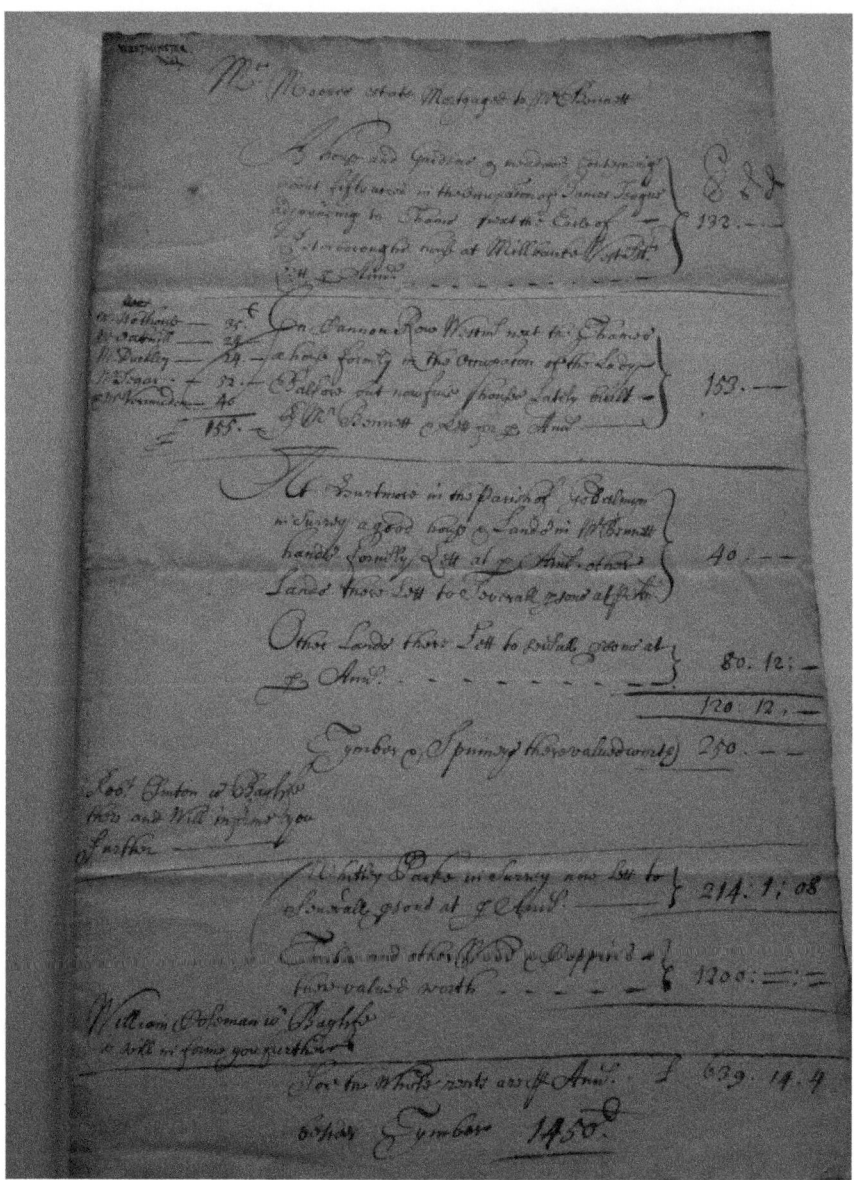

FIGURE 6.2 Moore's estate mortgage. Mr. Moore's estate mortgaged to Mr. Bennett, n.d. Source: London Metropolitan Archives, Clayton-Morris Collection, CLC/B/050/A/170 (photo by Julia Rudolph).

Lady Credit—easily identified with the mortgage, and Roxana as Mortgagee—distinctly conveyed contemporary ambivalence about the great potential, but also instability, of wealth amassed through investment and speculation. Credit was "the potent changeable lady," the scholar Laura Brown explains, who appeared in Defoe's essays and throughout the periodical press, and "dominate[d] the feminized representation of modern finance in the early eighteenth century" (2001: 97, 103). The kinds of danger that contemporaries attached to this association between credit and the female body can easily be understood by reflecting again on the image of Roxana pulling out her mortgages, all purchased with money made through prostitution. Here Defoe, like so many other writers, explored the ways in which commercial society promoted gender as well as social mobility, but also encouraged the commodification of women and men.

Many of these same concerns about gender norms and social mobility were addressed in eighteenth-century case reports and legal treatises. Indeed there are ways in which we might trace the impact of such literary and public discourses on the development of mortgage law itself. The focus of this chapter, however, is on the representation and interpretation of property law in literature and art. How were the operations of different facets of law, such as mortgage, entail or coverture, understood by novelists like Eliza Haywood or artists like William Hogarth? What roles did law play, and what purposes might it have served, in the expression of cultural norms and literary ideals? And finally how did the authority of juridical doctrine stand in relation to the fictionality of the novel or play? When was verisimilitude the goal, and when and why did authors seek to distort, challenge, or even change the law?

EQUITY OF REDEMPTION

"In his novel *Roxana*," the historian of banking Frank Melton avers, "Defoe presented [Sir Robert] Clayton as the only real figure amid fictional characters, to explain what he understood about private banking." Defoe—who was a tradesman, and a journalist concerned with politics and economy, as well as a novelist—depicted particular practices followed by Clayton, like the issuance of receipts and the formulation of interest tables, and clearly "refers to Clayton's specialty as investing in mortgage loans" (1986: 8).[2] Melton is surely right that Defoe's focus on this banker was deliberate: it reflected the author's awareness of the significance of Clayton's work during a critical period of development in mortgage practice and doctrine.

Clayton's career coincided with the chancellorship of Heneage Finch, 1st Earl of Nottingham and Lord Chancellor between 1675 and 1682, whose judicial decisions helped to establish new and ostensibly more reliable mortgage rules within English law in the later seventeenth century. Nottingham is more generally credited with beginning the work of regularizing and organizing equity law into a "system of principles and rules designed to supplement the common law, by emphasizing requirements of honesty and good faith in legal transactions and relations" (Yale 2004). These legal transactions included contracts and trusts as well as mortgages, and Nottingham's rulings had an impact in these areas too, in part because such agreements were quite often interrelated. It was in the mortgage dispute of *Newcomb v Bonham* (1681) that Nottingham set out his influential "general rule": "once a mortgage and always a mortgage." This rule became an established statement of the principle of equity of redemption, and this case functioned as an important precedent for subsequent generations of lawyers, legal scholars, and legal historians.[3]

"Equity of redemption" was a doctrine originating in the Court of Chancery that established that a mortgagor always retained an equitable right to redeem and regain his property and so, in effect, always remained the "true owner" of the property (Baker 2002: 313). By contrast, according to common law rules, if a mortgagor failed to pay monies borrowed at the agreed time he lost the property he had pledged to secure the loan, in a process known as foreclosure. As early as the fifteenth century mortgagors had turned to equity for relief from the severity of this penalty for default. Chancellors granted relief in particular cases where the monetary value of this penalty seemed excessive; or in cases where default occurred because of some kind of misfortune suffered by the mortgagor, or because of some kind of unfair advantage taken by the mortgagee. By the early seventeenth century, this relief had come to be generally expected, so that mortgagors could petition the Chancellor for the "usual clemency" (Turner 1931; Yale 1965: 32; Simpson 1986: 244). Over these two centuries—and continuing into the next—Chancellors worked out the equitable principles underlying this remedy, by first focusing on the parties' intentions in creating a mortgage. Chancellors emphasized the fact that a mortgage was created not to convey property but rather to secure a loan. Since the mortgagor's intention was to repay the loan, rather than convey the property, jurists concluded that he should always be able to regain his property if he eventually (within a reasonable time) repaid the money due (along with additional interest and costs). In making this distinction regarding intention, jurists relied on an insight about the consequences of a mortgagor's default: since a creditor could be made whole through repayment, they reasoned, but a debtor would suffer significant loss through foreclosure, the debtor could be protected without causing any harm to the lender.

By the last decades of the seventeenth century, then, the principle of a mortgagor's equity of redemption seemed to be well entrenched in English law. It rested on that understanding that when a mortgage was made the mortgaged property was understood to stand merely as security for the loan; and it was further stipulated that the lender obtained no "collateral advantage" to whittle away that property by postponing repayment or applying penalties thereafter.[4] Since mortgaged property was conceived of as security only, the lender's interest was "mere personalty," that is a right to the money. "But where a mortgage is made of an Estate, that is only considered as a Security for Money due," Lord Chancellor Hardwicke confirmed in 1740, "the Land is the Accident attending upon the other; and when the Debt is discharged, the Interest in the Land follows of course."[5] The mortgagor's equity of redemption was, by contrast, coming to be seen as a form of real property. "Like the trust," the legal historian John Baker asserts, the equity of redemption "had become an equitable estate" and the courts generally upheld this principle, safeguarding owners from loss of property (2002: 313, 314).[6]

Many commentators, then and now, have regarded this doctrine of the equity of redemption as an elegant solution to the problem of protecting both debtor and creditor rights. Claims about the implications of this solution have been extensive and have often echoed those earlier eighteenth-century debates about social mobility and economic change. Several historians have depicted such developments in mortgage law as an important part of that commercial change taking place in late seventeenth and eighteenth-century England; this was a legal doctrine, they say, that sanctioned the growth of the culture of borrowing by allowing for reliable expectations between parties. Other historians insist that the significance of mortgage doctrine lay in its tendency to promote the stability of landed property and to maintain the status and power of aristocratic interests (Schmidt 1990; Staves 1994; Sugarman and Warrington 1996). The relevant point, again, is that in this period mortgage was primarily a means of making money, a way for the wealthy to amass more wealth.

These broad scholarly debates over the interpretation of the law relating to mortgages have relied on the general assumption that the equitable doctrine worked, that debtors were protected, and creditors at least unharmed. Yet the scholarship has also demonstrated that this balance between creditor and debtor rights in mortgage was a fragile compromise:

it was complicated because of tensions between commercial and landed interests; it was complicated because of the novelty and growing complexity of mortgage agreements in the eighteenth century as they became implicated in the development of different kinds of financial instruments; and it was complicated because of particular demands and variations in women's property holding that developed in this period as well. It is not clear how well the doctrine worked, nor how far mortgagors were protected in practice.

Further research into the relevant case law, together with printed treatises and manuscript sources, promises to uncover the practical operation of the equity of redemption, and should enable us to assess how real the threat of foreclosure loomed in eighteenth-century England. As this chapter will demonstrate, however, it is also critical to explore the ways in which the threat of foreclosure was *perceived* by authors, artists and, by implication, their public. Literary examples reveal the kinds of fears and attitudes towards mortgage that were shared by contemporaries, and that formed an important context within which legal doctrine functioned. Primary among those fears were the notorious figures of the profligate husband and the prodigal son; essential to those attitudes were the sentimental figures of the ruined daughter, the worthy orphan and the desperate widow. These characters and their stories form an important part of the cultural operation of law.

PROFLIGATE HUSBANDS AND PRODIGAL SONS

In Defoe's novel, Roxana's troubles began when her husband succumbed to crushing debt. Although he had appeared to be an attractive match—a handsome sportsman, and son of an eminent businessman—Roxana's husband turned out to be "a weak, empty-headed, untaught Creature" ([1724] 2009: 48). In this work, and others, Defoe underscored the potential problems created by the common law doctrine of coverture, whereby a husband assumed legal dominion over any property that his wife had or acquired, and the system of primogeniture, whereby sons were favored over daughters, and older sons over younger ones, when determining the inheritance of landed estates.

Similar kinds of information about the operation of legal doctrines like coverture spread through a variety of sources in this era of an expanding print culture. Defoe's works were published at the same time that abridgments and popular manuals of law were becoming increasingly available. Texts like *A Treatise of Feme Coverts: Or the Lady's Law* (1732), and Giles Jacob's *Every Man his Own Lawyer* (1736), were aimed at the general reader and conceived as helpful guides to pursuing litigation or managing family affairs (Rudolph 2013). Like the novel, these texts were meant to be accessible and interesting to a broad audience of readers at various levels of socioeconomic status. As the author of a *Treatise of Feme Coverts* noted in a preface, his text not only included information about marriage and the "Laws and Statutes concerning Women in general," but it also included "some Things of Entertainment mix'd with the Law [since] our old Laws and Customs relating to Women, are many of them very merry, though the Makers of them might possibly be grave men."[7]

For those primarily seeking entertainment, still mixed with information about law, the new genre of the novel was likely to be more attractive and clearly reached a wider audience than these legal manuals. That was due in part to the fact that novels and other new forms of print like the newspaper and magazine, circulated in new ways. The coffee shops that proliferated in British towns, as they did in towns across eighteenth-century Europe, were an especially important venue for the wider consumption of print. By the middle of the century access to print was also provided by circulating libraries that had been established in London and in most provincial towns. Now instead of a luxury affordable only by the privileged and educated few, newspapers, magazines, and books were becoming popular and available. Readership, particularly for the novel, spanned the social scale. Scholars generally agree that by the middle of the eighteenth century literacy was rising, especially among women, and that it was increasingly common for middling and lower orders in urban areas to be literate consumers of print (Hunter 1990; Brewer 1997; Raven 2004). Moreover, the widespread interest in law helped to fuel this expanding print culture. Trial narratives and sensational stories about crime and family drama were especially popular, appearing in a variety of forms: in newspaper accounts, in periodical reviews, as stand-alone reports, in case collections, and in best-selling novels like Richardson's *Clarissa* or Defoe's *Moll Flanders*.[8]

All of these forms of print conveyed information about law, including technical doctrines regarding conveyances and contracts as well as more general rules regarding crime and punishment. At the same time many of these entertaining and educational texts articulated commonplace expectations and ideals for male as well as female behavior. For example, the stories of Roxana and Moll narrated by Defoe emphasized the vulnerability of wives and the culpability of men. Since a wife was placed, by the law of coverture, under the care and protection of her husband, the novelist suggested that male responsibility was paramount, and that much depended on a husband's character and resourcefulness. The theme of male responsibility, and attention to the critical connections among marriage, women's property and social mobility was a concern of painters as well. Thomas Gainsborough's landscape portrait of the newlyweds *Mr and Mrs Andrews* (1750) (Figure 6.3), for example, highlighted the wealth and aspirations of this couple. Robert Andrews stands, gun at his side, next to his seated wife; his estate

FIGURE 6.3 Mr and Mrs Andrews. Thomas Gainsborough, *c.* 1750. Source: Heritage Images / Getty Images.

was nicely augmented by the property she brought to the marriage, and this portrait of the couple within the landscape signaled their combined status as well as his mastery and control. This kind of focus on the role and responsibilities of the male householder was similarly explored in an influential contemporary literature on "oeconomy" and good governance. It was also at the center of the dramatic genre of prodigal husband plays that emerged in this period. In these works seventeenth- and eighteenth-century English playwrights investigated how "a man's sexual, economic, domestic, kinship and friendship ties became, upon marriage, both disconcertingly intertwined and a matter of increased public interest" (Panek 2013: 66).[9] While contemporaries certainly recognized the many pressures facing male householders, they also sharply criticized husbands' tendency to abuse their own power, and they cautioned against men's frequent moral, and legal, missteps (Defoe [1724] 2009).[10]

Indeed, the early eighteenth-century theater was increasingly becoming a place for moralizing instruction. Men like Richard Steele and Joseph Addison imparted lessons about virtue, civility, and improving sentiment through their plays, like *The Conscious Lovers* (1722) and *Cato* (1713), as well as their periodicals, like the *Tatler* (1709–1711) and *Spectator* (1711–1712) (Donohoe 2004). Many others contributed to an emerging genre of "reform comedy," and these playwrights frequently chose men and marriage as the focus of their moralizing tales. William Taverner's plays, and similar dramatic works like Colley Cibber's *The Careless Husband* (1704) or Charles Johnson's *The Wife's Relief or the Husband's Cure* (1711), exemplify the comedy of the age as described by their fellow playwright George Farquhar: each was "a well-framed tale handsomely told as an agreeable vehicle for counsel or reproof."[11] These authors satirized the domestic failures and corrupt behaviors of men of varied social status, chastising men equally whether they were born to aristocratic privilege or were consumed with new merchant pursuits. Such satire spoke to the diverse interests, and prejudices, of the dramatist's audience since the English theater, like English novels and popular law books, was becoming accessible to more men and women. This growing popularity of the theater was seen as a promising development, signaling the potential for moral outreach, but it also prompted anxiety about the suitability of the theater as a venue for improvement. The Theatre Licensing Act of 1737 was one expression of a concern about the need to control the dangerous messages emanating from the London stage (Donohoe 2004: 22–23). Taverner also pointedly articulated this kind of anxiety at the very opening of *The Artful Wife* (1718) by highlighting his characters' awareness that the theater, like clubs and shops and coffee houses, functioned not only as a place for instruction but also as a site of social mixing and luxurious display. Here the author slyly cautioned that the playhouse could be a setting for corruption as much as for ethical improvement.[12]

Taverner's *Artful Wife* is a good representative of the reform comedy because it depicted reformed masculinity—in this case a rake's moral awakening—through a popular romantic plot (Hume 1983). Moreover, it did so by critiquing the ways that men with different property interests took advantage of the privileges afforded them by law as well as custom, and it unmasked their selfish and corrupt behaviors. Taverner offered a vivid comparison between an indiscriminate, amoral seducer, Sir Francis Courtal, and a cuckolded merchant husband who cared only for business. In a characteristic scene Courtal advised one of his young female conquests not to expect marriage from him, but promised that he would provide even more passion and adulterous diversion once she was married to some other "grave citizen":

> I'll be your Friend, and visit you now and then, it's the Fashion ... Women of sense never marry the Man they like, but retain him as a Gallant.—Oh the Delight of a stolen Hour or two in a Hackney-Coach, *Spring Gardens*, or a lone House in the midst of a Garden, at *Chelsea, Fulham, or Kensington*! How delicious the Fruit will Taste!— While the good Man at home is thinking no harm, with his Head full of Freight, Bottom-Ree and Custom. (1718: 10–11)

Taverner frequently used the language of law and business while exposing men's depraved actions. Here reference to the law of contract, and to the law of maritime loans or bottomry, was key to his negative portrayal of both the profit-obsessed merchant husband and the aristocratic rake. In a later scene, Taverner further punctured the pretense of this fashionable rake by crafting a sharply critical analogy between "fashion" and "custom at common law" (1718: 29). Since Taverner was educated in civil law in Doctors' Commons, and maintained a law practice throughout his career as a dramatist, it is not surprising to find this preoccupation with legal terms and concepts in his texts (Brayne 2008). But Taverner must have been confident, too, that his audience would be adept at understanding the references to law as part of his play's moral instruction.

Clearly, questions about the relation between genteel and mercantile interests were an important part of contemporary reflection on the workings of coverture, and on the wider moral and legal implications of socioeconomic change. As authors voiced concerns about new opportunities that might ensnare "men of fashion" and "careless husbands" they explored the strengths and weaknesses of merchant and aristocratic values. Throughout the eighteenth century commentators worried that economic growth, and the new kinds of legal and financial transactions that accompanied the expansion of business ventures, inevitably provided new opportunities for men at all social levels to mismanage their assets, to gamble and to lose.

Thus many playwrights, novelists, and theorists agreed that incompetent, profligate men posed a danger to their wives, sisters, and daughters and were, more generally, a problem for the prosperity and longevity of their natal families. Profligate husbands were considered to be a particular threat to their wider communities since their selfish actions often led to family ruin which, in turn, brought new pressures to bear on local authorities. When deserted wives and children laid claim to public assistance they, perhaps even more than their absent men, were marked out as symbols of depravity. The malicious boys of Hogarth's *Four Stages of Cruelty* (1751) (Figure 6.4) and his *Industry and Idleness* (1747), or the wife-turned-prostitute of Defoe's *Roxana*, exemplified the dangerous consequences of patriarchal failure. Continued revisions to the poor laws, and additions to the harsh law of master and servant across the eighteenth century (and across the British Empire), were usually justified as attempts to redress these social ills caused by incompetent and recalcitrant men (Locke 1697; Mandeville 1723; Shesgreen 1976; Wind 1997; Steintrager 2001; Hay and Craven 2004, chs. 1–2).

The philosopher Mary Astell composed a sharp critique of the law of coverture precisely because it allowed such intense misery to be inflicted by profligate husbands:

> What tho' a Husband can't deprive a Wife of Life without being responsible to the Law, he may however do what is much more grievous to a generous Mind, render Life miserable, for which she has no Redress, scarce Pity which is afforded to every other Complainant. It being thought a Wife's Duty to suffer everything without Complaint.

FIGURE 6.4 First Stage of Cruelty. William Hogarth, 1751. Source: The Metropolitan Museum of Art, Harris Brisbane Dick Fund, 1932, 32.35(118) Courtesy www.metmuseum.org.

"If *all Men are born free*," Astell famously concluded this passage, "how is it that all Women are born slaves?" ([1700] 1996: 18). Astell denied that she was advocating any kind of radical solution to this problem of the profligate husband but was, rather, simply "exhorting Women, not to expect to have their own Will in any thing, but to be entirely Submissive, when once they have made choice of a Lord and Master, tho' he happen not to be so Wise, so Kind, or even so Just a Governor as was expected" (8). Here she expressed ideas about the inequity of the marriage contract that a novelist like Defoe or a playwright like Taverner also articulated. "I've considered the Articles of Agreement," one of Taverner's female protagonists asserted, before proceeding to dissect and reject traditional marriage vows, "and don't very well like 'em." (1718: 31).[13] Like Defoe, Astell envisioned women who learned resilience through adversity. Astell did not, however, wholly imagine women overturning social and legal norms. Yet this is what Defoe and others conceived in their fictions: women who rejected the strictures of the common law of property, who (as many women did) embraced the new opportunities for money-making, investing and property-accumulation, and who found success in commerce and credit (Froide 2016).

The profligate husband was closely related to the prodigal son, an even more common figure in Western literature and art. By the eighteenth century, the art historian Ellen D'Oench explains, "there was no biblical legend more firmly entrenched in high and low culture than that of the prodigal son" (D'Oench 1995: 10). The prodigal narratives commonly focused on a young man's fortunes after he inherited his patrimony, and followed his passage through the four phases of "departure, debauch, penitence and return" (D'Oench 1995: 4). The tale of the prodigal son examined the willful misuse of wealth by young men, and it often involved reference to the hazardous practice of mortgaging a family estate. This commonplace connection between prodigal and mortgage appeared in many kinds of texts as well as images. For example, the East India Company director, and economic writer, Josiah Child easily relied on this image and association while discussing key policies to promote national prosperity. Among arguments advanced in defense of his economic proposals, Child cautioned against the danger of borrowing at high rates by pointing to the salient image of

> a young gallant, that has newly mortgaged his land, and with the money thereby raised, stuffs his pockets, and looks big for a time, not considering that the draught of cordial he hath received, though it be at present grateful to his palate, does indeed prey upon his vital spirits, and will in a short time render the whole body of his estate in a deep consumption, if not wholly consumed. (Child 2003: 50; cf. 45)

The themes of consumption, waste and venery were other important elements of the prodigal's legend, and they played an even bigger part in dramatic and artistic representations of the story. Perhaps most famous are the prints in William Hogarth's series *The Rake's Progress* (1735) which chronicled the life of a shallow, vain and selfish young bachelor who inherits, and then loses, a fortune. This prodigal does not return home to penitence and reform but rather ends up mad and in debtor's prison. Early scenes depicted him drinking, whoring—with money spilling out of his pockets (plate III) (Figure 6.5)—and wedding a spinster in a clandestine marriage (plate V) (Figure 6.6), with an eye to squandering (mortgaging?) her estate too.

Hogarth's series was widely disseminated throughout England and Europe, and likely inspired other pictorial and literary examples of the prodigal tale. In fact this "picture-story format" was enormously popular, D'Oench explains, and "unprecedented numbers of inexpensive prodigal prints [circulated] during the years between 1750 and 1800" in England (1995: 10). Many English, and American, prints of the prodigal tale also circulated in North America in the eighteenth and nineteenth centuries. These series spoke to the same fears about dissipation, overwhelming debt, and the foreclosure of estate; they were especially compelling, one scholar suggests, to the newly propertied men of colonial America (Wolf 1979). The broad problem of colonial indebtedness obviously had political ramifications, for example shaping legislation enacted to protect British creditors, and these surely colored both artistic interpretation and the reception

FIGURE 6.5 Rake's Progress, plate III. William Hogarth, 1735. Source: The Metropolitan Museum of Art, Gift of Mrs. Carl Joseph Ulmann, 1929, 29.38.6, Courtesy www.metmuseum.org.

of the prodigal tale, especially in the era of the revolution. Finally, during the period of regency crisis in Britain a decade or so later prodigal prints were produced to advance a political message, underscoring troubling associations between corrupt household and state. A particularly scurrilous image depicted the Prince of Wales in the mode of Rake's Progress, coupled with the Whig politician Charles James Fox (depicted here as an old bawd), engaging in drunkenness, venery and debt, and posing a real danger to the nation (Figure 6.7: Thomas Rowlandson (?), Prodigal son [ca. 1785]).

Several other examples indicating the popularity of this tale of the prodigal son— and specifically the popular association made between prodigal and mortgage debt— appeared in the periodicals, dialogs, volumes of moral tales and sermons, and other collections that proliferated across the period.[14] *The Town Spy* (1704), for example, was published as a series of "diverting and ingenious" moral tales mainly designed for an urban audience. The first of its six dialogs recounted the miserable actions of a greedy father and spendthrift son, and incorporated mortgage in new ways in the prodigal tale. This story opened with a description of the father, Pinchgut, eagerly awaiting a trip to the scriveners where he, as creditor, anticipated delivery of a mortgage agreement to add to his wealth. Pinchgut invited his son, Scattergood, to join in witnessing the mortgage, and

FIGURE 6.6 Rake's Progress, plate V. William Hogarth, 1735. Source: The Metropolitan Museum of Art, Gift of Mrs. Carl Joseph Ulmann, 1929, 29.38.8 Courtesy www.metmuseum.org.

advised him to follow paternal example: "feed on Widows; have each Meal an Orphan serv'd to your Table, or a glibbery Heir, with all his Lands melted into a Mortgage" (5). Like the "glibbery Heir," Scattergood the prodigal preferred the tavern and the bawdy house, and rejected his father's life of grasping monied men with its "Pox of Attorny's Merchants and Scriveners" (5–6). The risks to a mortgagor were shown here to involve not only the demands of rapacious creditors, like Pinchgut, but also the interests of brokers, attorneys and other middlemen who were represented in this dialog by a third figure, Gnatho "the flatterer." Such brokers and money men would have been familiar characters to the reader, likely fellow patrons of the urban coffeehouse where these stories circulated. As this narrative demonstrated, foreclosure and the loss of estate were regarded as a certainty; the author recognized no real protection being afforded by the equity of redemption. In this particular version of the story, moreover, there was no satisfying filial repentance or moral resolution offered, and in fact the vices of Pinchgut the father appeared to equal or even surpass those of Scattergood the son. Equity and justice were, however, firmly contrasted with the single-minded pursuit of wealth, and the tale ended with a warning against all three "Devil's Factors": the miser, the spendthrift and the flatterer (26).[15]

FIGURE 6.7 Prodigal Son. Thomas Rowlandson, c. 1785. Source: Library of Congress.

As the prodigal tales and prints indicate, many eighteenth-century authors communicated a real worry not only about young men's dissolute behavior, but also about the potential for deceit, and for unfair advantage taken by creditors, brokers, and others in their dealings with young heirs. Several leading eighteenth-century mortgage cases demonstrated these same kinds of concerns. In the case of *Chesterfield v Janssen* (1750–1751) for example, Lord Chancellor Hardwicke uttered a strong caution against the dangerous avarice exhibited by both prodigal heir and predatory lender. In this case John Spencer, the necessitous and dissolute heir to the Duchess of Marlborough, sought credit by offering a bargain in which he bet against his own life. "The proposal was, that if any one would lend him L5000, he would oblige himself to pay L10,000 at or soon after the death of his grandmother, if he survived her, but to be totally lost if she survived him."[16] This prodigal found a willing lender in Janssen, who exacted further penalties when Spencer survived his grandmother and was, inevitably, unable to pay. In his notes on the case, Hardwicke reflected: "Those Bargains took their Rise from the extravagance and profligate expenses of the [future heirs] & the ambition of designing avaricious persons to take advantage of it." "This is become a publick mischief," he concluded, "the Ruin of many Families."[17] While Hardwicke's decision in this case provided an influential definition of equitable fraud, it also narrowly upheld the claims of the creditor to be paid "what should be due at law" regarding principal and interest on the loan.[18]

Growing numbers of legal abridgments and practice books for law students and lawyers, and for landed gentlemen and merchants, addressed such mischiefs by highlighting difficult cases, and drawing out specific lessons about time limits or about jurisdiction in mortgage disputes. These texts also offered detailed advice on how best to construct a mortgage agreement, or to redeem a mortgaged estate, in order to avoid common and dangerous pitfalls (Jacob 1713; Jacob 1718). One critical set of dangers was understood to stem from the lack of transparency in mortgaging estates, and indeed in conveyancing more generally. Some new legal protections were designed in this period so as to combat fraud committed by those men who deliberately withheld information when entering into agreements. As early as 1692 a statute against "clandestine mortgages"[19] appeared which denied "the benefit of equitable rules" to such debtors who mortgaged property without "notice of prior encumbrance" (Yale 1961: 66; Jacob 1715: 80–81; Hamburger 1983: 380). And early in the eighteenth century local deed registers were created in Middlesex and Yorkshire in order to prevent serious problems caused by those "ill disposed [men who] have it in their power to commit frauds and frequently do so, whereof persons have been undone in their purchases and mortgages, by prior and secret conveyances and fraudulent incumbrances" (Howell 1996: 5). Both of these remedies for fraud widened the potential for foreclosure because they entailed restrictions on the doctrine of the equity of redemption.

Similar kinds of concerns about fraud were also a focus of that broader public debate about the effects of commercial prosperity, and were expressed in contemporary popular pamphlets specifically regarding mortgage. For example a text entitled *A Precaution to Young Gentlemen and Others who Mortgage Estates* (1741) presented a clear warning about the dangers of mortgages for young, indebted, and incompetent heirs. Despite the apparent remedy of the equity of redemption, the author lamented, young heirs were prone to fall victim to unscrupulous creditors and to "skulking" solicitors, those "little decoys of the law" who made their money from others' economic misery.[20] Such fears about the defrauding of heirs were heightened precisely because mortgage was becoming an integral part of complex family property arrangements. They were another place, like trusts, where equity supplemented common law, and allowed for the provision of wives, daughters, and younger sons.

One more popular prodigal son text, a didactic poem entitled *The Unnatural Father, Or the Dutiful Son's Reward* (1775?), clearly conveyed such fears by effectively dramatizing the consequences of mortgaging family estates to support younger sons. In this florid tale, as in the slightly more sober report given by the *Precaution*, necessitous sons, unnatural fathers, covetous wives, and demanding mothers enacted a struggle between virtue and vice. The poem details the crimes of "a most stubborn, perverse and Wickedest youth" who "for a Harlot's sake killed a man." The youth's father, overly fond of this second, worthless son, mortgaged all his lands to raise money for a defense; the mortgage, however, only enabled his son to commit further crimes, and to run up further debts in pursuit of luxury and vice. Fortune and order were finally restored when the dutiful eldest son returned from exile, handsomely endowed with filial piety and a rich wife. This dutiful son was able to save his father, regain the family lands, and repair family status only because he made a profitable match: "For in process of time behold he found / A wealthy Fortune worth ten thousand pound / A virtuous wife right beautiful and fair."[21]

MARRIAGE MARKET AND MORTGAGES

In the *Unnatural Father*, and in almost all of the other examples discussed in this chapter, marriage figured as a regular part of the literary and legal analysis of mortgage. There are, in addition, several eighteenth-century stories about marriage negotiation where mortgage plays a pivotal role, and it is in these works that some of the most penetrating cultural attitudes towards law and property are expressed. *The City Jilt: Or the Alderman turned Beau; a Secret History* (1726), a short work written by the enormously popular and controversial writer Eliza Haywood, provides a first, striking example. Haywood's *City Jilt* explored some of this author's familiar themes: the economic value attached to female sexuality, the dangers posed by men who were focused on financial gain, and the wide potential for female agency. In this particular novel, the main opportunity for exercising that agency, and thereby controlling dangerous and destructive men, lay in the heroine's pursuit of a mortgage.

In *The City Jilt* Haywood narrated the story of Glicera, daughter and heir to a wealthy tradesman, who was courted and then abandoned by her suitor Melladore. Melladore's affections changed when he discovered that Glicera would not inherit a substantial fortune as expected. Seduction and breach of promise set in motion the rest of the dramatic action charting Glicera's quest for revenge. Haywood depicted the young woman's conscious manipulation of the governing system of sexual and financial exchange as Glicera attracted, encouraged and deliberately frustrated other suitors, including the old and enormously wealthy Alderman Grubguard. Mortgage was the key to her manipulation of Grubguard and, in turn, her humiliation of Melladore. It is revealed in the course of the story that riotous living, expensive litigation and misguided marriage had forced Melladore to mortgage his estate, and that the Alderman had become his mortgagee; Glicera, now employing deceit and fraud, promises the old man tantalizing sexual favors in exchange for transfer of the mortgage deed. She finally gains possession of the mortgage, and the ability to destroy Melladore, by tricking Grubguard into literally gambling it away (Haywood [1726] 1999).

Haywood's "revenge fantasy" challenged the social norms, economic motives and legal structures that allowed for the exploitation of women. Like other authors, artists, and legal thinkers, Haywood criticized the working of the eighteenth-century marriage market because it distorted individual, and familial, preferences. In this and other widely read texts, such as her periodical *The Female Spectator* (1744–1746), Haywood openly warned female readers about men who pursued women purely for financial gain. Moreover, like Defoe, Astell, and others, Haywood depicted a woman who rejected victimization and who exercised power. It is clear, however, that Haywood's texts presented a less tempered version of female power than appeared in these other authors' works, especially because Haywood challenged norms that equated female chastity with economic worth. Indeed Haywood explored the nature of female desire, and provided examples of women exercising sexual agency. Eliza Haywood did "more than demonstrate that romantic heterosexual relationships are fundamentally ones of obligation, debt and credit," Catherine Ingrassia explains. Haywood "places her characters in situations specifically defined by speculative investment ... [and] creates female subjects who derive pleasure and satisfy their desires from such financial activities" (1998: 86–87). Mortgage was one of these financial activities and Haywood highlights it here, building upon the familiar image of the mortgagor as prodigal son in order to challenge legal and social norms regarding contract and marriage.

Haywood's novels and other publications were popular, at least in part, because this author was willing to address such controversial subjects. While similar moves towards sentimentalism and didacticism characterized other early novels, Haywood's pointed message about women's choices was unconventional and often viewed as scandalous, or transgressive. This reputation for scandal was furthered by the notorious irregularity of her personal life. It was widely known that Haywood's early marriage had ended mysteriously, and that she had subsequently entered into open relationships with the writer Richard Savage and the playwright William Hatchett. Debate about the morality of fiction and the virtue of the woman writer erupted in the early eighteenth century, and Haywood became an important representative of the "immoral" woman novelist (Spencer 1996; Ingrassia 1998; Backscheider 2010). It is a mark of this author's commitment to dramatizing female agency and providing social critique that Haywood capitalized on her reputation for scandal: not only was she a prolific author, exceeding even someone like Daniel Defoe, who published in multiple genres for a growing audience, but she was also an engaged businesswoman who geared her production to the marketplace. Finally, and also like Defoe, Haywood demonstrated real knowledge of contemporary legal and financial practices. "The detail with which Haywood discusses mortgages, investments and various types of capital elevates the text above a figurative discussion of those activities," Ingrassia agrees. "She provides specific advice that can be used in actual personal interactions" (1998: 95).[22] Advice in *The City Jilt* included admonitions about the likelihood, and potential benefits, of mortgage foreclosure.

The threat of foreclosure, and its place in the course of marriage negotiations, was also explored in William Taverner's *The Artful Husband* (1717). This play offered a vision of female power that was different from Haywood's, however, and its message tended to reinforce more conventional eighteenth-century ideas about social value, age, and female sexual attraction. While Taverner's *The Artful Wife* advanced a fundamentally gentle reproof of a husband's failings, his *Artful Husband* afforded a sharper critique of female agency. In this play Taverner's central message lay in a contrast formed between the figures of a grasping widow, Lady Upstart, and a defrauded orphan-heiress Belinda, although much of the action revolved around the corrupt men—stockbrokers and fops—who courted Widow Upstart in search of her money. Among the suitors was Sir Harry Freelove, a self-indulgent young prodigal who had mortgaged his estate to Upstart's late husband. Harry's friends, espousing the wisdom of the marriage market, strongly advised him to find "a Wife whose Fortune would pay off the Mortgage, or remove the Apprehensions of a Foreclosure" (3).[23] This desired end was achieved by the close of the play, when it was revealed that Harry's wife was to be the beautiful young Belinda rather than old Widow Upstart. Belinda was the "artful husband" of the title: through cross-dressing disguise she successfully wooed the widow, and then used blackmail to extract the portion Upstart's late husband owed her, as well as the mortgage on Sir Harry's estate. After innumerable scenes of mistaken identity, Belinda at last explained to Sir Harry the reasons for her actions against Widow Upstart:

> Her late Husband being my Guardian, got Possession of ten thousand Pounds my Father left me; then turn'd me and my Servant that waited on me, out of doors ... knowing your Mortgage was obtain'd by Extortion, I made bold to get that, and there it is for you. And now, if you like me and my Fortune they are both at your Service. (67)

Redemption of the mortgage, and the orphan's portion, were both transferred to the gentleman. Rightful marriage of gentleman and heiress, Taverner insistently showed, properly ends in wealth secured, and retirement to a country estate.

CONCLUSION

In addition to the deep hostility expressed towards the widow-creditor Lady Upstart, *The Artful Husband* articulated many of those eighteenth-century concerns about new wealth and social mobility. In this plot mortgage served on the one hand to reaffirm gendered values, but on the other hand mortgage was used to challenge socioeconomic change. There was clearly suspicion about financial trickery, and fears that legal techniques might undermine stable values and relationships. Taverner's play, like Haywood's and Defoe's novels, and Hogarth's images, took part in ongoing debates about class, landed wealth, and the emergence of new social and professional roles—for both men and women—spurred on by economic change.

The literary examples discussed here particularly demonstrate contemporary anxiety about foreclosure, and the clear apprehension that a mortgagor was *not* protected by the equity of redemption. But these authors and artists who employed mortgage agreements as a plot device did not simply reflect contemporary attitudes. Their works actively contributed to the ongoing analysis of the nature of property during a period in which commercial expansion, the ubiquity of credit, and the rise of agricultural capitalism called into question legal doctrines and societal norms. Even more, artists like Hogarth, and authors like Haywood and Defoe, used their remarkable ability to represent, fictionalize—and at times distort—the definition of contract, mortgage, entail, and coverture in order to promote change in English law. Their works challenged established systems of marriage and inheritance, critiqued the subordination of women, and vilified corruption and fraud.

CHAPTER SEVEN

Wrongs

RUTH PALEY

THE ELASTICITY OF THE CONCEPT OF WRONGFULNESS

We all know what constitutes a wrong. Or at least we think we do. Actually the more one tries to define the concept the more difficult and subjective the exercise becomes. Most people would agree on certain fundamental human values such as the sanctity of life. Yet the continuing controversies sparked by debates about euthanasia and capital punishment demonstrate that even the act of killing can be subject to complex moral and legal arguments that render it impossible to draw universal firm distinctions between what is and is not regarded as a wrong. Similarly the continuing popularity of the legend of Robin Hood, who robbed the rich to give to the poor, testifies to an enduring belief that there are some circumstances in which theft and assault can be justified and that moral justice and legal justice may not always be the same thing.

Difficulties in interpreting the concept of wrong emerge clearly in the case of Daniel Clarke, who died at the hands of an enraged mob in 1769. That year was one of major economic hardship for the silk weaving industry which was concentrated in the Spitalfields area of London. The weavers banded together for self-protection in what was then known as a "combination"—what we would now call a union. The combination was in itself illegal. Its tactics were also illegal. In order to discourage their fellow weavers from accepting lower wages, members of the combination attacked and cut the silk from their looms—a crime that carried the death penalty and so necessarily had to be carried out under threat of violence by armed gangs. Substantial rewards were offered to those who would inform against them. Daniel Clarke was one of the few who were prepared to testify against the cutters. His evidence sent one of them, William Eastman, to the gallows. Just over a year later, on a bitterly cold and snowy April day he was chased down the street and pelted with bricks. The pelting continued after he had been cornered in a field, stripped, and forced into a pond with a noose round his neck. He died of his injuries.[1] Among his attackers were Eastman's brother-in-law and the widow of another man who had been executed as a cutter. She blamed Clarke for her husband's death even though he had not testified at that particular trial. In the eyes of the law Daniel Clarke had committed no wrong; in the eyes of his community he had betrayed them, and had probably been paid to do so. Even now, two hundred and fifty years later, it is likely that the social and political prejudices of those who read this story will influence the way in which they interpret the various wrongs committed by all the protagonists.

RIGHTING WRONGS AND PERFORMING JUSTICE

Nevertheless a belief and acceptance that English society was one that was bound by the rule of law, that the criminal law punished wrongs and was supposed to apply impartially to all, was (and still is) pervasive across both high and low culture. People from almost all ranks of society had access to legal knowledge and to legal processes and were not only prepared to use the law but appear to have believed that law and justice were virtually synonymous terms. In discussing the arrest for treason of the American banker and revolutionary sympathizer, Stephen Sayre (or Sayer), one continental observer wrote that in any other country being thrown from a window would have been the "most gentle punishment" that would have been offered to the defense attorney who interrupted Sayre's interrogation by forcing his way into the secretary of state's house. But "In England, where none are above the laws, where the first noblemen of the kingdom dare not infringe them, the case is quite otherwise." Indeed it was so much otherwise that Sayre subsequently prosecuted the secretary of state for false imprisonment and secured substantial damages (von Archenholz 1797: 242–243).[2]

At the very top of society, Parliament, or more specifically the House of Lords, was not just the legislature but also the venue for high-profile criminal trials. These may have been occasional but they were nevertheless major examples of what elsewhere in this volume Steve Banks calls justice performances. A fascination with revelations of wrongdoing in high places meant that the trials of peers for murder, of the duchess of Kingston for bigamy, the attempted impeachments of Dr. Sacheverall, Warren Hastings, and Henry Dundas became major socio-political occasions that enthralled elite and non-elite audiences alike. Even trials in the ordinary courts functioned as a sort of popular entertainment, but those in Parliament were even more theatrical. They even had all-ticket audiences: the tickets were issued to peers who then distributed them to friends, relatives, and clients.

The theatricality of such trials was evident before they had even started. Newspaper accounts of the trial of Laurence Shirley, 4th Earl Ferrers, in 1760 describe the arrival of Ferrers and of the judges in terms reminiscent of a ceremonial procession (Figure 7.1). He left the Tower, where he had been imprisoned, in his own landau, attended by "a large body of foot guards" and warders. From Bloomsbury onwards, he was joined by five coaches of gentlemen in the retinue of the Lord Chancellor, then by the Lord Chancellor himself in his state coach, followed "by a long train" of coaches containing the judges, masters in chancery and "other persons eminent in the law." The procession itself was flanked by numerous servants in livery. As it passed Charing Cross, several noblemen in their Parliament robes joined in, adding "great lustre and solemnity to the whole."[3]

Ferrers was about to be tried for murder. He was obsessively jealous of his wife, threatening to kill her should she ever leave him. His fellow peers were well aware that Ferrers was dangerously unstable because, quite apart from any other source of knowledge, proceedings in the Lords had assisted Lady Ferrers to escape from his custody and to obtain a legal separation. In the event it was not Lady Ferrers that he killed, but the steward entrusted with collecting monies on her behalf. In the modern world he would almost certainly be found unfit to plead but his lucid intervals and the stark definition of lunacy in the eighteenth century, which required a total inability to understand the difference between right and wrong, meant that he could not be deemed a lunatic. He was found guilty and sentenced to death. "Mother Proctor," who owned land adjacent to

FIGURE 7.1 A perspective view of the execution of Lord Ferrers. Anonymous, 1760. Source: © The Trustees of the British Museum.

the site of the gallows at Tyburn and rented out seats to spectators, was said to have made some £500 on the day of his execution (Angelo 1830).

As befitted a society event, those who attended trials in Parliament dressed up for the occasion. When the countess of Euston described the opening of impeachment proceedings against Henry Dundas, earl of Melville, in 1805, she wrote about being "very much struck with the magnificence of the effect produced by such a very large space entirely filled with well dress'd people." Lady Euston found amusement in the proceedings, commenting on the eccentric hat sported by Lord Pomfret and the laughter that erupted on the late arrival of Lord Kinnoull who clearly had not

> the smallest idea of what he was to do, or where he was to go, and the directing voices which sounded from all sides of "this way"—"That way"—"Here"—"There"—"Bow wow wow" put the poor little man perfectly out and he seated himself on the first vacant bench without going thro' any part of the ceremonial rules of proceeding.[4]

Some thirty years earlier, Archenholz had "had the pleasure of being a witness of the singular spectacle" of the duchess of Kingston's trial for bigamy "which very much resembled the pomp of sacred worship in catholic countries" and which drew "a prodigious concourse of people" to the proceedings in Westminster Hall. Boxes covered in fine cloth were erected for the royal family, foreign ministers, the ladies and members of the Commons:

> All were in high dress; the passages were guarded by soldiers ... the peers, almost 200 in number, the bishops and first magistrates of the kingdom in their robe, seated in a semi-circular form, in the body of the hall, making a grand and respectable group ... These six days were holidays for London. The peers met at ten o'clock, but the hall was filled with spectators at five o'clock in the morning. Ladies came there, even at three o'clock, by the very dawn of the day, magnificently dressed, and remained until five o'clock afternoon ... equipages were seen pouring in from the most distant corners of the kingdom. Persons offered by public advertisement, twelve, fifteen, and even twenty guineas, for a ticket of admission, and a certain lady is said to have declared in a company, that she would rather give fifty guineas than want the gratification of being present. (von Archenholz 1797: 250–253)

Ferrers' example was regularly used as evidence that the criminal justice system in Britain ensured that all were equal before the law. In reality the record of the House of Lords towards its members suggested that aristocratic criminals were treated very differently to the mass of the population and that they could quite literally get away with murder. Between 1680 and 1820 there were five trials of peers on charges of murder. One individual, Charles, 4th Baron Mohun, was actually tried and acquitted twice, in the face of overwhelming evidence of his guilt. Two (Edward Rich, 6th Earl of Warwick, and William, 5th Baron Byron) were convicted of the lesser charge of manslaughter, which essentially meant they would go free—again despite overwhelming evidence of guilt. Ferrers was the only peer to have been convicted and executed.

At a less elevated level of society, the twice yearly opening of the assizes provided another performance of justice. In the early 1820s, one admiring French observer described how,

> When the time for assizes is fixed, all England appears in motion. The lawyers set out with the judges on their respective circuits; the sheriffs ... the juries, the high constables, the coroners, the justices of the peace, the plaintiffs, the attornies, the witnesses, all hasten to the place where the assizes are to be held. The judges are received at the entrance of the town by the sheriff, and often by a great number of the richest inhabitants of the place; who come with them, or send their handsomest carriages, attended by servants in their richest liveries, in order to augment the pomp and ceremony of the train.
>
> They enter the city with trumpets sounding and bells ringing, and are preceded by the guards of the sheriff, from twelve to twenty in number, all dressed in full liveries, and armed with long pikes. These trumpeters and guards remain in their service all the time of their stay, accompany them every day to the court, and conduct them back again to their lodgings. (Cottu [1820] 2004)

The solemnity and natural drama of the occasion was reinforced by the attendance of the judges, clothed in their scarlet robes, at a service at the local church where they would hear the assize sermon, which almost always centered on the theme of justice. The first day of the assizes was usually dedicated to the formal business of reading the various commissions under which the judges were empowered to act, followed by an entertainment that ensured that the assizes were as much a major social as legal event.

FIGURE 7.2 The execution of the idle apprentice. William Hogarth, 1747. Source: The Metropolitan Museum of Art, Harris Brisbane Dick Fund, 1932, 32.35(48) Courtesy www.metmuseum.org.

OWNING JUSTICE

The crowds who flocked to watch these ceremonies played their own part in what was a highly participatory justice system (Figure 7.2). While the grand jury—a large panel who decided whether or not the defendant had a case to answer in much the same way as today's committing magistrates—was drawn largely from the gentry, the trial jury consisted of householders at a rather lower level of society. Members of the trial (or petty) jury played an active role in righting wrongs. The law specified certain criteria by which a crime became a capital offense. In the case of highway robbery it was necessary to prove that the victim had been put in fear. In the case of various thefts it was a matter of the value of the stolen goods: for example stealing goods worth 40s from a house was a capital offense; stealing goods worth less than that amount was not. Court records are full of verdicts where goods clearly worth far more than 40s (sometimes worth many hundreds of pounds) were declared by the jury, in a process known as pious perjury, to be worth 39s in order to save the defendant from the gallows (Beattie 1986a).

Because the system depended on private prosecution the prosecutors could be drawn from any level of society, as were the witnesses. Ordinary people were also involved because of the visibility of punishments: executions were public and the procession to the gallows had something of a fairground atmosphere; a similar atmosphere prevailed among the crowds who watched the public whipping of offenders. Perhaps the most participatory punishment of all was the use of the pillory, which encouraged the public to demonstrate their own opinion of the nature of the wrong that had been committed (Figure 7.3). The crowd did not simply observe an individual being pilloried, they expressed their own anger—or sometimes sympathy—in the choice of weapon that they chose to throw at the prisoner. When William Fuller, who led a somewhat bizarre career reaping rewards from inventing tales of Jacobite spies, was pilloried in the summer of 1702 he was "severely pelted with rotten eggs, dirt &c" (Luttrell 1857: 189). Another who was severely pelted was George Stokes, convicted of making a false accusation of sodomy (then a capital offense) in order to extort money.[5] James Eagan, convicted for his part in a conspiracy to secure the conviction and execution of two young men in order to claim a reward, fared even worse. He was pelted so severely that he actually died in the pillory.[6] Others whose crimes seemed less heinous were able to count on the sympathy of the assembled crowd. In 1716, just a year after an abortive Jacobite rebellion, two women sentenced to the pillory for singing and selling Jacobite songs profited from a sympathetic audience: a collection on their behalf raised £4.[7] William Gibson who was convicted of forgery handed out fliers insisting on his innocence and must have convinced the onlookers because he was spared a pelting.[8] Just occasionally someone was able to subvert the whole process. When Daniel Defoe was pilloried in 1703 he was apparently pelted with flowers. This was at least in part because he had been unjustly convicted of seditious libel—the pamphlet concerned, *The shortest way with dissenters*, was clearly

FIGURE 7.3 The pillory at Charing Cross. From an engraving by Rowlandson and Pugin in Ackermann's *Microcosm of London*, 1809. Source: © The Trustees of the British Museum.

meant to be ironic and could only be construed as seditious if taken literally. The merits of his cause apart, he took care to hire a suitable group of men to protect him. He also turned the occasion into a marketing opportunity, selling copies of his works to the crowd (Backscheider 1989).

Then too there was the everyday administration of justice for lesser offenses. The prosecution of offenses classified as misdemeanors regularly involved the practice of what we now call restorative justice—the payment of damages to the victim and, just as importantly, public apologies in person or even in the press. And, in London at least, a trip to the Old Bailey or to the courts of well-known lay magistrates like Sir John Fielding at Bow Street offered entertainment value to casual visitors. When the celebrated highwayman, Gentleman James MacLaine, was examined at Bow Street in the summer of 1750, the press reported that "a great number of persons of distinction" attended to hear what he had to say.[9]

ACCESSIBLE JUSTICE

Accessibility to the official or formal structures of the law was bolstered by the new technology of the day—print. The expansion of the publishing industry led to the publication of legal treatises and reports. Many of these were naturally aimed at practitioners, but a significant number were aimed at educating the wider public and figured among the best sellers of their time. Giles Jacob, for example, first produced his *New Law Dictionary* in 1729. His law dictionary, which explained forms of legal process as well as legal jargon, was still being revised and reissued by subsequent editors in the early nineteenth century. Of a rather different order were publications by Thomas Wood and William Blackstone, who both emphasized the importance of a knowledge of the law, including the criminal law, as a component of a proper gentlemanly education (Wood 1727; Blackstone [1765–9] 2016). Such knowledge was vital for middle- and upper-class men who would be expected to play a part in the criminal justice system as voluntary constables, jurymen, and magistrates, and who might also aspire to a seat in Parliament and thus become legislators. Giles Jacob also produced an overview of the legal system, *Every man his own lawyer*, which was first published in 1736. He emphasized his intention to teach "all manner of persons ... to know how to defend themselves and their estates and fortunes in all cases whatsoever" (Jacob 1736). By "all manner of persons" he presumably meant all manner of persons in the propertied world that he himself inhabited, as the price to be charged (it was advertised at 5 shillings, something in the order of half a week's wages for a skilled London artisan) suggests that this (and indeed other volumes by Jacob, which were priced at between 3 shillings and 6 shillings) would have been well out of reach of ordinary people.[10] Then too there were narrower manuals expressly aimed at educating magistrates and constables about the duties of their offices while magistrates and barristers produced guides aimed at explaining procedures for the prosecution of wrongdoers. Notable examples included Richard Burn's *Justice of the Peace and Parish Officer,* which went through many editions after its first publication in 1755; Samuel Glasse's *The magistrate's assistant* (1780); John Fielding's *Extracts from such of the penal laws as particularly relate to the peace and good order of this metropolis* (1768); and William Boscawen, *A treatise on convictions on penal statutes* (1792).

Print also transformed the techniques of criminal investigation. The traditional method of pursuing criminals was by raising the hue and cry—literally a loud cry to mobilize the local populace. With increasing numbers of printers and printing presses, and major

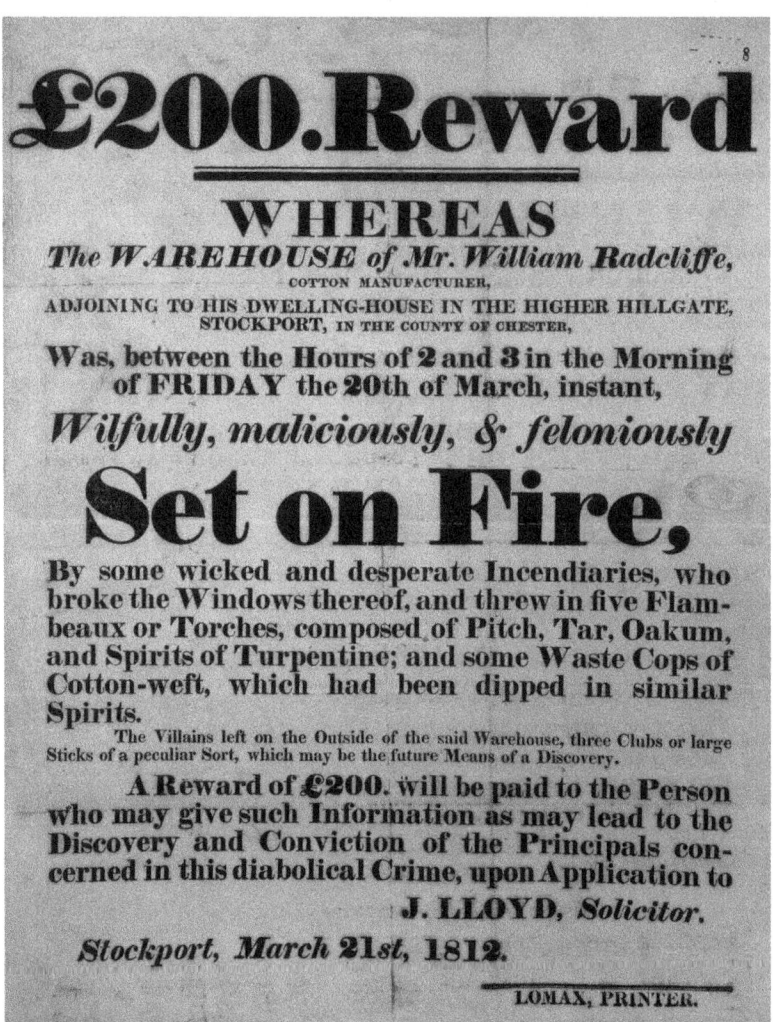

FIGURE 7.4 Reward Notice. Reward poster for arson at William Radcliffe's warehouse, 1812. Source: The National Archives, ref. HO40/1/1.

improvements to the roads facilitating the distribution of newspapers, broadsides, and pamphlets, it became possible to disseminate information more widely and more quickly than ever before (Figure 7.4). Newspapers now routinely carried information about stolen goods and offenders who had either fled from justice or were being held as part of an ongoing investigation. For those who were content to circulate information across a more restricted area local printers were available to run off handbills at short notice. The man who embraced the potential of these developments most vigorously was Sir John Fielding, the chief magistrate at Bow Street from 1754 to his death in 1780. Fielding turned Bow Street into a clearing house for information about crime and criminals and in 1772 he sought to build on his achievements by initiating a new scheme which he dubbed the General Preventative Plan. Between September 1772 and September 1773 he sent circular letters to clerks of the peace in England and Wales as well as to the mayors of corporate towns. He asked that the various provincial magistrates send descriptions of felons and suspected offenders to him at Bow Street. As he already received copies of the assize calendars he asked them to ensure that gaolers keep descriptions of offenders committed to their custody and add those descriptions to the assize calendars. His plan was to collate the information and then to redistribute it nationally in a form suitable for public display (Radzinowicz and Hood 1948–86). Given the lack of national newspapers, this would bring greater accessibility than any attempt to advertise in either the London or provincial press could possibly achieve. From 1773 the resultant circular—*The General Hue and Cry*, later *The Hue and Cry*—was funded by the government. It was initially issued weekly but by the later 1770s appeared on a monthly basis. Fielding promoted the scheme enthusiastically and it seems the provincial magistrates were also enthusiastic about a system that promised major benefits at no cost to themselves.

The pervasiveness of an interest in crime and the criminal law went far beyond the desire to encourage an understanding of the formal structures of prosecution and punishment or to catch criminals. The explosion of print culture in this period provided opportunities to create and serve new audiences. Alongside the more well-known advances of the burgeoning publishing industry—the development of the newspaper and of the novel—was the beginning of the true crime genre. The most famous were probably the *Old Bailey Sessions Papers*, printed transcripts (often verbatim) of the evidence given in trials at London's Old Bailey. Local printers occasionally published trial accounts in other parts of the country too: there is for example a fragmented run of *The Proceedings at the Assizes … for … Surrey*, but it seems that London was the only area populous enough to provide a sufficiently large market to ensure the viability of a long-term publication.

Both in London and elsewhere there was also a ready market for one-off pamphlet accounts of particularly notorious cases. One of the most fantastical *causes célèbres* of the century was the case of Mary Toft, who managed to convince not only a local doctor but a number of eminent doctors and other individuals in 1726 that she had given birth to rabbits. The hoax sparked several pamphlets, broadsides, and ballads, as well as a satirical poem by Alexander Pope and William Pulteney. In a mocking print by Hogarth, *The cunicularii, or, The wise men of Godliman in consultation* produced the same year, Toft was depicted in the throes of labor while her doctor surreptitiously accepts a rabbit from a butcher at the door and three of the most credulous of her supporters look on. Such was the lasting impact of the story that nearly forty years later Hogarth could expect his audience to recognize Mary Toft as one of the central characters in his *Credulity, superstition, and fanaticism* (1762). Once again in labor, she lies on the ground in front of the impassioned preacher, with rabbits running from beneath her skirts.

In 1753 the mystery surrounding the whereabouts of a young servant girl, Elizabeth Canning, sparked another controversy, propelling this otherwise obscure young woman into the national spotlight as, depending on one's point of view, either a victim of an attempt at what we now call sex trafficking or as the perpetrator of a wicked hoax. Elizabeth Canning, apparently a hardworking and reputable servant girl, disappeared on January 1, 1753. When she reappeared a month later, in a bedraggled and emaciated condition, she claimed to have been robbed, kidnapped, and kept as a prisoner in a house at Enfield Wash. She accused her captors of trying to force her into prostitution. Further details of the case are given by Dana Rubin in Chapter 5 of this volume, so it suffices here to mention that none of the stories—whether given by Canning herself, or by her supposed captors—were entirely consistent; nor is it possible to reconcile them to each other. The attempt to establish which tale amounted to "truth" split the public into fervent Canningites or anti-Canningites. It is a measure of the debate the case evoked that the British Library catalog contains entries for over 100 polemical pamphlets and reprints about it that were published between 1753 and 1754. Over and above these, there were newspaper articles, as well as ballads, engravings, and caricatures. Even after Canning had been convicted of perjury and transported to America, the resonances clearly continued, for in 1757 another supportive pamphlet charted her life after transportation.[11] So confused and contradictory was the evidence that neither then nor since has it been possible to solve the mystery of what really happened to Elizabeth Canning. Yet the story clearly has an enduring fascination, inspiring several modern published accounts and providing the basis for an updated and fictionalized version in Josephine Tey's 1948 novel, *The Franchise Affair*.

INVENTING THE MODERN FOLK HERO

The cases of Mary Toft and Elizabeth Canning, as well as the publication of accounts of criminal trials, highlight the beginnings of the true crime genre. One of the first authentic criminal biographies was produced by Daniel Defoe in 1724, *The history of the remarkable life of John Sheppard*. John—or Jack—Sheppard was something of a folk hero. It was not his criminal career that interested the public, because that was nothing out of the ordinary, consisting as it did of shoplifting, burglary, a bit of pickpocketing, and highway robbery. What was extraordinary about him was his ability to cock a snook at authority by escaping from custody. In the spring of 1724 he was arrested twice and escaped on both occasions from small local prisons. His third arrest led to his trial, conviction, and a death sentence, but he managed to escape again, this time from Newgate. Re-taken after a few days and returned to Newgate, he managed to escape from justice for a fourth time, climbing up the chimney and then breaking through the ceiling into the room above. This time he stayed free for a fortnight. When he was re-arrested the authorities took no chances. According to newspaper reports he was "double iron'd on both legs, handcuff'd, and chained down to the ground with a chain running through his irons, which is fastened on each side of him" and kept under constant observation. He was so famous that the crowds flocked to see him in gaol, providing the turnkeys with a windfall income—they were said to have made £200 by charging visitors to view him—and extra guards were required to secure the route that took him from Newgate to his death at the Tyburn gallows.[12]

Other celebrity criminals included Dick Turpin, Sixteen String Jack Rann, and Gentleman James MacLaine. Dick Turpin was executed for horse theft in 1739, the culmination of a criminal career that had involved various brutal crimes including deer stealing, murder, and highway robbery. His legendary status has resulted from the various fictional accounts of his life, including the legend of his daring ride to York which began to feature in chapbooks from about 1800. He was, however, moderately famous even in his own day and, like modern celebrities, took considerable care to control his image. He went to the gallows in new suit and hired mourners to follow him to the scaffold (Barlow 1973).

In the case of Sixteen String Jack and Gentleman James MacLaine, their very nicknames tell us something about the image they wished to project. MacLaine had some pretensions to gentility, being the son of one clergymen and brother of another. The story of his descent from being a respectable tradesman to crime via a stint as a servant after squandering his inheritance fascinated the public. He owed his nickname both to the quality of his clothing and to the courteous manner in which he treated his victims. The ordinary (or chaplain) of Newgate prison, perhaps worried about the social subversion inherent in regarding a highwayman in such a light, was dismissive of his claims to the nickname, remarking that "though he has been called the gentleman highwayman, and in his dress and equipage very much affected the fine gentleman, yet to a man acquainted with good breeding, that can distinguish it from impudence and affectation, there was very little in his address or behavior, that could entitle him to that character."[13] MacLaine did, however, have the additional advantage of being reputed to have carried out his crimes without violence. He also seems to have been a remarkably successful highwayman, for when he was arrested in July 1750, a search of his rooms found goods (including over twenty purses, all presumably stolen) worth nearly £200.[14] An account of his life appeared almost as soon as the conviction was announced. Men like these seemed to be more than mere thugs, as they were perceived to be bound by a code of honor.

Sixteen String Jack took his nickname from the eight strings that were used to tie each leg of his breeches. Not only was he well-dressed but he also attracted admiration for the way that he was able to defy authority and evade conviction. When he was examined at Bow Street in May 1774 on a charge of highway robbery he was reported to have "behaved with the most consummate assurance; had a remarkable large nosegay in his bosom, and his fetters decorated with ribbands." His behavior "was daring and shocking beyond example ... and ... excited equally improper emotions in the audience ... he was received with a general laugh and everything he said and did occasioned merriment." When he was subsequently acquitted at the Old Bailey, it was reported that this was the fourteenth time that he had escaped justice.[15] His luck ran out later that year; he was convicted and sentenced to death in October. Like MacLaine, copies of an account of his life, *The genuine life of John Rann*, were being advertised in the press before his execution.[16] Like Turpin, he was said to have gone to the gallows in a new suit.

A MIRROR ON SOCIETY

Jack Sheppard and James MacLaine both have a wider cultural significance. Sheppard was not only the subject of a work by Defoe but may also have been in part the inspiration for the highwayman Macheath in John Gay's *The Beggar's Opera* (1728). MacLaine's punishment continued after death as his body was sent to the College of Surgeons for anatomization. He not only contributed to medical knowledge but also appears in the background of the final picture of Hogarth's *Four Stages of Cruelty*—as a skeleton. The Royal College of Surgeons no longer holds the skeleton in its collection; it was probably destroyed in the blitz. It does, however, have the skeleton of a very much more ambiguous figure, Jonathan Wild, the self-styled thief-taker general of England (Figure 7.5). Wild managed to pose as a crime-fighting detective while running "a corporation of thieves" and a fencing operation as well as organizing many of the robberies that he claimed to have solved. He was hanged in 1725, but the idea of a criminal mastermind has fascinated authors ever since. Sherlock Holmes' arch enemy, Professor Moriarty, who first appeared in *The Valley of Fear* (1915), was explicitly based on Jonathan Wild, who had by then been dead for nearly two hundred years. To his contemporaries Wild's cultural significance was political as well as literary, his career did not merely provide an insight into the criminal underworld but into a much wider world of corruption. Within a month of Wild's execution, parallels between his career and that of the leading Whig politician Robert Walpole were made by the Tory *Mist's Weekly Journal*.[17] The identification of Wild with Walpole is also crucial to an understanding of *The Beggars*

FIGURE 7.5 Jonathan Wild. From the Newgate Calendar, 1824: Source: Hulton Archive/Getty Images Hulton Archive/Getty Images.

Opera. Long before he wrote *The Beggar's Opera*, Gay had remarked on the similarities between the characteristics required of a statesman and a highwayman: "I cannot indeed wonder that the characteristics requisite of a statesman are so scarce in the world since so many of those who possess them are every month cut off in the prime of their age at the Old Bailey" (Burgess 1966: 45). *The Beggar's Opera*, ostensibly about a criminal empire and drawing overt parallels between high and low life, was a runaway success when it was first produced in 1728. It is both a parody of high opera and a stinging satire on a society that rewards hypocrisy and moral bankruptcy rather than virtue and talent. Henry Fielding pursued the same theme even more viciously in his *Life and death of Jonathan Wild the Great* (1742) in which Wild the "great prig" stands for Walpole the "great Whig."

True crime was thus inherently mixed up with the origins of another literary form—the novel. Defoe passed off several of the works we now regard as novels as genuine autobiographies. These included his *Colonel Jack* (1722), *Moll Flanders* (1722) and *Roxana* (1724), whose realism was all the more convincing because of the ambiguous moral characters of their protagonists. Crime also figures in the novels of Tobias Smollett. Indeed in *The Expedition of Humphrey Clinker* (1771) Smollett provided an interesting but highly cynical account of what it was like to fall into the clutches of a busy metropolitan magistrate, clearly a thinly fictionalized version of Sir John Fielding. The suspiciously close relationship between the magistrate in question, Justice Buzzard, and the genteel highwayman, Mr. Martin, with its implications of corruption is further underlined by the description of Buzzard as "the thiefcatcher general of this metropolis," an oblique reference to Jonathan Wild.

PREVENTING WRONGS

While the true crime genre and the novel were still in their infancy, the publication of sermons was well established. It is difficult for modern readers to appreciate just how popular (and profitable) such publications were. Sermons by John Tillotson, archbishop of Canterbury from 1691 to his death in 1694, were still being published in the nineteenth century. Clergymen were extremely interested in the link between crime, immorality, and damnation. Beginning in the late seventeenth century, and continuing in various forms throughout the century, they were at the forefront of campaigns for moral reform. At the heart of such campaigns was the belief that men could be forced to be good—a fundamentally theological debate about whether man is intrinsically flawed or is capable of perfection. The early reformation societies were associated with high churchmen and thus inevitably had a political tinge, since high churchmen and Tories were virtually indistinguishable. They went beyond exhortations and became involved in the enforcement of the kind of laws and regulations that, in a system of private prosecution, were often ignored: prostitution, gambling and the stricter control (or even elimination) of licenses to sell alcohol. Naturally they were keen supporters in the mid-century of the Gin Acts, which aimed to reduce the consumption of gin by the twin expedients of increasing the tax on gin and by imposing a high license fee on retailers. They were also interested in penal reform. Despite the failure of earlier penal experiments they were convinced that prisons run on proper lines would become a powerful force for the redemption and reformation of convicts. Individuals kept in solitary confinement, with no distractions, would contemplate their sins, turn to God, and became useful members of society.

Several model prisons were built, including one at Cold Bath Fields on the site of what is now London's Mount Pleasant sorting office. Sadly, when Cold Bath Fields became enveloped in scandal at the turn of the century, the mental cruelty embodied in the ideas of penal reformers became obscured by politics and went unacknowledged. These new institutions, whose reformatory objectives were epitomized in their description as penitentiaries, were expensive to run and the insistence on treating all prisoners alike led to serious difficulties. When members of the radical political group, the London Corresponding Society, were imprisoned in Cold Bath Fields in the late eighteenth century they were appalled to find themselves mixing with, and being treated as, convicted felons. Clearly their concept of crime and wrongdoing was very different to that of the government who sought to convict them of treason. They claimed a new kind of special status—that they were political prisoners and as such should not be subjected to the same reformatory regime as criminals.

PROTEST AND RIOT

The protests of the London Corresponding Society serve as another reminder that the concept of just what constituted a wrong could and did vary from one social group to another. Sometimes such differing perceptions led to demonstrations that could all too easily be characterized as riots. The Riot Act with its requirement that the Act be read to the assembled populace and that they then be given an hour to disperse allowed a cooling off period, essentially recognizing that there was something of a continuum between a peaceful demonstration and one that had turned to violence. Rough music, considered elsewhere in this volume, provides one example of this (Banks 2014). Food riots—mass demonstrations that took place at times of rapid escalation in the price of staple foodstuffs (usually bread)—provide another. The purpose of the gathering was not to cause damage but to call magistrates and local officials to their duty: in other words, those assembling were doing so in the conviction that they were in the right both legally and morally. In general once orders were issued for prices to be lowered the gathering had served its purpose and the riot was over.

Depending on one's perspective the unruliness of the populace in such situations was either a wrong in itself, or the precise opposite—a means to prevent wrongdoing. But of course such demonstrations of popular concern could easily turn violent, especially if they were badly handled by the authorities. In 1769, the imprisonment of John Wilkes prompted a gathering in his support in St George's Fields in Southwark. Fearing disorder, the magistrates sent for the assistance of troops. Goaded by the crowd, the soldiers chased one individual, a man named William Allen, into a barn where they shot and killed him. It was then alleged that Allen was an innocent victim and as the news of his death spread, matters rapidly deteriorated. The Riot Act was read, but instead of dispersing the demonstrators began to pelt the soldiers with stones. They responded by shooting into and above the crowd. This eventually ensured that the crowd dispersed, but not before several people had been killed and others wounded.

Forty years later, on August 16, 1819, a far larger demonstration in and around what is now St Peter's Square, Manchester, led to a similar disaster. The sufferings caused by economic dislocation in the aftermath of the Napoleonic Wars, coupled with high food prices, encouraged demands for an extension of the franchise. In pursuit of demands for political reform, the Manchester Patriotic Union called a meeting to be addressed by the well-known radical orator Henry Hunt. Appalled by the size of the crowd who came to hear Hunt—modern estimates put it at some 60,000 to 80,000—and fearful that this was merely a prelude to either riot or insurrection, the magistrates ordered the arrest of Hunt and others with him on the speaker's stand. The only way such arrests could be effected was with military intervention. Whether the crowd began to attack the soldiers, or whether the soldiers began to attack the crowd in an attempt to destroy their flags and banners, remains a matter for debate. The magistrates, believing the former, ordered the soldiers to disperse the crowd. The resulting melee left fifteen people dead and hundreds injured. In an ironical reference to the battle of Waterloo, the events of that day became known as the Peterloo massacre—a nomenclature that reinforces the perception of wrongdoing by those who regarded themselves as the guardians of law and order rather than by the demonstrators.

REDEFINING WRONGS

One particular form of wrong perhaps deserves special mention. Since the days of classical civilization, and probably for centuries before that, the existence of slavery had rarely been questioned. Indeed, judging by the number of passages concerning the management of slaves in both the Old and New Testaments, the practice appears to have enjoyed biblical sanction.[18] However, the nature of slavery underwent a transformation in the late seventeenth and early eighteenth centuries. Not only did the terms slave and negro become synonymous but the concept of chattel slavery became pervasive. The slave was no longer simply a source of unpaid labor, his or her body was now also the property of the owner, in much the same way as a farmer might own cattle. Indeed an advertisement for a sugar plantation in 1791 referred to it having "a stock of negroes, cattle and appurtenances" as though all three formed a single category of assets.[19]

As a result of the work of men like Granville Sharp and Thomas Clarkson, attitudes to slavery were transformed in the second half of the eighteenth century. Sharp and Clarkson pioneered many of the techniques that political activists still use in our own day. One of those techniques was the use of a readily identifiable logo—a kneeling slave in chains asking "Am I not a man and a brother?" Another technique was to construct a test case to bring before the courts and establish legal rights and wrongs. Granville Sharp was involved in a number of legal actions to try to protect Africans in London from being re-enslaved by their masters. He did so in a conscious effort to reshape English law. In1765 he had become involved in the case of Jonathan Strong, a slave from Barbados who had been so badly beaten by his master, David Lisle, that a four-month stay in hospital was needed to restore him to health. When Lisle tried to reclaim him, Sharp was horrified to be advised that even in England the law favored the master's rights and became determined to secure a legal ruling in favor of other slaves. In February 1771 he was instrumental in the prosecution of Robert Stapylton for assaulting Thomas Lewis. Lewis was Stapylton's slave, but had left his service; Stapylton arranged to have him kidnapped and put on board a ship in order to return him to be sold in Jamaica. Sharp hoped that the verdict would amount to an unequivocal declaration that such an action was illegal. Instead the presiding judge, Lord Mansfield, managed to fudge the issue. Lewis' life history indicated that there was a break in Stapylton's alleged ownership, in that at one point Lewis had been captured by a Spanish privateer. Mansfield emphasized this capture to the jury and left it to them to decide whether Lewis really was Stapylton's property. They found that he was not, and convicted Stapylton of the assault (Oldham 1992).

Sharp had better luck the following year when the broadly similar case of James Somersett was heard—also in Mansfield's court. Like Lewis, Somersett had left his master, who, like Stapylton, arranged to have him kidnapped and put on board a ship in order to sell him in the West Indies. This time there was no break in the chain of ownership but Mansfield was still determined to avoid a definitive judgment. His carefully worded judgment concentrated on a very narrow point, the right to compel an individual to leave the country against his will. He ruled that such a right did not exist but stopped short of laying down the principle that slaves were free once they arrived in England. The ruling was, however, sufficiently ambiguous to enable Sharp to promote such a belief.

A legal victory, however ambivalent, was not enough to secure abolitionist aims. Instead Sharp and his fellow abolitionists had to find other means of engaging public sympathy. Their stock in trade became heart-rending stories of cruelty and the wrongs perpetrated throughout the slave trade. These included accounts of the violence inherent in slave trading practices in Africa. Allegations that previously free people were kidnapped and sold into slavery were disputed by slave traders but Clarkson's account of feuding Africans and the resultant massacre at Calabar in 1767—in which European slave traders were complicit—was easily verifiable (Clarkson 1788). A further propaganda coup for the abolitionists resulted from revelations about the fate of the slave ship *Zong*. This was even more horrifying than the massacre at Calabar. The *Zong* allegedly overshot its destination in Jamaica and became lost in the Caribbean. Water ran low and in order to save the crew, it was decided to kill the slaves who were packed into its hold. Accordingly, over 100 men, women and children were thrown overboard and drowned. The subsequent legal action was not a prosecution for murder but a civil action about whether the ship owners should or should not be compensated under the terms of their insurance policy. Even the most hardened of advocates of slavery must have found the details of the case unbearable. It certainly made it easier for the abolitionists to mobilize support and to channel that support into a series of petitions to Parliament.

Quite apart from the economic arguments concerning the impact of abolition on the fortunes of West Indian plantation owners, those who supported the slave trade contended that it brought wider economic benefits in that it provided a valuable training ground for sailors and hence for British domination of the seas. One of Clarkson's most significant achievements was his ability produce irrefutable evidence that participation in the slave trade, far from training sailors, was effectively a death sentence. A study of crew muster lists established that the death rate among crews on board slave trading vessels was in the order of 20 percent. Clarkson also produced a visual image that hit home—a plan of the slave ship *Brookes* that showed just how nearly 500 people could be packed into a small ship (Figure 7.6). Chained together, each individual had just 16 inches (40 cm) of space and could neither sit nor stand fully. Sir George Yonge MP deposed that he had once been on board a slave ship that was 200 slaves short of its full "cargo" and even so "the stench was intolerable."[20] Reproduced countless times in newspapers, pamphlets, and posters, the print became the most widely recognizable image of the realities of the transatlantic slave trade.

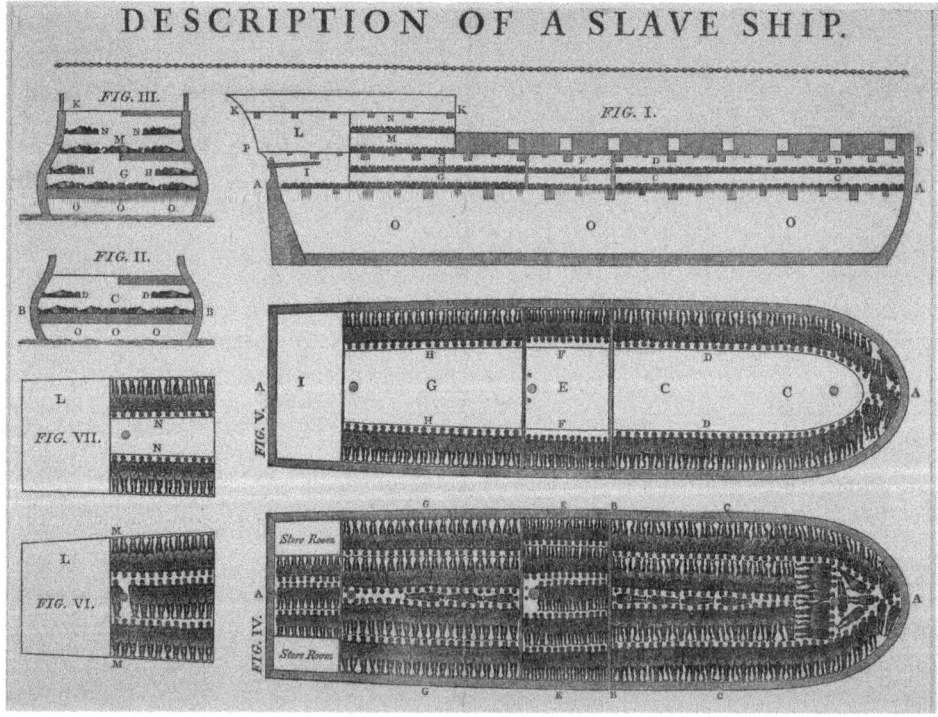

FIGURE 7.6 Plan and detail of the slave ship *Brookes*. Woodcut, 1789. Source: © The Trustees of the British Museum.

Another strand of the campaign was a boycott of slave-grown sugar and rum, introduced after the failure of William Wilberforce's abolition bill in April 1791. Consuming such products, "steeped in the blood of our fellow creatures" made the purchasers a party to slavery, for "The slave-dealer, the slave-holder, and the slave driver, are virtually the agents of the consumer, and may be considered as employed and hired by him to procure the commodity" (Fox 1792: 4). The campaign was publicized in a pamphlet that ran to at least twenty-four editions within just two years. It was produced in bulk with an eye to facilitating distribution. Initially single copies cost just a penny but fourteen copies could be had for a shilling and for those who wished to give them away, there was a bulk purchase price of 5s. per 100. By the time the twenty-fourth edition was published, the price had dropped still further: 1/2d., 13 for 6d. or 50 for 1s. 9d. The printers were also prepared to offer "an edition worked off with their names and residence in the title" to anyone buying 1,000 copies. Great numbers were reported to have joined the campaign.[21] One London society proposed a debate on the subject: "Which ought to be considered the most criminal, the merchants and planters who carry on the slave trade; or the people who encourage it by the consumption of sugar and rum?" The speakers were to include advocates of slavery, abolitionists and "an appeal from the suffering negroes." In the event the debate appears to have been a lively one that had to be adjourned to a second night, at which it was noted that several Africans would be present "in order to defend themselves and their fellow countrymen against the charge of their being a race of inferior beings."[22]

That individuals of African descent needed to prove themselves in this way provides a reminder that while many eighteenth-century abolitionists may seem to have been heroes, they were nevertheless heroes with feet of clay. By any modern definition of the word, the abolitionists were clearly racist. For Sharp the moral argument against slavery was as much about the moral welfare of the owners as about the welfare of the slaves. He believed that the possession of such power over another human being was dehumanizing and so an evil in itself; furthermore the sin of slavery was such that it would call down the wrath of God on the nation. Something of abolitionists' attitudes can be deduced from the "Am I not a man and a brother" image that was so successful in its day. Implicit in the image is an assumption that being black is co-terminous with slavery; primitive culture and lack of "civilized" Western values is suggested by the man's rudimentary clothing. Unable to help himself, he is forced to implore the assistance of (white) abolitionists. The idea that people of African descent were of inferior intellect was pervasive. David Hume was just one individual who suggested "the negroes and all other species of men ... to be inferior to the whites" (Hume 1994: 86n). When Dr. Johnson died in 1784 he made his black servant Francis Barber his residuary legatee, but he nevertheless placed control of the funds in the hands of trustees.[23] Frances Reynolds, sister of Sir Joshua, wrote that "It appears to me to be inconceivable, that the negro-race supposing their mental powers are on a level with other nations, could ever arrive at true taste when their eye is accustomed only to objects so diametrically opposed to taste as the face and form of negroes are!" (Reynolds 1785: 27).

Britain abolished the slave trade in 1807. Slavery in the British Empire (not including India, Ceylon and St Helena) was not abolished until 1833 and even then its effect was not immediate. The legislation acknowledged that a wrong was being committed, but in the eyes of Parliament the wrong was the expropriation of the slave owners' property. The sum of £20 million was set aside to compensate slave owners for the loss of their human assets. In the twenty-first century the wrong is perceived very differently, but calls for reparations to the countries and/or descendants of African slaves have so far gone unheeded.

THE CULTURAL CONTEXT

Human beings have an instinctive ability to label certain behaviors as either right or wrong, but making those choices is, at least in part, based on the social norms of the society in which we live as well as the influence of religion and of the peer groups (such as friends, family and co-workers) to which we belong. The values we imbue in childhood, our experiences, religious beliefs, education and gender will all influence our perception of what is and what is not ethical.[24] As we tackle the moral complexities of what is right or wrong in the twenty-first century it is as well to remember that our ancestors found it just as difficult to identify moral certainties. It is clear for example from many of his remarks in his famous *Commentaries* that William Blackstone struggled with the use of the death penalty, though as a judge he was part and parcel of the judicial system that inflicted it. He salved his own conscience (and the consciences of others) by explaining that those who held office within the criminal justice system were obliged to carry out capital sentences as a "an act of necessity, and even of civil duty" ([1765–9] 2016: Vol 4, 117).

In a society that lacked a strong and visible police force the delivery of justice depended on common understandings of what was and was not right and wrong. When those understandings broke down the result was often a popular demonstration that easily toppled over into riot, as in the case of Daniel Clarke. There were some spectacular instances of this. Riots broke out in 1749 in support of Bosavern Penlez, a young man whom it was widely believed had been unjustly arrested, convicted, and hanged for his part in an attack on a notorious brothel. The perception of wrong stretched to what was perceived to be unacceptable legislation: popular religious bigotry prompted riots in 1753 and 1780 against the Jewish naturalization bill and the Papists Act of 1778, respectively. Yet a realization that community-based ideals of justice were not always congruent with the definitions offered by the law did not destroy a fundamental belief in, and acceptance of, the rule of law: admiration for the exploits of gentlemanly highwaymen, for example, did not prevent acquiescence in their ultimate fate on the gallows. An abstract belief in the rule of law could be reconciled to the intricate and confusing realities of everyday life because there were ways of marrying the apparent rigidity of law to more flexible moral codes, enabling the delivery of justice to be shaped and, to a certain extent subverted, by cultural expectations: juries delivered verdicts that contradicted the evidence; crowds at the pillory demonstrated their disgust or occasionally approbation in their choice of weapons to throw, rioters ensured their grievances were heard by those with the power to remediate them. Concepts of right and wrong are after all as much cultural constructs as legal ones.

CHAPTER EIGHT

The Legal Profession

JAMES OLDHAM

In 1785, two things happened that are of importance to what we know about the practice of law in England in the late eighteenth century. First, the decisions of the Court of King's Bench, then the principal common law court that sat in Westminster Hall, began to be reported by Charles Durnford and Edward East (Figure 8.1). These reports were of excellent quality and, for the first time, the reports were published immediately after each law term ended (thus they came to be referred to as Term Reports). This near-contemporaneous publication was of great benefit to the practicing bar. As barrister Edward Bearcroft reportedly remarked in August 1789, "he had long ago left off taking notes"; instead, "he now relied on the Termly (*sic*) Reports, which made business very pleasant."[1] Yet it is worth noting that Durnford and East reported only the sittings of the full Court of King's Bench during the four annual law terms—Michaelmas, Hilary, Easter, and Trinity—each lasting approximately three weeks. The law terms were, collectively, the post-trial stage of civil litigation, when the full four-member court took up motions and reserved questions of law. No one was yet reporting the first stage of nearly all common law cases, the jury trial—and the vast majority of jury trials ended with the jury verdict, with no post-trial motions.

The second notable event of 1785 was the founding of *The Times* of London.[2] *The Times* has been published daily and continuously since its founding, and to the joy and grief of historians, the entire run is available online and is word-searchable. Over the past several years, I have perused, at least summarily, every single day's issue of *The Times* for a thirty-five year period, from 1785 to 1820, being particularly interested in assessing just how extensive law reporting was in the press during this period, how trustworthy it was, and how informative it was, especially as compared to the printed reports. Given the gaps, shortcomings, and delays associated with the printed reports[3]—as Bearcroft's delight at even termly publication might suggest—newspaper reports would have been an essential source of information for the legal profession in the eighteenth century, just as they now provide a crucial tool for the historian in uncovering details about the working lives of barristers and judges.

This chapter is a revised version of the 2012 Maurice and Muriel Fulton Lecture in Legal History, delivered at the University of Chicago Law School on May 2, 2012.

FIGURE 8.1 Court of King's Bench. Engraved by J. Black and published in Rudolph Ackermann, "The Microcosm of London," c. 1808–1811. Source: Court of Kings Bench / British Library, London, UK / © British Library Board. All Rights Reserved / Bridgeman Images.

THE POPULAR PRESS

Before turning to particulars about case reports and law-related stories that appeared in *The Times* during the reign of George III, it may be helpful to sketch the newspaper world in England in the second half of the eighteenth century. Historian Jeremy Black summarizes as follows:

> In 1760 London had four dailies and five or six tri-weeklies. A decade later there were at least five dailies, eight tri-weeklies and four weeklies published in the capital. In 1783 London possessed nine dailies and ten bi- or tri- weeklies. By 1790 the figures were 13 morning, one evening, seven tri-weekly and two biweekly papers; by early 1792 the number of dailies had risen to 14 and by the end of the year 16. In 1811 the total of papers in all categories published in London was 52, a number swelled by Sunday newspapers, the first of which, the *British Gazette and Sunday Monitor* was started in about 1779, and all of which were illegal due to sabbatarian legislation. (Black 1987)

By the 1770s, newspapers were read by a substantial and socially diverse portion of the population (Barker 1998). Studies of literacy show that by the beginning of the 1700s, almost everyone among the "commercial classes" in London was literate (Barker 1998: 27). Newspaper culture in England in the late eighteenth and nineteenth centuries was dramatically different than it is today in that newspaper reading was a social and public practice rather than an exclusively solitary activity (Barker 1998: 29). Pubs allowed newspapers to be jointly purchased, and to be read out aloud and discussed, thus providing access to newspapers even by the illiterate (Barker 1998; Garrad 2001). With regard to circulation numbers, politician Dennis O'Bryen wrote in a letter to Edmund Burke in 1782 that 25,000 papers were published daily in London, and each newspaper was read by ten people (Barker 1998: 23). As London had a population of approximately 750,000 in 1780,[4] if O'Bryen's estimate of 250,000 daily newspaper readers was correct, they would represent a third of London's population. This is consistent with historian David Lemming's (2009) estimates that approximately one-quarter of London's population read a newspaper in 1750 and approximately one-third did so in 1780.

There is a large literature dealing with the popular press in England during the eighteenth and nineteenth centuries (Black 1987; Barker 1998; Rea 1963; Werkmeister 1963).[5] As is well known, some of the newspapers then, as now, were published instrumentally for political purposes. Some were pro-government, some were radically opposed. Also, controversy over freedom of expression erupted in the courts in seditious libel cases, as, for example, the public clamor surrounding John Wilkes in the 1760s as the fortuitous folk hero favoring a free press (Oldham 1992). These realities might suggest that the popular press could not possibly be a reliable source of law or law-related news during the reign of George III. For several reasons, however, the reporting of legal cases and law-related issues in *The Times* became not only extensive but also largely trustworthy and often more informative than the the printed reports.

First, reading through the pages of *The Times*, it is clear that law reporting rather quickly became substantial and remained so for most of the reign of George III. In the early years of *The Times*, 1786–1790, the case descriptions from the common law courts (predominantly King's Bench) tended to be short summaries, usually averaging about one newspaper column in length. Several standard columns were fashioned—"Law Report," "Assize News," "Law Intelligence," and "Old Bailey Reports." In addition, freestanding separate reports of cases were published, sometimes in large numbers, plus occasional reports of Chancery, Admiralty, and Ecclesiastical cases. In these early years, the number of cases in the "Law Report" column ranged from approximately 50 to 100 per year; cases in the "Law Intelligence" column varied from very few to as many as twenty-one; assize cases were ten or fewer; and Old Bailey cases ran from seventeen to forty-one per year. Separate reports throughout the thirty-five-year period studied were widely variable in number—in some years none, in other years up to fifty.

Law reporting during the next three years, 1791–1793, produced more consistent coverage of the Old Bailey sessions, and greater attention to the assizes. The focus reverted to the London central courts in the years 1794–1799, with an average of 150 cases in the "Law Report" column. During 1800–1803, the law reporting was very active, covering in the aggregate approximately 210 to 230 cases per year. Reporting during 1804–1810 was widely variable, but 1811–1813 saw a return to high volume, and the remaining years to 1820 were again variable. Perhaps the peak years of coverage were 1817–1819, due principally to a sharp increase in cases from the assizes.

Secondly, there is both internal and external evidence to suggest that the law reporting in *The Times* was accurate. Most of the law reporting was made up of straightforward case summaries, leavened with descriptions of unusual or dramatic participants in legal proceedings, including occasionally the disgraceful behavior of the attorneys. It was no doubt true in the late eighteenth century, as it is today, that newspaper accounts of legal proceedings were not always unbiased and error-free. In the report in *The Times* of the 1799 case of *Bowles v. Atkinson*, Lord Kenyon (who succeeded Lord Mansfield as Chief Justice of King's Bench in 1788) "observed that he had just read in a newspaper [not *The Times*] an account of what he was supposed to have said in this case, and that the meaning of it was very mistaken indeed." And since *The Times* possessed its own note of what Lord Kenyon had said to the jury, that version was quoted in full.[6]

Yet many of the case reports in *The Times* can readily be cross-checked against high-quality printed reports of the same cases by Durnford and East, and also against surviving manuscript notes kept by judges, barristers, and court officers. Moreover, the Old Bailey cases can be compared to the reports in the Old Bailey Sessions Papers, just as John Langbein did for the years 1754–1756 by comparing the Sessions Papers reports with the detailed shorthand case notes kept by King's Bench Chief Justice Dudley Ryder (Langbein 1996). I have made many such comparisons for cases appearing in *The Times* in the late eighteenth and early nineteenth centuries, and it is my very strong conclusion that the reports in *The Times* are generally trustworthy.

Finally, and perhaps most importantly both for the legal profession of the late eighteenth century and the modern legal historian, the law reports in *The Times* include accounts of cases that do not appear elsewhere in print, as well as additional details about cases that do appear in the printed reports. One of England's circuit judges, David Bentley, in an introduction to his 1998 book, *English Criminal Justice in the Nineteenth Century*, has claimed that the case reports in *The Times* were "a far more valuable source" than the reports in the Old Bailey Sessions Papers because the reports of Old Bailey cases in *The Times* "contain material which the *Sessions Reports* omit … and include not only reports of Old Bailey trials but also of trials in the King's Bench" (2003: preface). It was not, of course, invariably true that the Old Bailey reports in *The Times* were superior—the quality of the Sessions Papers, in the late eighteenth century especially, was often quite good (Langbein 2003). Yet the Sessions Papers did not ordinarily include the judge's instructions to the jury, and this feature of the reports in *The Times* is indeed valuable.

In *The Times*'s coverage of the litigation in the common law courts, a great many of the reports were of jury trials, and for the first five years of the paper's existence, 1785–1790, these reports were unique. Regular printed reports of jury trials, or at *nisi prius* as they were called, did not emerge until the 1790s, when Peake published selected *nisi prius* cases from the years 1790–1812. Espinasse also reported *nisi prius* cases from the years 1793–1807, and was followed by Campbell (covering 1808–1816) and Starkie (1815–1822), both at *nisi prius*. Yet these reports did not make the reports in *The Times* superfluous or duplicative, since the printed reports encompassed only a small percentage of the jury trials that were conducted.[7] The majority of the trial-level cases that were reported in *The Times*—in some subject areas a very large majority—were entirely absent from the printed reports, even after *nisi prius* reporting began.

THE PRACTICES OF THE LEGAL PROFESSION

Most of the King's Bench business in the late eighteenth century was handled by a small, select group of barristers.[8] Within that group, Thomas Erskine, Vicary Gibbs, William Garrow, and Edward Law were the leaders. Edward Law would later become Lord Ellenborough, Lord Kenyon's successor as Chief Justice of King's Bench, but Erskine's dominance among the barristers is indicated not only by his frequent appearance in case reports in *The Times*, but also by the following notice that appeared in *The Times* on May 30, 1796:

Law Report

Court of King's Bench, May 28

The Court only sat about half an hour, and nothing of consequence occurred.

Mr. Erskine being at Portsmouth on his re-election for that place; and as he is retained as usual in all the business that was to have come before the Court, they could not proceed in his absence.[9]

Erskine's dominance can be illustrated by the extensive coverage by *The Times* of his courtroom speeches. A representative example is a case that came before the Court of King's Bench in 1804 in which the issue was whether a poetic song called *"Abraham Newland"* was entitled to copyright protection for the composer.[10] The problem was that the song occupied only a single sheet of paper. At the trial, Chief Justice Ellenborough "put the case of a newspaper, of a hand-bill, &c." He "observed that this was a case of some novelty," but on studying the copyright statute of 8 Anne, chapter 19, "he thought it clear that the Legislature did not mean to take under their protection a single sheet of paper, as answering the description of a book." He inspected other related statutes, and concluded that "the Legislature had considered a book as something that was stitched or bound up, and therefore as that which must consist of a number of sheets." The plaintiff, therefore, was nonsuited.

Several days later Erskine, who was acting as counsel for the plaintiff, filed a motion to set aside the nonsuit. In an argument that would resonate with the experience of most academics, he said that "Had the piece, which is the subject of this action, been varied in the type, it might have been made to extend beyond the compass of one sheet, and then it would not have been liable to the objection"; indeed, "This is a case on which a prodigious extent of property depends, not from the interest of the parties in the Poem itself, but from the interest all mankind must feel, in the protection to be extended to the productions of the human mind by British law."[11] Erskine cited "the great foundation of these actions," the case of *Millar v. Taylor*,[12] pointing out that at common law, the author of a book, *or any other literary composition*, was protected. Lord Ellenborough protested that no one at the time of *Millar v. Taylor* considered the question of whether a single sheet could be considered a book. Erskine, with his typical rhetorical flourish, responded by raising the fundamental question that had been at issue in *Millar v. Taylor*— whether copyright, "unimpeached at common law, be taken away by the statute of Queen Anne"—"Or is it consistent with the natural jurisprudence, to narrow, by legislation, the ancient rights of the British people?" He said that the Queen Anne statute was "for the encouragement of learning," and that it referred to *"Books and other writings."* Also, he pointed out that musical compositions were covered by the statute. And,

> If the voluminous extent of a production be the sole title to the guardianship the author receives from the law, the records of dullness will indeed receive a portion of reflected light, while the poetic fancy of the immortal *Gray* will be consigned to the church-yard in which his Elegy was composed, and the distant view of Eton College will recede forever from human observation.

Finally, he traced the etymology of the word "book" into Latin and Anglo-Saxon origins. In April 1804, according to the last report of the case to appear in *The Times*, Lord Ellenborough and his fellow judges appear to have been won over. A new trial was granted.[13]

The length of this particular case was, however, exceptional. Legal historians, John Langbein (1996) especially, have demonstrated the rapid pace of criminal trials in the Old Bailey during the late eighteenth century, due in significant part to the absence or limited role of lawyers for the defense. Less attention has been paid to the pace of trial in the flow of cases through the common law courts sitting in London and on Assize. Lord Ellenborough, Kenyon's successor as Chief Justice of the Court of King's Bench, gained some notoriety from the blistering pace with which he conducted jury trials. In the year 1812, for example, Ellenborough conducted trials in over 1,100 cases (Oldham 2004). Lord Brougham, in his "Historical Sketches," gave the following explanation:

> The whole City business was in the hands of [barristers] Gibbs, Garrow, and Park ... and it was a main object with them all to facilitate the dispatch of business. This they effected by at once giving up all but the arguable points of law, on which they immediately took the judge's opinion; and the maintainable questions of fact, on which they went to the jury. (1839: 3, 212)

In this way, Brougham claimed, "Fifteen or twenty important causes were thus disposed of in a morning, more to the satisfaction of the Court and the benefit of the Counsel than to the contentment of the parties or their attorneys" (284).

This is confirmed by occasional newspaper reports of activity in the courts. On February 10, 1791, for example, *The Times* reported that at Westminster Hall, "Lord Kenyon sat at *Nisi Prius* at twelve o'clock," and, "The bulk of the cases that were tried were undefended."[14] Several months later, *The Times* reported that at Guildhall, "Yesterday morning at 9 o'clock, Lord *Kenyon* sat at *nisi prius*, and tried about thirty causes before two o'clock."[15] If true, this meant that the average time per case was only ten minutes. Perhaps many of these were also undefended, or perhaps some were passed over because of the non-appearance of attorneys (Oldham 2013). Even more arresting, *The Times* reported that on July 4, 1791, "His Lordship sat at *Nisi Prius* about two o'clock and tried twenty-one issues before four"[16] — which would have been an incredible rocket docket, at the blazing speed of approximately six minutes per case.[17]

Statistics appeared sporadically in the newspapers that also demonstrated the high volume caseload in the civil trial docket for the Court of King's Bench, especially at the sittings for the City of London at the Guildhall. On June 21, 1791, *The Times* reported that at Guildhall as of June 20, "there were 103 causes in his Lordship's paper."[18] An even higher volume was reported for February 22, 1797—"Lord Kenyon sits this day at Guildhall, where there are 130 Causes entered for Trial."[19] The caseload did slacken at times, and may have customarily been lower at the sittings for Middlesex County at Westminster Hall. Thus, on February 14, 1800, it was reported that, "The number of causes entered at Westminster to be tried by Lord Kenyon is only sixty."[20]

Occasionally, the number of docketed special jury cases was noted. On June 27, 1796, *The Times* reported that, as of June 25, "There are near 40 Special Jury causes to be tried in the course of these sittings at Guildhall."[21] And on December 10, 1799, *The Times* reported that on that day, "the Special Jury Causes begin, and fifty-one stand in the paper for trial."[22]

The most common post-trial motion during the period under study was the motion for new trial. The increasing frequency with which new trials were requested troubled the courts. It was reported in *The Times* on November 12, 1792 that when a new trial motion was, for once, refused, the "learned counsel ... observed, that he had not made the application from having consulted his own judgment, but that he had been asked to do it." Lord Kenyon responded by saying that since he had known Westminster Hall, "new trials had increased twenty-fold," and "he was very uneasy about it." He said that, "New trials should not be granted when they can only serve to heap expenses on expenses, merely to try experiments, without the sober advice of counsel."[23]

Unsupportable new trial motions nevertheless persisted. In *Brier v. Kay* (1796), a jury had awarded 40 shillings damages for a trivial assault even though the trial judge had told the jury that the case was worth only a farthing, after which Serjeant Cockle moved for a new trial on the ground of excessive damages. Lord Kenyon refused the motion, saying that, "If they in such a case were to grant a new trial, it would make the granting of new trials ridiculous."[24]

More troublesome to the courts than new trial motions was the persistent practice of some attorneys to pad the pleadings in order to increase attorney fees. Occasionally the court tried to check this practice. In a trover action in 1790, *Koops v. Chapman*, the question was whether the plaintiff was subject to the bankrupt laws, and counsel for the plaintiff—Erskine, Mingay, and Lawes—were unable to present a persuasive case.[25] The solicitor for the plaintiff was Mr. Crossley, and according to *The Times*, the court ordered him "to pay the costs for delivering a declaration of eighty sheets, when the learned Judge declared, eight would have been sufficient."[26]

Perhaps the prize-winning case of inflated pleadings was *Cowan v. Berry*, tried in Easter Term 1798, in which the court seemed unable to take control. The case was a qui tam action involving the defendant's allegedly extensive, exploitative, unlawful gambling. The statutory penalties claimed by the plaintiff amounted to £1,330,000. According to a report in *The Times*, counsel for the defendant, James Mingay, claimed that the declaration "consisted of 480 counts, containing between 2 and 3000 sheets, and measuring in length upwards of 100 yards."[27] The vast sum of £1,330,000 was achieved by counting each loss suffered at play by each of thirty-two persons with whom the defendant played at the gaming tables as a violation of the statute of Queen Ann (9 Ann c. 14). These were then assembled, to produce penalties of £1,000 per day per person. Lord Kenyon said, "If this had been for the purpose of oppression, the court would set their face against it," but he would not "accede to the doctrine that the more offences a man has committed, that on that account the penalties ought to be remitted" (Oldham 2013: 184).

Yet another major frustration experienced by Lord Kenyon was the recurrent failure of attorneys, predominantly the solicitors, to attend to their cases when they were called. Here are late-eighteenth-century examples that were noted in the *The Times*:

Non-Appearance and Unpreparedness of Attorneys

Date	From The Times
Wednesday July 8, 1789	"Lord *Kenyon* sat only about an hour, as the attorneys were not prepared to go on with any more Causes."[28]
Thursday, November 11, 1789	"Yesterday when Lord Kenyon came into the Court of King's Bench, there was not one Counsel present."[29]

Thursday, July 20, 1791	"Lord Kenyon was obliged this morning to withdraw eight or nine records, because the attorneys did not attend with their witnesses."[30]
Friday, July 29, 1791	"As the Attorneys were not ready with their witnesses, Lord Kenyon was obliged to stop at ten o'clock."[31]
Tuesday, November 29, 1791	"Lord *Kenyon* came into Court at nine o'clock, and was obliged to sit a whole hour before he was able to go on. No Attorney or Witness attended, though the Counsel were all ready."[32]
Thursday, January 24, 1793	"The Court only sat about half a hour, and heard a few motions—counsel were not prepared to proceed to business."[33]
Thursday, December 10, 1795	"This morning the Lord Chief Justice, the Jury, and the Counsel waited almost a whole hour before they could proceed with a single cause, on account of the absence of the Attorneys and their Witnesses."[34]
Friday December 9, 1796	"Lord Kenyon, the Gentlemen of the Jury, and the Counsel attended this morning as usual, precisely at nine o'clock, and remained in Court upwards of an hour, without being able to do any business of consequence, because the Attorneys did not attend with their witnesses."[35]
Friday June 22, 1799	"Lord Kenyon was obliged to stop about half past 11 o'clock as the Attorneys were not ready to proceed in any more causes."[36]

Lord Kenyon seemed unable to deal effectively with this problem. He grumbled that, "Attorneys must have it impressed on their minds, that they must attend, and the only effectual way to do that, was *to touch their purses*."[37] He said "it was scandalous and infamous for Attorneys to charge their Clients for their non-attendance and he wished with all his heart that Clients would bring actions against such Attorneys for negligence, who were the ruin of many poor families."[38] Erskine sympathized, saying "that the only way of curing Attorneys and Witnesses of this evil, was to strike out every cause where the parties were not ready to proceed."[39] Kenyon eventually threatened to take such action. When attorneys and witnesses failed to appear at the sittings on December 10, 1795, "His Lordship gave notice that if the Attorneys were not ready with their witnesses tomorrow morning by nine o'clock, he would strike out one cause after another till he went through the whole list, except the Special Juries."[40] If this threat had any effect, it was only short-term. A year later, the attorneys and witnesses again were absent, and Lord Kenyon reverted to expressing indignation, lamenting "the expence parties were put to by the carelessness and neglect of those whom they had entrusted with the management of their affairs."[41]

THE GLORIOUS UNCERTAINTY OF THE LAW

Although most legal reports in *The Times* were reliable factual summaries of public trials, the reporters could not resist occasional editorial comment on the foibles and inefficiencies that seemed endemic to the legal profession (Figure 8.2). In its issue for November 11, 1791, for example, a brief story appeared about protracted litigation over a Dutch East Indiaman, the case of *Camden v. Home*.[42] According to *The Times*, the case "furnishes a fine illustration of the glorious uncertainty of the law." The first hearing was before the Court of Admiralty, which gave judgment. The losing party appealed to the Lords Commissioners of Appeal, who reversed the Court of Admiralty. The new losing party then applied to the Court of Common Pleas for relief, "who, after viewing the sentence of the Lords Commissioners, and hearing four arguments on it, were of opinion that they had put a wrong construction upon the Act of Parliament." The newly-defeated party then filed a Writ of Error in the Court of King's Bench,

> and that honourable Court, after hearing two arguments upon it, are of opinion that the Court of Common Pleas have no right to consider whether or no the Court of Appeal [the Lords Commissioners] had put a wrong construction on the Act of Parliament, and therefore the King's Bench were unanimously of opinion that the judgment of the Common Pleas ought to be reversed.[43]

FIGURE 8.2 Lawyers in Term. Attributed to William Dent, 1786. Source: Library of Congress.

Thus:

> [T]he first Court deliver a decision, the second Court says the decision of the first Court is wrong. The third Court says the decision of the second is wrong, and the fourth Court says the decision of the third is wrong!—We understand this business is to go to the House of Lords.[44]

Another "glorious uncertainty" case in the Court of King's Bench was reported in *The Times* two years earlier, on November 3, 1789, which also demonstrated that the editors were addressing a highly sophisticated readership. At issue in *Walpole v. Ewer* was the amount of recovery to be allowed under an English marine insurance policy on a Danish ship traveling from Bengal to Copenhagen. Bad weather on the voyage had partially damaged the ship, and the suit was brought to recover for the harm done.[45] Counsel for the plaintiff argued that recovery for this partial loss (known in the trade as "average loss") was permitted under Danish law, even though in England, recovery was only available for total loss. The court said that counsel "should produce an adjudged case in one of the superior Courts of Copenhagen, where this average loss was allowed"; however, "The parties concerned in this cause had written to Copenhagen for an account of the law on this subject; but received very different and contradictory accounts, so that the glorious uncertainty of the law is not peculiar to the English system."

As illustrated by *Camden v. Home*, above, the persistent uncertainty in the law was graphically shown in reports of seemingly unending delay in bringing litigated cases to a final resolution. In the 1795 case of *Wilkinson v. Wilkinson*,[46] the plaintiff and defendant were brothers "who were reported to have sunk a half a million of money in iron works," and the plaintiff accused his brother of having broken up some of the works. The Chief Justice of the Court of King's Bench, Sir Lloyd Kenyon, urged the parties to refer the case to an arbitrator, declaring that:

> A cause of this sort was so multifarious, that it would be impossible ever to get to the end of it at *Nisi Prius* [in a jury trial]. It was pursuing a shadow, and he was very clear that it ought to go to a reference. It appeared that there were three Bills in Chancery, each of them several thousand sheets long. His Lordship thought it was of some importance for the parties to understand that the Court of Chancery would not settle all these accounts for at least these fifty years, so that if it continued in that Court, it would descend as a legacy to their Executors, Administrators, &c.

To the modern eye, Lord Kenyon appears to have indulged in gross exaggeration merely as a means of urging the parties to go to arbitration. His remarks nevertheless bring to mind *Jarndyce v. Jarndyce*, the famous Chancery suit in Charles Dickens's *Bleak House* that ran through several generations, until the assets of the estate were exhausted by legal fees (Holdsworth 1928; Watt 2009). And reports in *The Times* of actual Chancery cases show that Lord Kenyon's remarks, even Dickens's imagined case, were not in the least unrealistic, at least not while Lord Chancellor Eldon was in office in the first two decades of the nineteenth century[47] (Figure 8.3).

Lord Eldon was not, however, entirely to blame. In *Creswell v. Byron*,[48] the Court of Chancery took up a dispute over whether buildings in Castle Yard on Oxford Road belonged to one Elizabeth Ford or to the creditors of John Burdon. The original Bill in Chancery had been filed over *seventy* years previously, in 1737, and, as a result "of the delays in the Court of Equity," John Burdon "has been a prisoner [in debtors' prison], and was obliged to take the benefit of the Insolvent Act to produce his liberation." After

FIGURE 8.3 Court of Chancery. Engraved by J. Black and published in Rudolph Ackermann, "The Microcosm of London," *c.* 1808–1811. Source: Heritage Images / Getty Images.

the case had been reviewed by Lord Chancellor Eldon at the hearing on August 8, 1805, one of the parties "very pathetically addressed the Court: he said he was in the vale of years, conflicting with distress and poverty, and had no means of asserting his own rights, and demanding the justice of his country." Lord Eldon said that, "It is a horrible thing to see a cause of this antiquity before us"—"The whole of the mischief seems to have arisen from giving the agents a percentage on the produce of the estate, so that it has been their interest to protract the sale for nearly a century." Notwithstanding, Lord Eldon ordered the case to stand over for further proceedings.

Other cases exhibiting less severe but still egregious delay were reported by *The Times.* On August 8, 1805, *The Times* introduced its report of the case of *Lord Radnor v. The Bishop of Bath and Wells* as follows: "This cause has been five and twenty years depending; in the conduct of it the present Chancellor [Lord Eldon], both as a junior and before the bar, has had a very considerable share."[49] And on August 10, 1805, a hearing before Lord Chancellor Eldon in the thirty-five-year-old case of *Purcell v. Macnamara* was reported by *The Times.*[50] Counsel for the plaintiff said that according to the mode by which the case had proceeded, "the remainder of the lives of their Client and the Defendant would be exhausted, during the examination of the accounts." They said that "There were two ways of preventing justice in this Court; the one, by increasing the expences of the cause;

the other, by contriving all means of procrastination; and when they both were combined redress seemed to be impossible." Counsel for the defendant gave the following galling (or possibly tongue-in-cheek) response, demonstrating yet again the glorious uncertainty of the law: "What was the advantage of precipitation, compared to the benefit to be derived from mature reflection on every part of the case?"

TRIAL BY JURY

During the eighteenth and nineteenth centuries, trial by jury was venerated as a fundamental pillar of the freedoms and protections enjoyed by Englishmen (Blackstone [1765-9] 2016), and many aspects of this trial procedure were illustrated by the law reports in *The Times*. Countless news stories could be offered, but I will give only two examples, both about the latter days of rules that had outlived their original justifications. The first is about jury deliberations. There was a longstanding rule that when a case was submitted to a jury, the jury was to be confined without food or drink until they reached a unanimous decision. As William Blackstone stated in his *Commentaries*:

> The jury, after the proofs are summed up, unless the case be very clear, withdraw from the bar to consider of their verdict: and, in order to avoid intemperance and causeless delay, are to be kept without meat, drink, fire, or candle, unless by permission of the judge, till they are unanimously agreed. (Blackstone [1765-9] 2016: Vol. III, 349)

This would seem inhumane today, but in the late eighteenth and early nineteenth centuries, juries often rendered their verdicts in open court without any deliberation (especially in criminal cases at the Old Bailey) after trials lasting only fifteen or twenty minutes (Langbein 1978). Yet at times, juries were seriously deliberative, and the ancient rule of confinement with no comforts (other than a chamber pot) wore thin. In *The Times* on January 27, 1792, it was noted that, "The very respectable Special Jury who tried the cause of *Revett* against *Braham* did not eat or drink for the space of seventeen hours."[51] By contrast, perhaps in a fit of editorial excess, the report added:

> The Juries at the Old Bailey after eating an excellent breakfast begin their business at nine in the morning and are discharged punctually at three in the afternoon, when they have a sumptuous dinner. One would suppose this would be sufficient for the most craving appetites, but it is not, for at eleven o'clock they are plentifully supplied with bread and negus, and at one o'clock they have a fresh supply of coffee or porter. It might be supposed that common decency would prevent men from stuffing their bellies when they are deciding upon the lives of their fellow creatures.

Even if the report in *The Times* of Old Bailey jury feasting were largely true, the jurors were required to be sequestered until they reached a verdict, a practice that continues to the present day. Naturally this was not without protest. At the Old Bailey sessions on Saturday, October 31, 1812, the trial jury resumed hearing a case that had been suspended the previous evening, and after extensive additional testimony, Baron Thompson of the Court of Exchequer, one of the two judges conducting the Old Bailey trials for the sessions, announced that the Court must adjourn until the following Monday, and the jury "must be kept together till then." This provoked the following colloquy, according to *The Times*[52]:

FIGURE 8.4 The trial of M. D'Eon by a jury of matrons. Anonymous, 1786. Source: © The Trustees of the British Museum.

The Jury complained very much of the hardship of not being allowed to go home to their families, particularly on the Sabbath day; and asked if they could not be permitted to do so, attended by an officer of the Court.

Mr. Baron Thompson said, it was wholly out of his power to grant such a liberty. The law was peremptory as to their being kept together, and from everybody else.

The Jury said, that this confinement amounted to an imprisonment of four days, and might be prejudicial to the health of some of them who were used to air and exercise.

The Lord Mayor (sitting with Baron Thompson as the second judge at the Old Bailey sessions) said the Jury would have a large, airy room, and Baron Thompson "added, that on the trial of Mr. Hardy, the Jury were thus necessarily, and as a part of their duty in the administration of justice according to the laws of England, confined 9 days."

The second illustration of a jury practice that was anachronistic by the late eighteenth century is the continuing use of juries composed entirely of women—the "jury of matrons," as it was called (Figure 8.4). For centuries, juries of women had been empaneled whenever a female defendant in a criminal prosecution had been convicted and sentenced to death, but she "pleaded her belly," that is, she claimed to be pregnant. If she were not only pregnant but also "quick with child," her death sentence would be respited until after the child was born, when, in theory at least, she would be "called down to her former sentence."[53] The practice originated at a time when the medical profession had very little understanding of what physical evidence would accurately confirm not only pregnancy, but "quickening," which was once viewed as the moment when human life began (Oldham 1985). The theory was that the woman's death sentence did not justify taking a second life, so that after quickening, the hanging would be delayed.[54]

By the late eighteenth century, the medical profession was gaining pregnancy expertise and was increasingly called upon to consult in these cases, yet the jury of matrons persisted into the late nineteenth century (Oldham 1985). *The Times* for November 6, 1786 reported that at the conclusion of the sessions at the Old Bailey, twenty-seven prisoners had been sentenced to death, one of whom was Eleanor Kirwan, for forging a seaman's will. She, however, "pleaded pregnancy; upon which a jury of matrons were empaneled, who found the fact, upon which judgment was respited." Nearly two years later, another report printed the sentence of death that had been read out to two prisoners who had been convicted of coinage, then classified as high treason.[55] One of the prisoners was a woman, Christian Murphy, who said she was with child, but, in an unusual outcome, "A Jury of matrons found she was with child, but not with quick child." Her sentence was "to be burned with fire."

Additional reports of the appointment of juries of matrons appeared during the 1790s,[56] but change was on the way. *The Times* reported on July 17, 1798 that at the General Sessions of the Peace for Canterbury, Margaret Hilton was convicted of having willfully poisoned her husband,

> but pleading pregnancy, a Jury of matrons, assisted by some Gentlemen of the faculty, were appointed to ascertain the fact, and, after a consultation of two hours, returned a verdict that she was quick with child: she was accordingly respited for three months, but [she was] desired not to indulge the most distant idea of mercy on this side of the grave.[57]

The jury of matrons was occasionally used in civil cases as well as criminal. According to William Blackstone, "when a widow feigns herself with child, in order to exclude the next heir, and a suppositious birth is suspected to be intended; then upon the writ *de ventre inspiciendo* [to inspect the belly], a jury of women is to be impaneled to try the question whether she be with child or not" (Blackstone 1765–69: Vol. III, 362).

A late eighteenth-century example of the invocation of a jury of matrons in a civil action occurred in July 1792 in *Ex Parte Brown*.[58] The case involved the estate of Henry Arthur Fellows, Esq., whose will left large sums of money to several children whom, according to *The Times*, "Martha Brown had the address to make him [Fellows] believe she had by him." Also, Fellows left a codicil to his will providing

> that if Mrs. Brown should be pregnant, and bear a child after his death, within a time so limited that it was probable he was the father of it, that the child, on attaining the age of 21 years, was to have £10,000 and the instant it was born the interest of that money was to be applied to its maintenance and education.

The petitioner was the Earl of Portsmouth, who sued as next friend (and father) to an infant named Newton Wallop (who was, in Blackstone's words, "the heir presumptive"). The petitioner requested that the Lords Commissioners [of Chancery] "issue the writ *de Ventre Inspiciendo* to Martha Brown, in order to inspect and examine whether she was now pregnant." The writ would call for the empaneling of a jury of matrons, who would physically inspect the woman, as in the criminal cases, and if found to be pregnant, she was to be kept under watch day and night, until the birth did or did not occur. The petition claimed that Mrs. Brown was the wife of Captain Ulysses Brown, an officer in the service of the East India Company, and that Mrs. Brown was a person of ill fame, who kept several houses of ill fame—and that she "gained a great ascendance over Mr. Fellows, and pretended she had children by him." Counsel for the Petitioner, the Solicitor

General (Sir John Scott, later Lord Eldon) and Mr. John Mitford (who later became Attorney General) argued that the writ *de ventre inspiciendo* was a legitimate common law writ, but it had not been intended to be issued on facts such as those before the Lords Commissioners. The Chief Baron (Sir James Eyre) nevertheless decided upon a qualified order—if within fourteen days the woman were to consent and actually permit "two midwives to be named by the petitioner to inspect her, and to examine whether she was pregnant or not, by such modes of examination as such midwives should think necessary," then the writ would be withheld; otherwise, the writ was to be issued.

CONCLUSION

The case reports in *The Times* are, on the whole, trustworthy, and valuable. A great many of the case reports that appear in the newspaper pages, indeed most of them, appear nowhere else in print. These reports significantly enhance our understanding of the principles established and followed in the evolving common law of the late eighteenth and early nineteenth centuries, and as well of the realities, not all of them admirable, of the practice of law of the time. The reporters' firsthand accounts of jury trials, including speeches to the judges by counsel and jury instructions from the trial judges, are almost virtual reality, as if the reader has been admitted to the courtroom while the trial is in progress. One can almost see, as if "live," the judges' personalities and philosophies in play, and the comfortable, largely congenial small world of litigation, especially on the plea side, as practiced by several dozen barristers and the twelve central court judges. We can understand, as well, that popular dependency on and dissatisfaction with the practicing bar are constants across the ages.

NOTES

Preface

1. Laurence Rosen, *Law as Culture: An Invitation* (Princeton, NJ: Princeton University Press, 2006), 199–200.
2. Pierre Legrand, *Fragments on Law-as-Culture* (Deventer: W E J Tjeenk Willink, Schoordijk Institute, 1999), 5.
3. Malcolm Andrews, *Landscape and Western Art* (Oxford History of Art) (Oxford: Oxford University Press, 1999), 53.

Introduction

1. See further Prest 2008.
2. In "The Representation of Chaos," at the beginning of his oratorio *The Creation* (1798), Joseph Haydn (1732–1809) uses "vague and fragmentary musical themes," "ambiguous harmonies" and "denied [listener] expectations" to suggest the primal absence of such laws (Temperley 1991: 83).
3. 1 Will. & Mary, sess. 2, c. 2, reprinted in Williams 1970: 26.
4. 12 & 13 Will. III, c. 2, reprinted in Williams 1970: 56.
5. 12 & 13 Will. III., c. 2, reprinted in Williams 1970: 56, 58.
6. 51 Geo. III, c. 1.
7. On "economic inequality," see, e.g., Israel 2010: 96–98.
8. The Battle of Copenhagen was the occasion of Vice Admiral Horatio Viscount Nelson's "Nelsonian blindness" or "Nelsonian dishonesty," or "contrived ignorance," traditionally referred to by trusts and tax lawyers (see, e.g., *Twinsectra Ltd v. Yardley and Others* [2002] UKHL 12, para [112]; [2002] 2 A.C. 164, 195F-G (Lord Millett)) "[T]urning to Captain Foley, a massive man and who was a foot taller … [Nelson] said, according to Southey, 'You know, Foley, I have only one eye—and I have a right to be blind sometimes,' and putting his small telescope to his blind eye, he exclaimed, 'I really do not see the signal!'" The signal was Signal No. 39, Admiral Sir Hyde Parker's command to Nelson to "leave off action" (Pope 1972: 410–411).
9. The argument for the necessity for representation in Parliament, as a corollary to taxation, is forever associated (see Wood 2006: 608) with the writings of the Massachusetts lawyer James Otis (1725–1783), whose "public career was [sadly] ended in 1769 when John Robinson, a commissioner of the customs whose accusations of treason he had publicly denied, hit him over the head in a Boston coffee house" (Boorstin 1966: 361).
10. Something recognized contemporaneously by Jonathan Swift, in *Gulliver's Travels* ([1735] 2005). See Stubbs 2016: 11–12.
11. This was in the 1780s, when counsel was still not allowed to address the jury directly (ibid.) Beattie states that defense counsel may date only from the early 1730s (Beattie 1986a: 356n).
12. 1 Will. and Mar. c. 18.
13. Hoppit 2000: 33.
14. 47 Geo. III, c. 36; Langford 1989: 516–518; Baker 2002: 477.

15. Holding 40 shillings of freehold was the electoral qualification in the shires of England, though not in the boroughs, in which there were wide differences. The 40-shilling qualification, which dated from the fifteenth century, lasted until the Representation of the People Act 1832 (or what has since been known as "the great Reform Act" of that year).
16. 5&6 Ann., c. 11.
17. 39&40 Geo. III, c. 67.
18. 9 Geo. I, c. 22.
19. (1765) 95 ER 807.
20. Citing Bill of Rights, art. 10.
21. 1 Geo. I, c. 5, reprinted in Williams 1970: 414.
22. 4 Geo. I, c. 11.
23. 25 Geo. II, c. 37.
24. 60 Geo. III, c. 1; 60 Geo. III, c. 2; 60 Geo. III, c. 4; 60 Geo. III, c. 6; 60 Geo. III, c. 8; 60 Geo. III, c. 9.
25. (1783) 99 ER 629.
26. (1772) 98 ER 499.
27. (1772) 98 ER 499, 510.
28. Quoted in Hoppit 2000, 459.
29. The dedication to the wordbook of *Judas Maccabaeus* reads: "PRINCE WILLIAM, DUKE OF CUMBERLAND, THIS FAINT PORTRAITURE OF A Truly Wise, Valiant, and Virtuous COMMANDER, As to the Possessor of the like Noble Qualities, IS, With most profound Respect and Veneration, INSCRIBED. By His ROYAL HIGHNESS'S *Most Obedient, and most devoted Servant*, The AUTHOR" (Morell 1747).
30. On magistrates more generally see Hay and Rogers 1997, ch. 9; Lemmings 2011: 33.
31. Quoted in Langford 1989: 303.
32. Ibid.
33. J.S. would like to dedicate his contribution to the work on the Introduction to happy memories of many undergraduate conversations on the eighteenth century with Jeffrey Gillie, of Southampton, a long-lost friend, who originally showed J.S. this reference.
34. Summarizing Boswell 1762–1763, 252.
35. See the "notorious" 1725 case of *Everet v. Williams,* noted at (1893) 9 LQR 197, and characterized in our own time by Lord Sumption JSC in 2016 as "the notorious case in which two highwaymen sought an account of the division of their profits," in which "the court not only dismissed the action but fined the plaintiff's solicitors for the indignity visited upon it" (see *Patel v. Mirza* [2016] UKSC 42 [228]; [2016] 3 WLR 399, 460E).

Chapter 1

1. 5 Eliz. I, c. 4, ss 3–7. The Justices could direct labor to get in the harvest: see ss 22–23.
2. 5 Eliz. I, c. 4, s 26.
3. 4 Geo. IV, c. 34. Chase 2000: 111–112.
4. 13 & 14 Car. II, c. 12.
5. Cobbett, *Political Register* (February 20, 1834).
6. N.L.W. MS. Chirk B 42c/3 (Denbighshire Quarter Sessions), Great Sessions 4/33/4/16, July 3, 1686.
7. Geo. 3, c. 68.
8. *Steel v. Houghton* (1788) 126 ER 32.
9. In Tewkesbury, for example, a bushel comprised nine gallons.
10. *Bath Journal*, December 26, 1768.
11. *London Post*, June 20–23, 1701.

12. *Applebee's Original Weekly Journal*, February 25, 1721.
13. *London Post*, July 28, 1749.
14. *Daily Journal*, March 13, 1833.
15. *Common Sense or the Englishman's Journal*, June 25, 1737.
16. *Lloyd's Evening Post*, October 5, 1764.
17. *Cumberland Chronicle*, December 13, 1777.
18. *Grubb St Journal*, September 23, 1731.
19. *Northampton Mercury*, May 6, 1751.
20. *Northampton Mercury*, September 2, 1751.
21. *Northampton Mercury*, July 2, 1770.
22. *Northampton Mercury*, May 28, 1808.
23. *Worcester Herald*, April 12, 1845.
24. *Illustrated Police News*, July 1, 1876.
25. PRO, Treasury Solicitor, Papers, TS, 11/169.
26. Place MSS, 27803, 53.
27. *Daily Post*, July 3, 1730.
28. *Fragmenta historicum graecorum*, ed. Karl Müller (Paris 1841–51) 3.461 no. 130.
29. *Mason v. Jennings* (1680) 83 ER 209.
30. *Daily Gazetteer*, 1736.
31. *The Pindar of Wakefield: Being the Merry History of George a Greene, the Lusty Pindar of the North* ... (London, 1632, S. T. C. 12213). See Capp 1977.
32. *London Chronicle*, June 21, 1761.
33. *The Remembrancer*, July 9, 1748.
34. *Northampton Mercury*, August 19, 1765.
35. *London Evening Post*, April 12, 1737.
36. *Exeter Flying Post*, October 2, 1817. See Radford 1933.
37. Welsh National Library Court of Great Sessions 4/753/3 Indictment of James David.
38. *The Advertiser*, July 29, 1756.
39. *London Evening Post*, January 12, 1738.
40. *London Daily Advertiser*, April 22, 1751.
41. Northants CRO QS Grand File, 1767.
42. *Bath Chronicle*, October 28, 1784.

Chapter 2

1. Thanks to the participants in the workshop held at the University of Warwick on July 6–7, 2015. Dr. Ruth Paley, History of Parliament Trust, suggested the potential significance of the Tonson connection. Thanks also to Rebecca Probert and Gary Watt for insightful and helpful comments. I have benefited in innumerable ways from conversations with my wife Angela, the chapter's dedicatee.
2. Montesquieu's *L'Esprit des Lois* was published anonymously, in October 1748, in Switzerland, by Barrillot (Shackleton 1961: 241). The first complete English translation, by Thomas Nugent, appeared in 1750.
3. (1703) 1 ER 417.
4. (1703) 87 ER 808, 815.
5. (1765) 19 St Tr col 1029, col 1066.
6. Despite intimidation by the Duke of Bedford, on Trentham's behalf, "Handel ... would in any case have felt a natural sympathy for the Whigs—as the party of government

7. Thomas Hudson (*bap*. 1701–1779) made at least two Handel portraits, the other in 1756 (Simon 1985: facing 37; Miles 2008).
8. Non-naturalized Crown subjects, i.e., aliens, were not competent to hold a legal estate before 1870 (Baker 2002: 467, referring to 33 and 34 Vict., c.14, s 2).
9. This citation is from the Loeb Classical Library Edition (1930), vol. 3: 217–329.
10. Act of Uniformity 1558 (1 Eliz 1, c. 2).
11. Introduction.
12. McCreesh's reconstruction uses a chorus of thirty-eight singers and an orchestra of fifty-six players. In Handel's day, the five vocal soloists probably "continued to sing in the choruses" (Butt 2009: 146).
13. But see Burrows 2012: Plate 7.
14. "The Royal Opera House, Covent Garden, is the third theater to occupy this site, both its predecessors having been destroyed by fire" (Sheppard 1970: 71). The theater in which *Solomon* was first performed burned down in 1808. Its successor, and predecessor to the present theater, burned down in 1856.
15. Licensing Act 1737, ie: 10 Geo 2, c. 28, s 5.
16. A conversation with a volunteer at Handel and Hendrix in London, on November 8, 2017, suggested this insight (see https://handelhendrix.org/ (accessed December 4, 2017)).
17. "Was ever singer so blessed as Giulia Frasi," asks Dean, "with five of the loveliest airs Handel ever wrote, not to mention the trio and three duets?" (Dean 1959: 526).
18. Swanston's theological intent is sometimes underappreciated (Smith 1995).
19. "God save King George. / Long live King George. / May the King live for ever!" (Quoted in King 2001: 13). It is interesting that, when the oratorio *Esther* (Anon. 1732) was first publicized, "the chorus was advertised as being placed as if for a 'Coronation Service'" (Butt 2009: 146).
20. Burrows 2012: 428.
21. Ibid.
22. Handel may have seen the painting or an engraving thereof as a connoisseur collector "of upwards of 145 prints and paintings, plus his own portraits" (McGeary 2009: 306).
23. Burrows 2012: 429.
24. *Delany v Tenison* (1758) 1 ER 1559.
25. Carolyn Watkinson, in the recording directed by Sir John Eliot Gardiner (Philips 475 7561 (2 CD)), hauntingly vindicates Handel's choice.
26. 1 Will & Mar, c. 6, s 3. ss 2–4. See also Act of Settlement 1701 (12&13 Will III, c. 2), s 2.
27. 34 *Halsbury's Laws* 810.
28. Lora 2009.
29. Charles Yorke (1722–1770), ultimately a rather tragic figure, became Lord Chancellor for three days in 1770. Presumably (though the writer has not yet been able to check) he is the 'C. Yorke' referred to in the report of *Delany v Tenison* (1758) 1 ER 1559, 1568.
30. 12 Will. 3, c. 4 (Blackstone [1765–9] 2016: II:200). These disabilities will not be lifted until the 1778 Catholic Relief Act (18 Geo. III, c. 60), which will provoke the 1780 Gordon Riots (see Lecky 1893: 306–326). Generally, on the political and social position of English Catholics in the period to 1745, see Glickman (2009).
31. (1608) 77 ER 1342, 1343.
32. See Burrows 2012: 428; Elster 1989, ch. III, latter on the biblical Solomon.

Chapter 3

1. *Hart v. Durand* (1795) 145 ER 1006.
2. *Hansard's Parliamentary History*, Vol. 15, col. 3.
3. *Lord Strange v. Smith* (1755) 27 ER 175.
4. *Merry v. Ryves* (1757) 28 ER 584.
5. *Dashwood v. Lord Bulkeley* (1804) 32 ER 832, at 242.
6. See *The Lord Raymond's Case* (1734) 25 ER 661; *Smith v. Smith* (1745) 26 ER 977.
7. *Mr. Justice Eyre v. Countess of Shaftsbury* (1722) 24 ER 659.
8. *Sullivan v. Sullivan, falsely called Oldacre* (1819) 161 ER 728.
9. Ibid.
10. Ibid.
11. *Hansard's Parliamentary History*, Vol. 15, col. 61.

Chapter 4

1. See below on the influence of the East India Company on employment contracts.
2. Mapping the Republic of Letters Project, Stanford University, with data from the Electronic Enlightenment Project, Oxford University; http://republicofletters.stanford.edu/casestudies/locke.html (last accessed February 2, 2016).
3. Though certain rules of discourse had to be followed: e.g., Goodman 1994.
4. In part due to the abolition of the Printing Act 1695: see Barker 2000.
5. See below on the Statute of Frauds.
6. English School, *Scene in a London Coffee House* (*c.* 1695)
7. The fact that agreements above a certain amount had to be in writing also contributed to the improved enforcement and this will be discussed later.
8. This will be discussed in more detail below in connection with the influence of the East India Company. See also Broadberry and O'Rourke 2010.
9. For more details on the new Company in Scotland see Lawson 1993.
10. Standard form contracts originated in the fifteenth century, in the upper Italian provinces, where notaries would develop generic forms for a particular industry which would often become an industry norm as they were nothing more than a summary of what was common practice (rather than a rule of law) within the industry (Pappenheim 1918).
11. In the Court of Bridewell in January 1698/9: Davies 2007: 15.
12. Printed in Newcastle (date estimated between 1700 and 1800).
13. Though see the section on marriage above.

Chapter 5

1. Herrup 1999: 6.
2. Ibid.
3. Masciola 2003; Donnachie 2004.
4. *Old Bailey Proceedings Online*, February 1733, trial of Sarah Malcolm, alias Mallcombe (t17330221-52).
5. Ibid.
6. Hay 1975: 61; Thompson 1990.
7. Langbein 2003. For more on the issues of criminal process and mitigation, see Beattie 1986b, chs. 7 and 8; Cockburn and Green 1988; Green 1985, especially ch. 7; Herrup 1987; King 1984; King 2000, ch. 7; Linebaugh 1992; Sharpe 1983.

8. Edelstein 2014.
9. A decline in a belief in witchcraft and magic among educated elites has long been attributed to the Enlightenment. For more on witchcraft and law, see Shapiro 1983 and Gaskill 2000.
10. Slavery and the legal apparatus that supported it stand as one of the biggest contradictions within Enlightenment thought. For more on slavery in England and throughout the Empire, see Rabin: 2014.
11. Smith [1583] 1982: 114.
12. de la Rochefoucauld 1774: 83.
13. Langbein 2003: 35–36. Defendants were not sworn until 1898: Langbein 2003: 52–53.
14. For more on the development of counsel for the defense, see Langbein 2003.
15. Beattie 1986b: 344–345; Green 1985: 273, 285–287; Langbein 1978: 284–300.
16. Langbein 1978: 288.
17. de la Rochefoucauld 1774: 84.
18. For a more extensive discussion of the relationship between the judge and the jury during the eighteenth century, see Beattie 1986b: 397, 413–415, 424–427; Green 1985, ch. 7; Hay 1975.
19. The Licensing Act (1662) required the approval of government censors for all printed works and limited publishing by granting a monopoly to the Stationers' Company: Patterson 1968; Patterson and Lindberg 1991.
20. New studies show that crime literature appealed to a fairly wide audience of "readers" and "hearers" that included the wealthy and educated as well as artisans and laborers. On literacy and reading in early modern England, see Barry 1995; Brewer 1997.
21. Cockburn 1985.
22. The form and function of crime literature is the subject of a wide range of scholarship. Bell 1991; Faller 1987; Faller 1993; McKenzie 2003; McKenzie 2007; Linebaugh 1992; Sharpe 1983; Singleton 1970; Watt 1957.
23. Harris 1999: 17.
24. For more on jury discretion, see authors cited in footnote 7 above.
25. Beattie 1986b: 140.
26. Blackstone justified "pious perjury" as an adjustment for inflation: Blackstone 1769: 4, 239. For more on the practice, see Beattie 1986b: 424–425.
27. Beattie 1986b: 91–99, 406, 420, 424–430.
28. King 2000, chs. 7–8.
29. For more on mobility and vagrancy, see Fumerton 2006.
30. Walker 1967. See also Eigen 1995.
31. Rabin 2004.
32. Wrightson 1980.
33. Green 1985: 287; Green 1988: 394–395.
34. Langbein 2003: 266–273.
35. One could argue that the novel evolved as a forum best suited to explore and develop ideas about identity, subjectivity, and selfhood: Bender 1987; Cox 1980; Lynch 1998; Mascuch 1997; Preston 1970.
36. Starr 1971: v.
37. Defoe's interest in crime is the subject of much literary criticism including Bell 1985; Bell 1991; Faller 1993; Faller 1987; Starr 1971; and Watt 1957.
38. Defoe 1722: 155.
39. Ibid., 155.

40. Ibid., 233.
41. Ibid.
42. Ibid.
43. Ibid.
44. For more on character, see Beattie 1977; Cockburn 1985; King 1984; King 2000.
45. John Moer, *OBSP*, January 1716. Moer was acquitted.
46. TNA: Assizes, Northern Circuit, 1743: Assi 45/22/4/48B.
47. Old Bailey Proceedings Online, April 1750, trial of Richard Sweetman (t17500425-7).
48. Old Bailey Proceedings Online, October 1772, trial of Valentine Dudden (t17721021-57).
49. Old Bailey Proceedings Online, July 1721, trial of Richard Grantham (t17210712-57).
50. Old Bailey Proceedings Online, September 1722, trial of John Garton (t17220907-57).
51. TNA: Assizes, Northern Circuit, 1758, Assi 45/26/2/95G.
52. TNA: Assizes, Northern Circuit, 1729, Assi 45/18/6/57.
53. TNA: Assizes, Northern Circuit, 1737, Assi 45/21/2/57.
54. Mandeville 1725: 16.
55. Ibid., 17.
56. Barker-Benfield 1992.
57. King 2000: 231–234.
58. Langbein 1978: 28.
59. Blackstone 1769, vol. 4, 394. An offense "within clergy" refers to the benefit of clergy, the privilege of exemption from trial by a secular court allowed to or claimed by clergymen arraigned for felony.
60. The work on sensibility is tremendously rich and provocative. Some of the most helpful insights for this study emerged from Armstrong 1987; Barker-Benfield 1992; Benedict 1994; Brissenden 1974; Mullan 1988; Pinch 1996; Todd 1986; Van Sant 1993.
61. Pinch 1996: 2.
62. Todd 1986: 9.
63. Pinch 1996: 11.
64. Todd 1986: 2.
65. Notes made by Dudley Ryder on cases at the Home Circuit assizes, 1754–55, 4. For more on Ryder's Notebook and his Assize Diary, its reliability, and its uses for legal historians, see Langbein 1983.
66. Ibid.
67. Beattie 1986b: 113–124; Jackson 1996, 133–150.
68. Ibid.
69. Madan 1785: 13.
70. Ibid., 137–139.
71. Dawes 1782: 3.
72. Ibid., 54.
73. Ibid., 3.
74. Ibid., 4.
75. Dolan 1994; Walker 2003. For more on gender order, see Amussen 1988; Fletcher 1995; Mendelsohn and Crawford 1998; Shoemaker 1998.
76. Masciola 2003: 26.
77. Rabin 2004.
78. Lanser 1999: 297–306. For more on single women, see Froide 2005 and Hufton 1984.
79. Hecht, 1955; Hill 2001; Kent 1989; Meldrum 2000.

80. Daniel Defoe articulated many of these attitudes in his pamphlet on the subject published in 1725: Defoe 1725.
81. Nussbaum 1995.
82. *Old Bailey Proceedings Online*, February 1753, trial of Mary Squires Susannah Wells (t17530221-47).
83. Mayall 1992: 26.
84. *Old Bailey Proceedings Online*, February 1753, trial of Mary Squires Susannah Wells (t17530221-47).
85. Ibid.
86. Ibid.
87. Ibid.
88. *Old Bailey Proceedings* Online, February 1753, trial of Mary Squires Susannah Wells (t17530221-47).
89. Ramsay 1753: 3–4.
90. Ibid., 20–21.
91. Fielding [1753] 1988: 309, 294.
92. A gypsy was defined as "a member of a wandering race (by themselves called Romany)," who first arrived in England at the beginning of the sixteenth century, "believed to have come from Egypt," *Oxford English Dictionary*. For more on gypsies, see Mayall 2004.
93. Hill 1753: 15.
94. Fielding 1753: 21.
95. Mayall 1997: 62.
96. Fisher 2004 uses cases from the Old Bailey that featured non-English subjects in his study of London's diversity in the eighteenth century. The place of racial and ethnic difference in the criminal courts and their impact on conviction rates and sentencing is the subject of Peter King's newest work: King 2013; King forthcoming.
97. Burke 1790: 245–246.
98. Ibid.
99. Paine 1791–1972: 117.

Chapter 6

1. See also Brockman account records, British Library, Add MS 42679.
2. Cf Defoe [1724] 2009: 187.
3. *Newcomb v. Bonham* (1681) 23 ER 266; *Bonham v. Newcomb* (1684/5) 86 ER 488; see also the statement repeated in his ruling in *Howard v. Harris* (1681) 23 ER 288, and in Carter 1728: 3.
4. *Jennings and Ward* (1705) 23 ER 935; *Manning v. Burges* (1663) 22 ER 687; *Lutton v. Rodd* (1675) 22 ER 922; Simpson 1986.
5. *Richards v. Syms* (1740) 27 ER 568.
6. Cf also Sugarman and Warrington 1996; Yale 1965; Simpson 1986.
7. *A Treatise of Feme Coverts: or, the Lady's Law. Containing all the Statutes and Laws relating to Women* (London 1732), vi–vii.
8. Salmon 1720–31; *The Proceedings Upon the Bill of Divorce Between His Grace the Duke of Norfolke and the Lady Mary Mordant* (London 1700); Lemmings 2012; McKenzie 1998; Gladfelder 2008.
9. See also Harvey 2012, ch. 2; Shepard 2006, ch. 7.

10. Cf. Defoe 1726 (a set of instructive essays aimed at merchants, where Defoe squarely attributed such failures in household and business economy to the widespread incidence of male vanity and weakness: ch. XI, 171, 174). Panek 2013: 72.
11. Farquhar, George, *Discourse Upon Comedy* (1702) quoted in Donohoe 2004, 19; Hume 1983, Ill. 5–14.
12. See further Brewer 1997, chs. 3–4, 330, 333, 353.
13. See Hume 1983.
14. In addition to the works discussed here see, for example, Goodman 1689; Cennick 1754; Whitefield 1741; Flower 1785.
15. See Twining 2000: 158–159 on the "polyvalent" moral of this parable.
16. *Chesterfield (Earl of) v. Janssen* (1751) 28 Eng Rep 82, 82.
17. Hardwicke Papers, British Library, Add MSS 36063 f 97.
18. *Chesterfield (Earl of) v. Janssen* (1750) 26 ER 191; Lobban 1997.
19. 4 & 5 W. & M. c.16.
20. *A Precaution to Young Gentlemen and Others who Mortgage Estates* (London, 1741), 6, 9.
21. *The Unnatural Father, Or the Dutiful Son's Reward* (London, 1775?), 6.
22. Cf. Backscheider 1999: xxiv.
23. Cf. his satirical take on this idea, in Taverner 1718, 5.

Chapter 7

1. http://www.oldbaileyonline.org, t17691206-31; t17710703-59.
2. For a fuller account of the arrest of Sayre, see Alden 1983: 70–91.
3. *Whitehall Evening Post*, April 15–17, 1760.
4. Suffolk (Bury St Edmunds) RO, HA 513/26/18, letter III.
5. *London Evening Post*, March 15–17, 1733.
6. *Public Advertiser*, March 9, 1756.
7. *Newsletter*, January 21, 1716.
8. *Craftsman*, June 15, 1734.
9. *Old England*, August 4, 1750.
10. *London Evening Post*, July 17–20, 1736.
11. *Virtue triumphant, or, Elizabeth Canning in America Being a circumstantial narrative of her adventures, from her setting sail for transportation, to the present time; in whose miraculous preservation the hand of providence is visible* (London, 1757).
12. *British Journal*, November 7, 1724; *Weekly Journal*, November 7, 1724.
13. *The ordinary of Newgate's account of the behaviour, confession, and dying words, of the twelve malefactors who were executed at Tyburn On Wednesday the 3d of October, 1750.*
14. *General Advertiser*, July 30, 1750; *Penny London Post*, September 19–21, 1750.
15. *General Evening Post*, 31 May-June 2, 1774; *Public Advertiser*, June 7, 1774; *Morning Chronicle*, July 9, 1774.
16. *London Chronicle*, November 3, 1774.
17. *Mist's Weekly Journal*, June 12, 1725.
18. See for example Leviticus 25, 44–46; Exodus 21, 2–6; Ephesians 6, 5; Timothy 6, 1–2.
19. *St James Chronicle*, May 21–23, 1791.
20. *Parliamentary Register*, xvi. 235.
21. *World*, December 17, 1791.
22. *Gazetteer*, February 16 and March 1, 1792.
23. TNA, PROB 11/19.

24. There is extensive literature, both in the field of social science and in that of philosophy, on this subject. For an introduction to some of the themes, see Bidney 1959, 51–76; Herskovits 1973; Hanfling 2003, 25–41.

Chapter 8

1. *The Times*, August 2, 1789, 3.
2. First known as *The Daily Universal Register*, the newspaper became *The Times or Daily Universal Register* on January 1, 1788, later becoming merely *The Times*.
3. For a full discussion of the gaps, shortcomings, and delays, see Oldham 2013, xiii–xxxix.
4. See Barker 1998, citing Law 1972.
5. For specific attention to press coverage of criminal trials, see Devereaux 2003; Devereaux 2007; King 2007.
6. *The Times*, July 10, 1799, 3. (Lord Kenyon gave sensible commentary on the obligations of a seller of a house to disclose to the buyer any defects, differentiating between what everyone must know [that dry rot will invade timbers in a wet climate] and latent defects.)
7. Lord Ellenborough was Chief Justice of King's Bench from 1802–1818. His trial notes survive, and these were a main source for an earlier study of mine. See Oldham 2004. Among other things, I calculated the percentage of cases in Ellenborough's trial notes that also appeared in the printed *nisi prius* reports. The percentages over Ellenborough's years ranged from 5 percent to 16 percent, with most of the years in single digits: Oldham 2004, 233.
8. A portion of this section appears in Oldham 2013, liii–lvi.
9. *The Times*, May 30, 1796, 4.
10. *Hale* [later corrected to "Hime"] *v. Dale*, *The Times*, January 24, 1804, 3.
11. *Hime v. Dale*, *The Times*, January 27, 1804, 3.
12. (1769) 98 ER 201.
13. *Hime v. Dale*, *The Times*, April 21, 1804, 3. In addition to the report in *The Times*, this case is summarized in *Campbell's Reports* in a footnote to another case involving the same "single sheet" issue, *Clementi v. Golding* (1809) 170 ER 1069. Abraham Newland, the subject of the song in *Hime v. Dale*, was Chief Cashier of the Bank of England from 1782–1807, and, "His signature on Bank of England notes became so familiar that they were known as Abraham Newlands": McConnell 2004. Counsel for the plaintiff in *Hime v. Dale*, William Garrow, attempted a second argument—that the poem was "a gross and nefarious libel upon the solemn administration of justice in Britain," quoting the following stanza: "The world is inclined / To think Justice blind; / Yet what of all that? / She will blink like a bat / At the sight of friend *Abraham Newland!* / Oh! *Abraham Newland!* Magical *Abraham Newland!* / Tho' Justice 'tis known / Can see thro' a mill stone, / She can't see through *Abraham Newland!*." Chief justice Ellenborough was not persuaded, nor was Justice Lawrence, who said that, "The argument used by Mr. Garrow on this fugitive piece as being a libel, would as forcibly apply to *The Beggar's Opera*, where the language and allusions are sufficiently derogatory to the administration of public justice." According to Campbell's report, "the cause was not again carried down to trial." 170 ER 1069, 1071, n. (b).
14. *The Times*, February 11, 1791, 3. See also Oldham 2004 for a mid-nineteenth-century memoir by a Lincoln's Inn barrister that, "Formerly at the sittings during Term at Guildhall, in the City of London, only undefended causes were taken, such as actions on

bills of exchange, promissory notes, and other similar inquiries—where, in fact, the proof of the handwriting of the parties constituted the whole of the evidence to be produced."

15. *The Times*, June 28, 1791, 3.
16. *The Times*, July 5, 1791, 3.
17. Other reports were less dramatic, showing nevertheless very rapid case handling. See *The Times* for May 26, 1792 at 3 (twenty-five cases tried by Lord Kenyon by 3:00 o'clock p.m., which would be fifteen minutes per case, assuming a 9:00 o'clock a.m. start time); July 18, 1800, three (six special jury causes were disposed of before 11:00 o'clock a.m., or twenty minutes per case, again assuming a 9:00 o'clock a.m. start time).
18. *The Times*, June 21, 1791, 3.
19. *The Times*, February 23, 1797, 3.
20. *The Times*, February 15, 1800, 3.
21. *The Times*, June 27, 1796, 3.
22. *The Times*, December 10, 1799, 3.
23. *The Times*, November 12, 1792, 4.
24. *The Times*, April 18, 1796, 3.
25. *The Times*, December 15, 1790, 4.
26. Ibid.
27. *The Times*, April 28, 1798, 3.
28. *The Times*, July 9, 1789, 3.
29. *The Times*, November 12, 1789, 3.
30. *The Times*, July 21, 1791, 3.
31. *The Times*, July 30, 1791, 3.
32. *The Times*, November 30, 1791, 3.
33. *The Times*, July 8, 1793, 3.
34. *The Times*, December 11, 1795, 4.
35. *The Times*, December 10, 1796, 3.
36. *The Times*, June 24, 1799, 3.
37. *The Times*, July 21, 1791, 3.
38. *The Times*, November 30, 1791, 3
39. Ibid.
40. *The Times*, December 11, 1795, 4.
41. *The Times*, December 10, 1796, 3.
42. *The Times*, November 11, 1791, 3
43. This phase of the case was included in the printed law reports: (1791) 100 ER 1076.
44. The case does not appear in the printed judicial records of the House of Lords.
45. *The Times*, November 3, 1789, 3.
46. *The Times*, October 7, 1795, 2.
47. Lord Eldon was said by some to be the inspiration for the protracted case in *Bleak House*. Jeremy Bentham referred to Eldon as "Lord Endless" because of the difficulty Eldon had in making up his mind. See Smith 2004.
48. *The Times*, August 9, 1805, 3. The case also appears in the printed law reports—see (1791) 29 ER 584; (1807) 33 ER 525.
49. *The Times*, August 8, 1805, 3. Needless to say, facts that today would clearly present conflicts of interest were not of concern to the legal community of this earlier time.
50. *The Times*, August 10, 1805 3. Other phases of this case were reported by *The Times* on December 20, 1803 and February 23, 1808. The case also appears multiple times in the standard printed reports. The phase of the litigation reported by *The Times* on August 10, 1805

was also reported at (1805) 32 ER 1127. Other phases, both before and after August 1805, are reported at (1803) 32 ER 379, (1804) 33 ER 64, (1806) 33 ER 455, and (1811) 34 ER 168.
51. *The Times*, January 29, 1792, 2.
52. *The Times*, November 2, 1812, 3.
53. Many years ago, I studied and wrote about this unusual chapter of trial by jury: Oldham 1985. See also Forbes 1988.
54. This delay usually allowed the woman to petition for a royal pardon, conditional on transportation to the colonies, which was usually granted: Oldham 1985.
55. *The Times*, September 19, 1788, 3.
56. See, e.g., *The Times*, January 20, 1790, 3 ("A Jury of Matrons found, that Mary Talbot was with quick-child, in consequence of which her execution was ordered to be stayed till the next Sessions").
57. *The Times*, July 17, 1798, 3.
58. *The Times*, July 28, 1792, 3, also reported at 19 ER 794 (sub nom. *Ex Parte Wallop*). See also Oldham 1985.

BIBLIOGRAPHY

REFERENCE WORKS

Broadberry, Stephen and O'Rourke, Kevin. 2010. *The Cambridge Economic History of Modern Europe, Vol. 1*. Cambridge: Cambridge University Press.
Donohue, Joseph (ed). 2004. *The Cambridge History of British Theatre, Volume 2: 1660–1895*. Cambridge: Cambridge University Press.
Goldie, Mark, and Wokler, Robert (eds.). 2006. *The Cambridge History of Eighteenth-Century Political Thought*. Cambridge: Cambridge University Press.
Landgraf, Annette, and Vickers, David (eds.). 2009. *The Cambridge Handel Encyclopedia*. Cambridge: Cambridge University Press.
Pappenheim, Max. 1918. *Handbuch des Seerechts*, Vol. 3. Leipzig: Duncker & Humboldt.
Sheppard, F.H.W. (ed.). 1970. *Survey of London*, Volume 35: *The Theatre Royal Drury Lane and The Royal Opera House Covent Garden*. London: Athlone Press and University of London.

PRIMARY SOURCES

Achenwall Gottfried. 1752. *Staatsverfassung der Europaeischen Reiche im Grundrisse*. Joh. Wilhelm Schmidt, Univ. Buchhandel.
Angelo, Henry. 1830. *Reminiscences of Henry Angelo*. London: Henry Colburn and Richard Bentley Publishers.
Anon. 1704. *The Town Spy*. London.
Anon. 1724. *AN EPISTLE TO Mr. HANDEL, UPON HIS OPERAS OF FLAVIUS and JULIUS CAESAR*. London: J. Roberts. Eighteenth Century Collections Online. Gale Group (accessed October 30, 2017).
Anon. 1732. *Esther, An Oratorio: Or, Sacred Drama. As it is Performed at The King's Theatre in the Haymarket. The Musick Formerly Compos'd by Mr. Handel, and now Revised by Him, With Several Additions. The Additional Words by Mr. Humphreys*. London: T. Wood. Eighteenth Century Collections Online, Gale Group (accessed November 30, 2017).
Anon. 1741. *A Precaution to Young Gentlemen and Others who Mortgage Estates*. Cog.
Anon. 1748a. *Joshua. A Sacred Drama. As it is Perform'd at the Theatre-Royal in Covent-Garden. Set to Musick by George-Frederick Handel, Esq.* London: J. and R. Tonson and S. Draper. Eighteenth Century Collections Online. Gale Group (accessed November 25, 2017).
Anon. 1748b. *Susanna. An Oratorio. As it is Perform'd at the Theatre-Royal in Covent-Garden. Set to Musick by George-Frederick Handel*. London: J. and R. Tonson and S. Draper.
Anon. 1749. *Solomon. An Oratorio. As it is Perform'd at the Theatre-Royal in Covent-Garden. Set to Musick by Mr. Handel*. London: Tonson and Draper.
Anon. 1775. *The Unnatural Father, Or the Dutiful Son's Rewar*. London.
Anon. 1800. *Britons Strike Home! A New Song*. London: J Ginger.

Aristotle. [*c.* 350 BC] 2004. *The Nicomachean Ethics*. Translated and edited by J.A.K. Thomson, H. Tredennick and J. Barnes. London: Penguin.

Armstrong, John. [1736] 1739. *The Oeconomy of Love*. London, 3rd edition.

Astell, Mary. [1700] 1996. "Some Reflections Upon Marriage." In Patricia Springborg (ed.) *Astell: Political Writings*. Cambridge: Cambridge University Press.

Austen, Jane. [1811] 1994. *Sense and Sensibility*. London: Penguin Popular Classics.

Austen, Jane. [1813] 2006. *Pride and Prejudice*. Edited by Vivien Jones. London: Penguin Classics.

Austen, Jane. [1814] 1966. *Mansfield Park*. Harmondsworth: Penguin English Library.

Austen, Jane. [1815] 1985. *Emma*. Harmondsworth: Penguin Classics.

Austen, Jane. [1818] 1975. *Persuasion*. Edited by R.W. Chapman. London: Folio Society.

Backscheider, Paula R. (ed.) 1999. *Selected Fiction and Drama of Eliza Haywood*. Oxford: Oxford University Press.

Blackstone, William. [1765–9] 2016. *Commentaries on the Laws of England* (4 vols.). Edited by Wilfrid Prest. Oxford: Oxford University Press.

Bolingbroke, Viscount (Henry St John). [1749] 1997. "The Idea of a Patriot King." In David Armitage (ed.), *Bolingbroke: Political Writings*. Cambridge: Cambridge University Press.

Boswell, James. [1762–1763] 1974. *Boswell's London Journal*. Edited by Frederick A. Pottle. London: Book Club Associates.

Boswell, James. [1791] 1980 *Life of Johnson*. Edited by R.W. Chapman and J.D. Fleeman. Oxford: Oxford University Press.

Brougham, Henry, Lord. 1839. *Historical Sketches of Statesmen Who Flourished in the time of George III*, 3 vols. London: Charles Knight & Co.

Burgess, C.F. (ed.). 1966. *Letters of John Gay*. Oxford: Clarendon Press.

Burke, Edmund. [1790] 2009. *Reflections on the Revolution in France*. Oxford: Oxford University Press.

Burney, Fanny. [1796] 1972. *Camilla*. Oxford: Oxford University Press.

Care, Henry. 1691. *English Liberties: or, the Free-Born Subject's Inheritance*. London: Sarah Harris.

Carter, Samuel. 1728. *Lex Vadiorum The Law of Mortgages*. London.

Cennick, John. 1754. *The Lost Sheep, Piece of Silver and Prodigal Son*. Dublin.

Centlivre, Susanna. [1718] 1969. *A Bold Stroke for a Wife*. London: Edward Arnold.

Chicken, Edward. 1764. *The Collier's Wedding*. Newcastle.

Child, Josiah. 2003. "A New Discourse on Trade." In Henry Clark (ed.) *Commerce Culture and Liberty: Readings on Capitalism before Adam Smith*. Indianapolis: Liberty Fund.

Clarkson, Thomas. 1788. *An Essay on Slavery and Commerce of the Human Species*. London. 2nd edition.

Colman, George, and Garrick, David. [1766] 1928. "The Clandestine Marriage." In John Hampden (ed.), *Eighteenth Century Plays*. London and Toronto: J.M. Dent.

Congreve, William. [1700] 1967. *The Way of the World*. Chicago: University of Chicago Press.

Cottu, Charles. [1820] 2004. *On the Administration of the Criminal Code in England*. Clark, NJ: Law Book Exchange reprint.

Cowper, William. 1785. "The Task, Book VI ('The Winter Walk at Noon')." In H.S. Milford and Norma Russell (eds.), *Cowper: Poetical Works*. London: Oxford University Press.

Crabbe, George. [1807] 1988. "The Parish Register." In Norma Dalrymple-Champneys and Arthur Pollard (eds.), *George Crabbe: The Complete Poetical Works*: Vol. 1. Oxford: Clarendon Press.

Dawes, Manassaw. 1782. *An Essay on Crimes and Punishments with a View of, and Commentary Upon, Beccaria, Rousseau, Voltaire, Montesquieu, Fielding and Blackstone.* London.

Defoe, Daniel. 1710. *Essay upon Publick Credit.* London.

Defoe, Daniel. 1722. *Moll Flanders.* London.

Defoe, Daniel. 1724–1726. *A Tour through the Whole Island of Great Britain.* Edited by Pat Rogers, London: Penguin, 1971.

Defoe, Daniel. [1724] 2009. *The Fortunate Mistress: Or, A History of the Life and Vast Variety of Fortunes of … Roxana.* Edited by Melissa Mowry. Toronto: Broadview Press.

Defoe, Daniel. 1725. *Everybody's Business, Is Nobody's Business; Or, Private Abuses, Publick Grievances: Exemplified in the Pride, Insolence, and Exorbitant Wages of our Women-Servants, Footmen, etc.* London.

Defoe, Daniel. 1726. *The Complete English Tradesman.* London.

de la Rochefoucauld, François. [1774] 1988. *A Frenchman's Year in Suffolk: French Impressions of Suffolk Life in 1784.* Edited and translated by Norman Scarfe. Woodbridge: The Boydell Press.

Downes, Henry. 1708. *The Necessity and Usefulness of Laws and the Excellency of our Own.* London: H Hills. *Eighteenth Century Collections Online.* Gale Group (accessed November 21, 2017).

Edgeworth, Maria. [1801] 1994. *Belinda.* Edited by Kathryn Kirkpatrick. Oxford: Oxford University Press.

Ferrier, Susan. [1818] 1997. *Marriage.* Edited by Kathryn Kirkpatrick. Oxford: Oxford University Press.

Fielding, Henry. [1742] 2003. *Joseph Andrews.* Edited by Judith Hawley. London: Penguin Classics.

Fielding, Henry. [1749] 1996. *Tom Jones.* Oxford: Oxford University Press.

Fielding, Henry. [1750/1751] 1988. "An Enquiry into the Causes of the late Increase of Robbers." In Malvin Zirker (ed.), *An Enquiry into the Causes of the Late Increase of Robbers and Related Writings.* New York: Oxford University Press.

Fielding, Henry. [1753] 1988. "A Clear State of the Case of Elizabeth Canning." In Malvin Zirker (ed.), *An Enquiry into the Causes of the Late Increase of Robbers and Related Writings.* New York: Oxford University Press.

Fitz-Adam, Adam. 1756. *The World.* Dublin: George Falkner.

Flower, Joseph. 1785. *The Prodigal Son: A Poem.* Bath.

Fox, William. 1792. *An Address to the People of Great Britain, on the Propriety of Abstaining from West India Sugar and Rum.* London. 10th edition.

Gay, John. [1728] 1986. *The Beggar's Opera.* Edited by Bryan Loughrey and T.O. Treadwell. London: Penguin.

Goldsmith, Oliver. [1759] 1934. *The Bee,* no. 7. 1759, "Custom and Laws Compared," reprinted in *The Citizen of the World and the Bee.* Edited by Austin Dobson. London: J.M. Dent.

Goldsmith, Oliver. [1770] 1984. "The Deserted Village." In Roger Lonsdale (ed.), *The New Oxford Book of Eighteenth Century Verse.* Oxford: Oxford University Press.

Goodman, John. 1689. *The Penitent Pardoned: Or a Discourse of the Nature of Sin and the Efficacy of the Nature of Repentance under the Parable of the Prodigal Son.* London.

Goodwyn, E.A. n.d. *Selections from Norwich Newspapers 1760–1790.* Ipswich: Privately Printed.

Grose, Francis. 1787. *A Provincial Glossary, with a Collection of Local Proverbs, and Popular Superstitions*. London: S. Hooper.

Hamilton, Elizabeth. [1800] 1992. *Memoirs of Modern Philosophers*. London: Routledge/Thoemmes Press.

Hardwicke, Lord. [1744] 1952. "The King and the Ministry, 1744–46 … Notes of Audience [January 5, 1744]." In W.C. Costin and J Steven Watson (eds.), *The Law and Working of the Constitution: Documents 1660–1914* [Vol. 1]. London: Adam and Charles Black.

Harrington, James. [1700] 1992. "A System of Politics." In John Greville Agard Pocock (ed.), *The Commonwealth of Oceana* and *A System of Politics*. Cambridge: Cambridge University Press.

Hawkins, Sir John. 1776. *A General History of the Science and Practice of Music*, 2 vols. New York: Dover 1963.

Haym, Nicola Francesco. 1724. *Giulio Cesare in Egitto. Drama. Da Rappresentarsi Nel Regio Teatro di Haymarket, per La Reale Accademia di Musica*. London: Thomas Wood.

Haywood, Eliza. [1726] 1999. "The City Jilt; or, The Alderman Turn'd Beau: A Secret History." In Paula R. Backscheider (ed.) *Selected Fiction and Drama of Eliza Haywood*. Oxford: Oxford University Press.

Haywood, Eliza. [1751] 1986. *The History of Miss Betsy Thoughtless*. London: Pandora.

Hill, John. 1753. *The Story of Elizabeth Canning considered by Dr. Hill*. London.

Hobbes. [1651] 1955. *Leviathan or the Matter, Forme and Power of a Commonwealth Ecclesiasticall and Civil*. Oxford: Basil Blackwell.

Hume, David. 1739–1740. *A Treatise of Human Nature*. London.

Hume, David. [1739–1740] 1978. "Of the Laws of Nations." In L.A. Selby-Bigge (ed.), *A Treatise of Human Nature*, 2nd edn. Oxford: Clarendon Press.

Hume, David. [1778] 1983. *The History of England from the Invasion of Julius Caesar to The Revolution in 1688*. W.B. Todd (ed.). Indianapolis: Liberty Fund, available electronically at http://oll.libertyfund.org/titles/1868 (accessed February 19, 2016).

Hume, David. 1994. *Hume: Political Essays*. Edited by Knud Haakonssen. Cambridge: Cambridge University Press.

Huntington, W. 1795. *Living Testimonies: or, Spiritual Letters on Divine Subjects* [Vol. 2]. London: T. Bensley.

Jacob, Giles. 1713. *The Compleat Court-Keeper, Or Land-Stewards Assistant*. London.

Jacob, Giles. 1715. *A Review of the Statutes*. London.

Jacob, Giles. 1718. *Lex Mercatoria, Or the Merchant's Companion*. London.

Jacob, Giles. 1736. *Every Man his Own Lawyer*. London.

Kant, Immanuel. [1784] 1991. "An Answer to the Question: 'What is Enlightenment?'." In Hans Reiss (ed.), *Kant: Political Writings*, 2nd edn. Cambridge: Cambridge University Press.

King, James. 1784. *A Voyage to the Pacific Ocean*, Vol. 3. London: W. and A. Strahan.

Lillo, George. [1731]. 1928. "The London Merchant." In John Hampden (ed.), *Eighteenth Century Plays*. London and Toronto: J.M. Dent.

Locke, John. [1689] 1980. *Second Treatise of Government*. Edited, with an introduction, by C.B. Macpherson. Indianapolis: Hackett Pub. Co.

Locke, John. [1689] 2003. "A Letter Concerning Toleration." In I. Shapiro (ed.), *Two Treatises of Government* and *A Letter Concerning Toleration*. New Haven, CT: Yale University Press.

Locke, John. [1690] 2003. "Of Property." In I. Shapiro (ed.), *Two Treatises of Government* and *A Letter Concerning Toleration*. New Haven, CT: Yale University Press.

Locke, John. [1697] 1997. "Essay on the Poor Laws." In Mark Goldie (ed.), *Locke: Political Essays*. Cambridge: Cambridge University Press.
Luttrell, Narcissus. 1857. *A Brief Historical Relation*, 6 vols. Oxford: Oxford University Press.
Madan, Martin. 1785. *Thoughts on Executive Justice*. London.
Mandeville, Bernard. 1723. *Essay on Charity Schools*. London.
Mandeville, Bernard. 1725. *Enquiry into the Causes of the Frequent Executions at Tyburn*. London.
Marshall, William. 1818. *The Review and Abstract of the County Reports to the Board of Agriculture*: Vol. 4, *Midlands Department*. New York.
Milton, John, Harris, James, and Jennens, Charles. 1740. *L'Allegro, Il Penseroso, ed Il Moderato. In Three Parts. Set to Musick by Mr. Handel*. London: J. and R. Tonson. *Eighteenth Century Collections Online*. Gale Group (accessed November 20, 2017).
Montesquieu, Charles Louis de Secondat, Baron de. [1721] 1993. *Persian Letters*. Translated by Christopher Betts. London: Penguin Books.
Montesquieu, Charles Louis de Secondat, Baron de. [1748/1750] 1949. *The Spirit of the Laws*. Translated by Thomas Nugent. New York: Hafner Publishing.
Morell, Thomas. 1747. *Judas Macchabaeus. A Sacred Drama. As it is Perform'd at the Theatre-Royal in Covent-Garden. The Musick by Mr. Handel*. London: John Watts.
Morell, Thomas. 1748. *Alexander Balus. An Oratorio. As it is Perform'd at the Theatre-Royal in Covent-Garden. Set to Musick by George-Frederick Handel, Esq*. London: John Watts. *Eighteenth Century Collections Online*. Gale Group (accessed November 20, 2017).
Moser JJ. 1752. *Grundsätze des Europäischen Völker-Rechts in Kriegs-Zeiten*. Verlag Johann Georg Gotter.
Paine, Thomas. [1791–1792] 2008. "Rights of Man." In Mark Philp (ed.), *Rights of Man, Common Sense, and Other Political Writings*. Oxford: Oxford University Press.
"Philogamus." 1739. *The Present State of Matrimony: Or, The Real Causes of Conjugal Infidelity and Unhappy Marriages*. London.
Pope, Alexander. [1733–1734] 2006. "An Essay on Man." In Pat Rogers (ed.), *Alexander Pope: The Major Works*. Oxford: Oxford University Press.
Ramsay, Allan. [1753] 1762. "A Letter to the Right Honorable the Earl o —f," reprinted in *The Investigator. Containing the Following Tracts: I. On Ridicule. II. On Elizabeth Canning. III. On Naturalization. IV. On Taste*. London.
Reynolds, Francis. 1785. *Enquiry Concerning the Principles of Taste and of the Origins of Our Ideas of Beauty*. London.
Richardson, Samuel. [1747–48] 1985. *Clarissa, or, The History of a Young Lady*. London: Penguin Classics.
Rogers, John. 1749. *The Necessity of Divine Revelation, and the Truth of the Christian Revelation Asserted, in Eight Sermons*. London: W. Innys. *Eighteenth Century Collections Online*. Gale Group (accessed November 24, 2017).
Rousseau Jean-Jacques. [1754] 1984. *A Discourse on Inequality*. Translated by Maurice Cranston. London: Penguin.
Salmon, Thomas (ed). 1720–31. *State Trials and Proceedings upon High Treason and Other Crimes and Misdemeanors, from the Reign of King Richard II to the End of the Reign of King George I*, 9 vols. London.
Shebbeare, John. 1754. *The Marriage Act*. London.
Shelley, Percy Bysshe. [1819] 2009. "The Mask of Anarchy: Written on the Occasion of the Massacre at Manchester." In Zachary Leader and Michael O'Neill (eds.), *Percy Bysshe Shelley: The Major Works*. Oxford: Oxford University Press.

Sheridan, Frances. [1769] 1999. *Memoirs of Miss Sidney Biddulph*. Oxford: Oxford University Press.
Sheridan, Richard Brinsley. [1775] 1906. *The Rivals*. London: J.M. Dent.
Smith, Adam. [1776] 1976. *An Inquiry into the Nature and Causes of the Wealth of Nations*. Edited by R.H. Campbell and A.S. Skinner (textual ed. W.B. Todd), 2 vols, Oxford: Clarendon Press.
Smith, Adam. [1790]. 1976. *The Theory of Moral Sentiments*. Edited by D.D. Raphael and A.L. MacFie. Oxford: Clarendon Press.
Smith, Charlotte. [1792] 2001. *Desmond*. Toronto: Broadview Press.
Smith, Thomas. [1583] 1982. *De Republica Anglo*rum. Edited by Mary Dewar. Cambridge: Cambridge University Press.
Smollett, Tobias. [1751] 1964. *The Adventures of Peregrine Pickle*. Oxford: Oxford University Press.
Smollett, Tobias. [1762] 1973. *The Life and Adventures of Sir Launcelot Greaves*. Edited by David Evans. London and elsewhere: Oxford University Press.
Smollett, Tobias. [1771] 1995. *The Expedition of Humphry Clinker*. Ware: Wordsworth Classics.
Stebbing, Henry. 1754. *A Dissertation on the Power of States to Deny Civil Protection to the Marriages of Minors Made without the Consent of their Parents or Guardians*. London: C Davis.
Swift, Jonathan. [1735] 2005. *Gulliver's Travels*. Edited by Ian Higgins and Claude Rawson. Oxford: Oxford World's Classics.
Taverner, William. 1717. *The Artful Husband*. London.
Taverner, William. 1718. *The Artful Wife*. London.
Taylor, John. 1639. Pseud Mary Makepeace. *Divers Crabtree Lectures. Expressing the Severall Languages that Shrews Read to Their Husbands, Either at Morning, Noone, Or Night. With a Pleasant Relation of Shrewes Munday, and Shrewes Tuesday, and why They Were So Called. Also a Lecture Betweene a Pedler and His Wife in the Canting Language*. London: J. Sweeting.
Thomson, James. [1736] 1984. "Liberty." In Roger Lonsdale (ed.), *The New Oxford Book of Eighteenth Century Verse*. Oxford: Oxford University Press.
Thomson, James. 1740. *Alfred: A Masque. Represented before Their Royal Highnesses the Prince and Princess of Wales at Cliffden, On the First of August, 1740*. London: A. Millar.
Voltaire. 1733. *Letters Concerning the English Nation*. Edited by Nicholas Cronk. Oxford: Oxford University Press, 1994.
Voltaire. [1759] 2005. *Candide, or Optimism*. Edited and translated by Theo Cuffe. London: Penguin.
von Archenholz, Johann W. 1797. *A Picture of England*. London.
Whitefield, George. 1741. *The Prodigal Son: A Lecture*. London.
Wood, Thomas. 1727. *Some Thoughts Concerning the Study of the Laws of England*, 2nd edn. London: J. Stagg.
Woodforde, James. 1999. *The Diary of a Country Parson 1758–1802*. Edited by John Beresford. Norwich: Canterbury Press.

SECONDARY SOURCES

Books

Adkins, Roy A. 2004. *Trafalgar: The Biography of a Battle*. London: Little, Brown.
Alden, John R .1983. *Stephen Sayre: American Revolutionary Adventurer*. Baton Rouge & London: Louisiana State University Press.

Amussen, Susan. D. 1988. *An Ordered Society: Gender and Class in Early Modern England*. New York: Columbia University Press.

Armstrong, Nancy. 1987. *Desire and Domestic Fiction: A Political History of the Novel*. Oxford: Oxford University Press.

Axon, William E.A. 1884. *Cheshire Gleanings*. London: Simpkin, Marshall and Co.

Backscheider, Paula R. 1989. *Daniel Defoe*. Baltimore, MD: Taylor & Francis.

Baker, J.H. 2002. *An Introduction to English Legal History*, 4th edn. London: Butterworths LexisNexis.

Banks, Stephen. 2014. *Informal Justice in England and Wales, 1760–1914: The Courts of Popular Opinion*. Woodbridge: Boydell and Brewer.

Barker, Hannah. 1998. *Newspapers, Politics, and Public Opinion in Late Eighteenth Century England*. Oxford: Clarendon Press.

Barker, Hannah. 2000. *Newspapers, Politics and Public Opinion in the Eighteenth Century*. Harlow: Longman.

Barker-Benfield, G.J. 1992. *The Culture of Sensibility: Sex and Society in Eighteenth-Century Britain*. Chicago: University of Chicago Press.

Barlow, Derek. 1973. *Dick Turpin and the Gregory Gang*. Chichester: Phillimore.

Bate, Jonathan. 2003. *John Clare: A Biography*. London: Picador.

Battestin, Martin C, and Battestin, Ruthe R. 1989. *Henry Fielding: A Life*. London and New York: Routledge.

Beattie, John M. 1977. "Crime and the Court in Surrey 1736–1753." In James. S Cockburn (ed.), *Crime in England, 1550–1800*. Princeton, NJ: Princeton University Press.

Beattie, John M. 1986a. *Crime and the Courts in England 1660–1800*. Oxford: Clarendon Press.

Beattie, John M. 1986b. *Crime and the Courts in England, 1660–1800*. Princeton, NJ: Princeton University Press.

Beauman, Francesca. 2011. *Shapely Ankle Preferred: A History of the Lonely Hearts Ad*. London: Chatto & Windus.

Bell, Ian. A. 1985. *Defoe's Fiction*. London: Croom Helm.

Bell, Ian. A. 1991. *Literature and Crime in Augustan England*. London: Routledge.

Bender, John. 1987. *Imagining the Penitentiary: Fiction and the Architecture of the Mind in Eighteenth-Century Engl*and. Chicago: University of Chicago Press.

Benedict, Barbara. 1994. *Framing Feeling: Sentiment and Style in English Prose Fiction, 1745–1800*. New York: AMS Press.

Benner, Erica. 2017. *Be Like the Fox: Machiavelli's Lifelong Quest for Freedom*. London: Allen Lane.

Bentley, David. 2003. *English Criminal Justice in the Nineteenth Century*. London: Bloomsbury Academic.

Bew, John. 2012. *Castlereagh: A Life*. Oxford: Oxford University Press.

Black Jeremy. 1987. *The English Press in the Eighteenth Century*. Philadelphia, PA: University of Pennsylvania Press.

Black, Jeremy. 2001. *Eighteenth-Century Britain, 1688–1783*. Basingstoke: Palgrave.

Boorstin, Daniel J. 1966. *The Americans: The National Experience*. London: Weidenfeld & Nicolson.

Brewer, John. 1997. *The Pleasures of the Imagination: English Culture in the Eighteenth Century*. London: HarperCollins.

Brewer, John. 2004. *A Sentimental Murder: Love and Madness in the Eighteenth Century*. London: HarperCollins Publishers.

Brissenden, R.F. 1974. *Virtue in Distress: Studies in the Novel of Sentiment from Richardson to Sade*. London: Macmillan.
Brooks, Christopher W. 1998. *Lawyers, Litigation and English Society since 1450*. London: Hambledon.
Brown, Laura. 2001. *Fables of Modernity: Literature and Culture in the English Eighteenth Century*. Ithaca, NY: Cornell University Press.
Burrows, Donald. 2012. *Handel*, 2nd edn. New York: Oxford University Press.
Cannon, John. 1984. *Aristocratic Century*. Cambridge: Cambridge University Press.
Capp, Bernard. 2003. *When Gossips Meet: Women, Family and Neighbourhood in Early Modern England*. Oxford: Oxford University Press.
Carlson, Marvin. 2014. *Theatre: A Very Short Introduction*. Oxford: Oxford University Press.
Chase, Malcolm. 2000. *Early Trade Unionism: Fraternity, Skill and the Politics of Labour* Aldershot: Ashgate.
Clarke, Norma. 2009. *Queen of the Wits: A Life of Laetitia Pilkington*. London: Faber & Faber.
Clayton, Antony. 2003. *London's Coffee Houses: A Stimulating Story*. Whitstable: Historical Publications.
Cockburn, James. S. 1985. *Calendar of Assize Records, Home Circuit Indictments, Elizabeth I and James I*, Vol. 1. London: HMSO.
Cockburn, James S., and Green, Thomas A, (eds.), 1988. *Twelve Good Men and True: The Criminal Trial Jury in England, 1200–1800*. Princeton, NJ: Princeton University Press.
Colley, Linda. 1992. *Britons: Forging the Nation 1707–1837*. New Haven, CT: Yale University Press.
Colley, Linda. 2014. *Acts of Union and Disunion*. London: Profile.
Cook, Hera. 2004. *The Long Sexual Revolution: English Women, Sex, and Contraception 1800–1975*. Oxford: Oxford University Press.
Cowan, Brian. 2005. *The Social Life of Coffee: The Emergence of the British Coffeehouse*. New Haven, CT and London: Yale University Press.
Cox, Stephen. 1980. *"The Stranger Within Thee": Concepts of the Self in Late-Eighteenth Century Literature*. Pittsburgh: Pittsburgh University Press.
D'Oench, Ellen. G. 1995. *Prodigal Son Narratives 1480–1980*. New Haven, CT: Yale University Art Gallery.
Dabhoiwala, Faramerz. 2012. *The Origins of Sex: A History of the First Sexual Revolution*. London: Allen Lane.
Davies, Maud. [1909] 2013. *Life in an English Village: An Economic and Historical Survey of the Parish of Corsley in Wiltshire*. East Knoyle: The Hobnob Press.
Dean, Winton. 1959. *Handel's Dramatic Oratorios and Masques*. London: Oxford University Press.
Deutsch, Otto. 1955. *Handel: A Documentary Biography*. London: Adam and Charles Black.
Dickinson, H.T. 1970. *Bolingbroke*. London: Constable.
Dolan, Frances. 1994. *Dangerous Familiars: Representations of Domestic Crime in England, 1550–1700*. Ithaca, NY: Cornell University Press.
Duckworth, Alistair M. 1971. *The Improvement of the Estate: A Study of Jane Austen's Novels*. Baltimore, MD and London: Johns Hopkins University Press.
Duman, Daniel. 1982. *The Judicial Bench in England 1727–1875: The Reshaping of a Professional Elite*. London: Royal Historical Society.
Dunn, John. 1984. *Locke*. Oxford: Oxford University Press.
Eigen, Joel. 1995. *Witnessing Insanity: Madness and Mad-Doctors in the English Court*. New Haven, CT: Yale University Press.

Ellis, Markman. 2004. *The Coffee-House: A Cultural History*. London: Phoenix.
Engelsing, Rolf. 1974. *Der Bürger als Leser: Lesergeschichte in Deutschland 1500–1800*. Stuttgart: Metzler.
Elster, Jon. 1989. *Solomonic Judgements: Studies in the Limitations of Rationality*. Cambridge: Cambridge University Press.
Evans, Mary. 1987. *Jane Austen and the State*. London and New York: Tavistock.
Faller, Lincoln. 1987. *Turn'd to Account: The Forms and Functions of Criminal Biography in Late Seventeenth and Early Eighteenth-Century England*. Cambridge: Cambridge University Press.
Faller, Lincoln. 1993. *Defoe and Crime: A New Kind of Writing*. Cambridge: Cambridge University Press.
Fideler, Paul A, 2006. *Social Welfare in Pre-Industrial England: The Old Poor Law Tradition*. Basingstoke: Macmillan.
Fisher, Michael. 2004. *Counterflows to Colonialism: Indian Travelers and Settlers in Britain, 1600–1857*. Delhi: Permanent Black.
Fleischacker, Samuel. 2004. *A Short History of Distributive Justice*. Cambridge, MA: Harvard University Press.
Fletcher, Anthony. 1995. *Gender, Sex, and Subordination in England, 1500–1800*. New Haven, CT: Yale University Press.
Franklin, Michael J. 2011. *Orientalist Jones: Sir William Jones, Poet, Lawyer, and Linguist, 1746–1794*. Oxford: Oxford University Press.
Froide, Amy. 2005. *Never Married: Singlewomen in Early Modern England*. Oxford: Oxford University Press.
Froide, Amy. 2016. *Silent Partners: Women as Public Investors During Britain's Financial Revolution 1690–1750*. Oxford: Oxford University Press.
Fumerton, Patricia. 2006. *Unsettled: The Culture of Mobility and the Working Poor in Early Modern England*. Chicago: University of Chicago Press.
Furber, Holden. 1976. *Rival Empires of Trade in the Orient, 1600–1800 (Europe and the World in the Age of Expansion)*, Vol. 2. Oxford: Oxford University Press.
Garrad, John. 2001. *Democratisation in Britain: Elites, Civil Society, and Reform since 1800*. Basingstoke: Palgrave Macmillan.
Gaskill, Malcolm. 2000. *Crime and Mentalities in Early Modern England*. Cambridge: Cambridge University Press.
Gatrell, Vic. 2006. *City of Laughter: Sex and Satire in Eighteenth-Century London*. London: Atlantic Books.
Gillis, John. 1985. *For Better, for Worse: British Marriages 1600 to the Present Day*. Oxford: Oxford University Press.
Gilman, Todd. 2014. *The Theatre Career of Thomas Arne*. Newark, DE: University of Delaware Press.
Glickman, Gabriel. 2009. *The English Catholic Community 1688–1745: Politics, Culture and Ideology*. Woodbridge: Boydell.
Goodman, Dan. 1994. *The Republic of Letters: A Cultural History of the French Enlightenment*. Ithaca, NY: Cornell University Press.
Goodwin, George. 2016. *Benjamin Franklin in London: The British Life of America's Founding Father*. London: Weidenfeld & Nicolson.
Graves, Michael A.R. 1985. *The Tudor Parliaments: Crown, Lords and Commons, 1485–1603*. London: Longman.
Gray, Kevin, and Gray, Susan Francis. 2009. *Elements of Land Law*, 5th edn. Oxford: Oxford University Press.

Gray, Kevin, and Gray, Susan Francis. 2011. *Land Law*, 7th edn. Oxford: Oxford University Press.
Green, Thomas A. 1985. *Verdict According to Conscience: Perspectives on the English Criminal Trial Jury, 1200–1800*. Chicago: University of Chicago Press.
Griffiths, Paul, Fox, Adam and Hindle, Steve (eds.), 1996. *The Experience of Authority in Early Modern England*. Basingstoke: Macmillan.
Gutman, Robert W. 1999. *Mozart: A Cultural Biography*. London: Secker and Warburg.
Harris, Ellen T. 2014. *George Frideric Handel: A Life with Friends*. New York: WW Norton.
Harris, James A. 2015. *Hume: An Intellectual Biography*. Cambridge: Cambridge University Press.
Harvey, Karen. 2012. *The Little Republic: Masculinity and Domestic Authority in Eighteenth-Century Britain*. Oxford: Oxford University Press.
Hay, Douglas and Craven, Paul. 2004. *Masters, Servants and Magistrates in Britain and the Empire 1562–1955*. Chapel Hill, NC: University of North Carolina Press.
Hay, Douglas and Rogers, Nicholas. 1997. *Eighteenth-Century English Society: Shuttles and Swords*. Oxford: Oxford University Press.
Hecht, J.J. 1955. *The Domestic Servant Class in the Eighteenth Century*. London: Routledge & Kegan Paul.
Henriques, Henry Straus Quixano. 1908. *The Jews and the English Law*. Oxford: H. Hart.
Herrup, Cynthia. 1987. *The Common Peace: Participation and the Criminal Law in Seventeenth-Century England*. Cambridge: Cambridge University Press.
Herrup, Cynthia. 1999. *A House in Gross Disorder: Sex, Law, and the 2nd Earl of Castlehaven*. Oxford: Oxford University Press.
Herskovits, Melville J. 1973. *Cultural Relativism: Perspectives in Cultural Pluralism*. New York: Vintage.
Hill, Bridget. 2001. *Women Alone: Spinsters in England, 1660–1850*. New Haven, CT: Yale University Press.
Hilton, Boyd. 2006. *A Mad, Bad, and Dangerous People?* Oxford: Clarendon Press.
Hinton, Michael. 1994. *The Anglican Parochial Clergy: A Celebration*. London: SCM Press.
Hogwood, Christopher. 2007. *Handel*. Revised edition. London: Thames & Hudson.
Holdsworth, William. 1928. *Charles Dickens as a Legal Historian*. New Haven, CT: Yale University Press.
Holdsworth, Sir William. 1938. *A History of English Law*, Vol. 10. London: Methuen.
Hont, Istvan. 2010. *Jealousy of Trade*. Cambridge, MA: Harvard University Press.
Hoppit, Julian. 1987. *Risk and Failure in English Business, 1700–1800*. Cambridge: Cambridge University Press.
Hoppit, Julian. 2000. *A Land of Liberty? England 1689–1727*. Oxford: Clarendon Press.
Hoskins, William George. 1957. *The Midland Peasant: The Social and Economic History of a Leicestershire Village*. London: Macmillan.
Houlbrooke, Ralph (ed.). 1989. *English Family Life, 1576–1716: An Anthology from Diaries*. Oxford: Basil Blackwell.
Howarth, David. 1970. *Trafalgar: The Nelson Touch*. London: World Books.
Hume, Robert, D. 1983. *The Rakish Stage: Studies in English Drama 1660–1800*. Carbondale, IL: Southern Illinois University Press.
Hunt, Margaret. 1996. *The Middling Sort: Commerce, Gender and the Family in England, 1680–1780*. Berkeley, CA: University of California Press.
Hunter, David. 2015. *The Lives of George Frideric Handel*. Woodbridge: Boydell Press.
Hunter, J. Paul. 1990. *Before Novels: The Cultural Contexts of Eighteenth-Century English Fiction*. New York: Norton.

Hunter, Sir William Wilson. [1900] 1912. *A History of British India*, Vol. 2. Harlow: Longmans, Green and Co. 1912 (originally published in 1900).
Hurley, David Ross. 2001. *Handel's Muse: Patterns of Creation in his Oratorios and Musical Dramas, 1743–1751*. Oxford: Oxford University Press.
Ingrassia, Catherine. 1998. *Authorship Commerce and Gender in Early Eighteenth-Century England*. Cambridge: Cambridge University Press.
Israel, Jonathan. 2010. *A Revolution of the Mind: Radical Enlightenment and the Intellectual Origins of Modern Democracy*. Princeton, NJ and Oxford: Princeton University Press.
Jackson, Mark. 1996. *New-Born Child Murder: Women, Illegitimacy and the Courts in Eighteenth-Century England*. Manchester: Manchester University Press.
Jacob, W.M. 1996. *Lay People and Religion in the Early Eighteenth Century*. Cambridge: Cambridge University Press.
Jardine, Lisa. 2008. *Going Dutch: How England Plundered Holland's Glory*. London: HarperPress.
Jarrett, Derek. 1965. *Britain 1688–1815*. London: Longmans.
Keates, Jonathan. 2016. *Messiah: The Composition and Afterlife of Handel's Masterpiece*. London: Head of Zeus.
King, Peter. 2000. *Crime, Justice, and Discretion in England, 1740–1820*. Oxford: Oxford University Press.
King, Peter. Forthcoming. *Ethnicity, Crime and Justice 1700–1830*.
Landau, Norma. 1984. *The Justices of the Peace, 1679–1760*. Berkeley, CA: University of California Press.
Langbein, John. H. 2003. *The Origins of Adversary Criminal Trial*. Oxford: Oxford University Press.
Langford, Paul. 1989. *A Polite and Commercial People: England 1727–1783*. London: Guild Publishing.
Langford, Paul. 1991. *Public Life and the Propertied Englishman 1689–1798*. Oxford: Clarendon Press.
Langford, Paul. 2000. *Eighteenth-Century Britain: A Very Short Introduction*. Oxford: Oxford University Press.
Lawson, Philip. 1993. *The East India Company: A History*. London: Routledge.
Lecky, William Edward Hartpole. 1893. *A History of England in the Eighteenth Century*: Vol. 4. New York: Appleton.
Lemmings, David. 2011. *Law and Government in England during the Long Eighteenth Century: From Consent to Command*. Basingstoke: Palgrave Macmillan.
Lemmings, David (ed.) 2012. *Crime, Courtrooms and the Public Sphere in Britain, 1700–1850*. Farnham: Ashgate.
Lenman, Bruce. 1984. *The Jacobite Risings in Britain 1689–1746*. London: Methuen.
Linebaugh, Peter. 1992. *The London Hanged: Crime and Civil Society in the Eighteenth Century*. London: Allen Lane.
Lobban, Michael. 1991. *The Common Law and English Jurisprudence 1760–1850*. Oxford: Clarendon Press.
Loughlin, Martin. 1992. *Public Law and Political Theory*. Oxford: Clarendon Press.
Loughlin, Martin. 2010. *Foundations of Public Law*. Oxford: Oxford University Press.
Loughlin, Martin. 2013. *The British Constitution: A Very Short Introduction*. Oxford: Oxford University Press.
Lynch, Deidre S. 1998. *The Economy of Character: Novels, Market Culture, and the Business of Inner Meaning*. Chicago: University of Chicago Press.

McClelland, J.S. 1996. *A History of Western Political Thought*. London and New York: Routledge.
McKenzie, Andrea. 2007. *Tyburn's Martyrs: Execution in England, 1675–1775*. London: Hambledon Continuum.
McIntosh, Michael K. 1991. *A Community Transformed: The Manor and Liberty of Havering, 1300–1620*. Cambridge: Cambridge University Press.
MacMahon, Darrin M. 2006. *The Pursuit of Happiness: A History from the Greeks to the Present*. London: Allen Lane.
McPhee, Peter. 2012. *Robespierre: A Revolutionary Life*. New Haven, CT and London: Yale University Press.
Maitland, F.W. 1908. *The Constitutional History of England*. Edited by H.A.L. Fisher. Cambridge: Cambridge University Press.
Marlow, Joyce. 1971. *The Peterloo Massacre*. London: Panther.
Marshall, Dorothy. 1974. *Eighteenth Century England*, 2nd edn. Harlow: Longman.
Mascuch, Michael. 1997. *Origins of the Individualist Self: Autobiography and Self-Identity in England, 1591–1791*. Cambridge, MA: Polity Press.
Mayall, David. 2004. *Gypsy Identities 1500–2000: From Egipcyans and Moon-men to the Ethnic Romany*. London: Routledge.
Meldrum, Tim. 2000. *Domestic Service, and Gender, 1660–1750: Life and Work in the London Household*. London: Longman.
Melton, Frank T. 1986. *Sir Robert Clayton, Robert and the Origins of English Deposit Banking 1658–1685*. Cambridge: Cambridge University Press.
Mendelsohn, Sarah and Crawford, Patricia. 1998. *Women in Early Modern England: 1550–1720*. Oxford: Oxford University Press.
Miller, John. 1983. *The Glorious Revolution*. London: Longman.
Moore, Wendy. 2013. *How to Create the Perfect Wife: Georgian Britain's Most Ineligible Bachelor and his Quest to Cultivate the Ideal Woman*. London: Orion Publishing.
Morrill, John. 2000. *Stuart Britain: A Very Short Introduction*. Oxford: Oxford University Press.
Mudge, B.K. 2004. *When Flesh Becomes Word: An Anthology of Early Eighteenth-Century Libertine Literature*. Oxford: Oxford University Press.
Muldrew, Craig. 1998. *The Economy of Obligations*. Basingstoke: Palgrave Macmillan.
Mullan, John. 1988. *Sentiment and Sociability: The Language of Feeling in the Eighteenth Century*. Oxford: Clarendon Press.
Murray, Penelope, and Wilson, Peter (eds.). 2004. *Music and the Muses: The Culture of 'Mousikē' in the Classical Athenian City*. Oxford: Oxford University Press.
Neeson, J.M. 1993. *Commoners: Common Right, Enclosure and Social Change in England 1700–1820*. Cambridge: Cambridge University Press.
Nussbaum, Felicity. 1995. *Torrid Zones: Maternity, Sexuality, and Empire in Eighteenth-Century English Narratives*. Baltimore, MD: Johns Hopkins University Press.
O'Donovan, Katherine. 1985. *Sexual Divisions in Law*. London: Weidenfeld & Nicolson.
Oldham, James. 1992. *The Mansfield Manuscripts and the Growth of English Law in the Eighteenth Century*. Chapel Hill, NC: University of North Carolina Press.
Oldham, James. 2004. *English Common Law in the Age of Mansfield*. Chapel Hill, NC: University of North Carolina Press.
Oldham, James (ed.) 2013. *Case Notes of Sir Soulden Lawrence 1787–1800*. London: Selden Society.
Outhwaite, R.B. 1995. *Clandestine Marriage in England, 1500–1850*. London: Hambledon Press.

Outhwaite, R.B. 2006. *The Rise and Fall of the English Ecclesiastical Courts, 1500–1860*. Cambridge: Cambridge University Press.

Outram, Dorinda. 2013. The *Enlightenment—New Approaches to European History*, 3rd edn. Cambridge: Cambridge University Press.

Parker, Stephen. 1990. *Informal Marriage, Cohabitation and the Law, 1750–1989*. Basingstoke: Macmillan.

Patterson, Lyman R. 1968. *Copyright in Historical Perspective*. Nashville, TN: Vanderbilt University Press.

Patterson, Lyman R. and Lindberg, Stanley W. 1991. *The Nature of Copyright: A Law of Users' Rights*. Athens, GA: University of Georgia Press.

Perry, Thomas W. 1962. *Public Opinion, Propaganda, and Politics in Eighteenth-Century England: A Study of the Jew Bill of 1753*. Cambridge, MA: Harvard University Press.

Phillips, Mark Salber. 2013. *On Historical Distance*. New Haven, CT and London: Yale University Press.

Phillipson, David. 1973. *Smuggling: A History 1700–1970*. Newton Abbot: David and Charles.

Phillipson, Nicholas. 2010. *Adam Smith: An Enlightened Life*. London: Allen Lane.

Pike, L.O. 1894. *A Constitutional History of the House of Lords*. London: Macmillan and Co.

Pinch, Adela. 1996. *Strange Fits of Passion: Epistemologies of Emotion, Hume to Austen*. Palo Alto, CA: Stanford University Press.

Pocock, Tom. 2002. *Battle for Empire: The Very First World War 1756–63*. London: Caxton.

Pope, Dudley. 1972. *The Great Gamble*. London: Chatham, 2001.

Porritt, Edward. [1903] 1963. *The Unreformed House of Commons: Parliamentary Representation before 1832*. New York: Augustus M. Kelley.

Porter, Enid. 1969. *Cambridgeshire Customs and Folklore*. London: Routledge.

Porter, Roy. 1991. *English Society in the Eighteenth Century*. Revised edition. London: Penguin.

Poser, Norman S. 2013. *Lord Mansfield: Justice in the Age of Reason*. Montreal: McGill-Queen's University Press.

Prest, Wilfrid. 2008. *William Blackstone: Law and Letters in the Eighteenth Century*. Oxford: Oxford University Press.

Preston, John. 1970. *The Created Self: The Reader's Role in Eighteenth-Century Fiction*. New York: Heinemann.

Probert, Rebecca. 2009. *Marriage Law and Practice in the Long Eighteenth Century: A Reassessment*. Cambridge: Cambridge University Press.

Probert, Rebecca. 2012. *The Changing Legal Regulation of Cohabitation: From Fornicators to Family, 1600–2010*. Cambridge: Cambridge University Press.

Rabin, Dana. 2004. *Identity, Crime, and Legal Responsibility in Eighteenth-Century England*. New York: Palgrave Macmillan.

Radzinowicz, Leon and Hood, Roger. 1948–86. *A History of the English Criminal Law and its Administration from 1750*, 5 vols. London: Sweet and Maxwell.

Rahe, Paul A. 2009. *Montesquieu and the Logic of Liberty*. New Haven, CT and London: Yale University Press.

Randall, Adrian. 1991. *Before the Luddites: Custom, Community and Machinery in the English Woollen Industry 1776–1809*. Cambridge: Cambridge University Press.

Randall, Adrian. 2006. *Riotous Assemblies*. Oxford: Oxford University Press.

Rea, Robert. 1963. *The English Press in Politics, 1760–1774*. Lincoln, NE: University of Nebraska Press.

Riding, Jacqueline. 2016. *Jacobites: A New History of the '45 Rebellion*. London: Bloomsbury.

Riding, Jacqueline, Burrows, Donald, and Hicks, Anthony. 2001. *Handel House Museum Companion*. London: Handel House Trust.

Robertson, John. 2015. *The Enlightenment: A Very Short Introduction*. Oxford: Oxford University Press.

Rodger, N.A.M. 1988. *The Wooden World: An Anatomy of the Georgian Navy*. London: Fontana.

Rooke, Deborah W. 2012. *Handel's Israelite Oratorio Libretti: Sacred Drama and Biblical Exegesis*. Oxford: Oxford University Press.

Roth, Cecil. 1964. *A History of the Jews in England*, 3rd edn. Oxford: Clarendon Press.

Rubenhold, Hallie. 2009. *Lady Worsley's Whim: An Eighteenth-Century Tale of Sex, Scandal and Divorce*. London: Vintage Books.

Rudolph, Julia. 2013. *Common Law and Enlightenment in England, 1689–1750*. Woodbridge: Boydell.

Schmitt, Carl. [1928] 2008. *Constitutional Theory*, trans. Jeffrey Seitzer. Durham, NC: Duke University Press.

Sedgwick, Romney. 1970. *The House of Commons 1715–1754*, Vol. 1. London: HMSO and History of Parliament Trust.

Shackleton, Robert. 1961. *Montesquieu: A Critical Biography*. Oxford: Oxford University Press.

Shapiro, Barbara. 1983. *Probability and Certainty in Seventeenth-Century England: A Study of the Relationships between Natural Science, Religion, History, Law, and Literature*. Princeton, NJ: Princeton University Press.

Sharpe, J.A. 1983. *Crime in Seventeenth-Century England: A County Study*. Cambridge: Cambridge University Press.

Shepard, Alexandra. 2006. *Meanings of Manhood in Early Modern England*. Oxford: Oxford University Press.

Shoemaker, Robert. 1998. *Gender and English Society, 1650–1850: The Emergence of Separate Spheres?* London: Longman.

Simon, Jacob (ed.). 1985. *Handel: A Celebration of his Life and Times 1685–1759*. London: National Portrait Gallery.

Simpson, A.W.B. 1986. *A History of The Land Law*, 2nd edn. Oxford: Clarendon Press.

Smith, Ruth. 1995. *Handel's Oratorios and Eighteenth-Century Thought*. Cambridge: Cambridge University Press.

Smither, Howard E. 1977. *A History of the Oratorio*, Vol. 2. *The Oratorio in the Baroque Era: Protestant Germany and England*. Chapel Hill, NC: University of North Carolina Press.

Sobba Green, Katherine. 1991. *The Courtship Novel, 1740–1820: A Feminized Genre*. Lexington, KY: The University Press of Kentucky.

Sokol, Mary. 2011. *Bentham, Law and Marriage: A Utilitarian Code of Law in Historical Contexts*. London: Continuum International Publishing Group.

Somerset, Anne. 2012. *Queen Anne: The Politics of Passion*. London: HarperPress.

Spaeth, Donald A. 2000. *The Church in an Age of Danger: Parsons and Parishioners 1660–1740*. Cambridge: Cambridge University Press.

Spector, Céline. 2011. *Montesquieu: Pouvoirs, Richesses et Sociétés*. London: Hermann Éditeurs.

Starr, George. 1971. *Defoe and Casuistry*. Princeton, NJ: Princeton University Press.

Stevenson, John. 1979. *Popular Disturbances in England, 1700–1870*. London: Longman.

Stone, Lawrence. 1990. *Road to Divorce: England 1530–1987*. Oxford: Oxford University Press.

Stubbs, John. 2016. *Jonathan Swift: The Reluctant Rebel*. London: Viking.

Swanston, Hamish. 1990. *Handel*. London: Geoffrey Chapman.
Sykes, Norman. 1934. *Church and State in England in the XVIIIth Century*. Cambridge: Cambridge University Press.
Tate, William Edward. 1967. *The English Village Community and the Enclosure Movements*. London: Gollancz.
Temperley, Nicholas. 1991. *Haydn:* The Creation. Cambridge: Cambridge University Press.
Thomas, Keith. 2009. *The Ends of Life: Roads to Fulfilment in Early Modern England*. Oxford: Oxford University Press.
Thompson, Edward P. 1990. *Whigs and Hunters: The Origin of the Black Act*. London: Penguin.
Thompson, Edward P. 1991. *Customs in Common*. Harmondsworth: Penguin.
Todd, Janet. 1986. *Sensibility: An Introduction*. London: Methuen.
Tombs, Robert. 2014. *The English and Their History*. London: Allen Lane.
Trudgill, Eric. 1976. *Madonnas and Magdalens: Origins and Development of Victorian Sexual Attitudes*. London: William Heinemann.
Turner, James Grantham. 2002. *Libertines and Radicals in Early Modern London: Sexuality, Politics and Literary Culture, 1630–1685*. Cambridge: Cambridge University Press.
Turner, Richard. W. 1931. *The Equity of Redemption: Its Nature, History and Connection with Equitable Estates Generally*. Cambridge: Cambridge University Press.
Uglow, Jenny. 2003. *The Lunar Men: The Friends Who Made the Future 1730–1810*. London: Faber & Faber.
Uglow, Jenny. 2015. *In These Times: Living in Britain Through Napoleon's Wars 1793–1815*. London: Faber & Faber.
Underdown, David. 1985a. *Revel, Riot and Rebellion: Popular Beliefs and Culture in England 1603–1660*. Oxford: Oxford University Press.
Underhill, Nicholas. 1978. *The Lord Chancellor*. Lavenham: Terence Dalton.
Van Sant, Ann Jessie. 1993. *Eighteenth-century Sensibility and the Novel: The Senses in Social Context*. Cambridge: Cambridge University Press.
Vickery, Amanda. 2009. *Behind Closed Doors: At Home in Georgian England*. New Haven, CT: Yale University Press.
Walker, Garthine. 2003. *Crime, Gender and Social Order in Early Modern England*. Cambridge: Cambridge University Press.
Walker, Nigel. 1967. *Crime and Insanity in England, 2 vols., Vol. 1: The Historical Perspective*. Edinburgh: Edinburgh University Press.
Watt, Gary. 2009. *Equity Stirring: The Story of Justice Beyond Law*. Oxford: Hart Publishing.
Watt, Ian. 1957. *The Rise of the Novel: Studies in Defoe, Richardson and Fielding*. London: Chatto & Windus.
Weitzman, Steven. 2011. *Solomon: The Lure of Wisdom*. New Haven, CT and London: Yale University Press.
Werkmeister, Lucyle. 1963. *The London Daily Press, 1772–1792*. Lincoln, NE: University of Nebraska Press.
Williams, Basil. 1960a. *The Whig Supremacy 1714–1760*, 2nd edn., revised by C.H. Stuart. Oxford: Clarendon Press.
Williams, E. Neville. 1970. *The Eighteenth-Century Constitution 1688–1815: Documents and Commentary*. Cambridge: Cambridge University Press.
Williams, Raymond. 1960b. *Culture and Society 1780–1950*. London: Chatto & Windus.
Witte, John. [1997] 2012. *From Sacrament to Contract: Marriage, Religion and the Law in the Western Tradition*. Louisville, KY: Westminster John Knox Press.

Young, Percy M. 1949. *The Oratorios of Handel*. London: Dobson.
Zaretsky, Robert. 2015. *Boswell's Enlightenment*. Cambridge, MA: Belknap Press.

CHAPTERS IN BOOKS AND ENCYCLOPEDIA ENTRIES

Bailey, Joanne. 2010. "Family Relationships." In Elizabeth Foyster and James Marten (eds.), *A Cultural History of Childhood and Family in the Age of Enlightenment*. London: Bloomsbury.
Barry, Jonathan. 1995. "Literacy and Literature in Popular Culture: Reading and Writing in Historical Perspective." In Tim Harris (ed.), *Popular Culture in England, c. 1500–1850*. New York: Palgrave.
Best, Terence. 2009. "Deidamia, HWV 42." In Annette Landgraf and David Vickers. (eds.), *The Cambridge Handel Encyclopedia*. Cambridge: Cambridge University Press 184.
Bidney, David. 1959. "The Philosophical Presuppositions of Cultural Relativism and Cultural Absolutism." In Leo R. Ward (ed.), *Ethics and the Social Sciences*. Notre Dame, Ind: University of Notre Dame Press.
Brown, Roger Lee. 1981. "The Rise and Fall of the Fleet Marriage." In R.B. Outhwaite (ed.) *Marriage and Society*. London: Europa Publications.
Butt, John. 2009. "Chorus." In Annette Landgraf and David Vickers (eds.), *The Cambridge Handel Encyclopedia*. Cambridge: Cambridge University Press,145.
Clausen, Hans Dieter. 2009. "*Samson*, HWV 57." In Annette Landgraf and David Vickers (eds.), *The Cambridge Handel Encyclopedia*. Cambridge: Cambridge University Press, 563.
Crick, Bernard. 2003. "Introduction: So Many Machiavellis." In Niccolò Machiavelli (ed.), *The Discourses*, edited and translated by Bernard Crick, Leslie J. Walker and Brian Richardson. London: Penguin.
Cummings A.J.G. 1987. "The Harburgh Company and its Lottery." In R.P.T. Davenport-Hines and Jonathan Liebenau (eds.), *Business in the Age of Reason*. London: Frank Cass.
Foyster, Elizabeth and Marten, James. 2010. "Introduction." In Elizabeth Foyster and James Marten (eds.), *A Cultural History of Childhood and Family in the Age of Enlightenment*. London: Bloomsbury.
Gerrard, Christine. 1994. "Mythologizing the Monarch: Ideas of a Patriot King." In *The Patriot Opposition to Walpole: Politics, Poetry, and National Myth, 1725–1742*. Oxford: Clarendon Press.
Gladfelder, Hal. 2008. "Defoe and Criminal Fiction." In John Richetti (ed.). *The Cambridge Companion to Defoe*. Cambridge: Cambridge University Press.
Glowotz, Daniel. 2009. "*Alexander Balus*, HWV 65." In Annette Landgraf and David Vickers (eds.), *The Cambridge Handel Encyclopedia*. Cambridge: Cambridge University Press, 22.
Gowing, Laura. 2014. "Marked Bodies and Social Meanings." In Carole Reeves (ed.), *A Cultural History of the Human Body in the Enlightenment*. London: Bloomsbury.
Green, Thomas A. 1988. "Retrospective." In James S. Cockburn and Thomas A. Green (eds.), *Twelve Good Men and True: The Criminal Trial Jury in England, 1200–1800*. Princeton, NJ: Princeton University Press.
Harris, Michael. 1999. "Murder in Print: Representations of Crime and the Law, c. 1660–1760." In Rosamaria Loretelli and Roberto De Romanis (eds.), *Narrating Transgression: Representations of the Criminal in Early Modern England*. Frankfurt: Peter Lang.
Harrison, Christopher. 1997. "Manorial Courts and the Governance of Tudor England." In Christopher W. Brooks and Michael Lobban (eds.), *Courts and Communities in Britain, 1150–1900*. London: Hambledon Press.
Hay, Douglas. 1975. "Property, Authority, and the Criminal Law." In Douglas Hay, Peter Linebaugh, John G. Rule, E.P. Thompson, and Cal Winslow (eds.), *Albion's Fatal Tree: Crime and Society in Eighteenth-Century England*. New York: Pantheon Books.

Hicks, Anthony. "Solomon: Vision of a Golden Age" (CD booklet note, Carus 83.242, 2007).
Hogg, Katharine. 2009. "Foundling Hospital, The." In Annette Landgraf and David Vickers (eds.), *The Cambridge Handel Encyclopedia*. Cambridge: Cambridge University Press, 242.
Hont, Istvan. 2006. "The Early Enlightenment Debate on Commerce and Luxury." In Mark Goldie and Robert Wokler (eds.), *The Cambridge History of Eighteenth-Century Political Thought*. Cambridge: Cambridge University Press.
Hurley, David Ross. 2009a. "*Susanna*, HWV 66." In Annette Landgraf and David Vickers (eds.), *The Cambridge Handel Encyclopedia*. Cambridge: Cambridge University Press, 623.
Hurley, David Ross. 2009b. "*Solomon*, HWV 67." In Annette Landgraf and David Vickers (eds.), *The Cambridge Handel Encyclopedia*. Cambridge: Cambridge University Press, 596.
Hurley, David Ross. 2009c. "Frasi, Giulia." In Annette Landgraf and David Vickers (eds.), *The Cambridge Handel Encyclopedia*. Cambridge: Cambridge University Press, 244–245.
Ingram, Martin. 1997. "Juridical Folklore in England Illustrated by Rough Music." In Christopher W. Brooks and Michael Lobban, (eds.), *Communities and Courts in Britain, 1150–1900*, London: Hambledon Press.
Landgraf, Annette, and Vickers, David. 2009. "Oratorio." In Annette Landgraf and David Vickers (eds.), *The Cambridge Handel Encyclopedia*. Cambridge: Cambridge University Press, 454.
Lanser, Susan. "Singular Politics: The Rise of the British Nation and the Production of the Old Maid." In Amy Froide and Judith Bennett (eds.), *Singlewomen in the European Past, 1250–1800*. Philadelphia: University of Pennsylvania Press, 1999.
Lemmings, David. 2003. "Ritual, Majesty and Mystery: Collective Life and Culture among English Barristers, Serjeants and Judges, c. 1500–1830." In W. Wesley Pue and D. Sugarman (eds.), *Lawyers and Vampires: Cultural Histories of Legal Professions*. Oxford: Hart.
Lemming, David. 2009. "Introduction: Law and Order, Moral Panics, and Early Modern England." In David Lemmings and Claire Walker (eds.), *Moral Panics, The Media and the Law in Early Modern England*. Basingstoke: Palgrave Macmillan.
Linebaugh, Peter. 1975. "The Tyburn Riot against the Surgeons." In Douglas Hay, Peter Linebaugh, John G. Rule, E.P. Thompson, and Cal Winslow (eds.), *Albion's Fatal Tree: Crime and Society in Eighteenth Century England*. London: Allen Lane.
Lora, Francesco. 2009. "Zadok the Priest, HWV 258." In Annette Landgraf and David Vickers (eds.), *The Cambridge Handel Encyclopedia*. Cambridge: Cambridge University Press, 679.
McGeary, Thomas N. 2009. "18. Handel the Art Collector." In Annette Landgraf and David Vickers (eds.), *The Cambridge Handel Encyclopedia*. Cambridge: Cambridge University Press, 306.
McKenzie, Andrea. 1998. "Making Crime Pay: Motives, Marketing Strategies and the Printed Literature of Crime in England 1670–1770." In Greg T. Smith, Allyson N. May and Simon Devereaux (eds.), *Criminal Justice in the Old World and New: Essays in Honor of J.M. Beattie*. Toronto: Centre of Criminology, University of Toronto.
Malcolmson, Robert. 1980. "'A Set of Ungovernable People': The Kingswood Colliers in the Eighteenth Century." In John Brewer and John Styles (eds.), *An Ungovernable People: The English and Their Law in the Seventeenth and Eighteenth Centuries*. London: Hutchinson.
Morgan, David H. 1975. "The Place of Harvesters in Nineteenth-century Village Life." In Raphael Samuel (eds.), *Village Life and Labour*. London: Kegan Paul.
Neal, Larry. 1994. "The Finance of Business During the Industrial Revolution." In Roderick Floud and D.N. McCloskey (eds.), *The Economic History of Britain since 1700*, Vol. 1, 2nd edn. Cambridge: Cambridge University Press.

Price J.M. 1987. "*Sheffield v Starke*: Institutional Experimentation in London–Maryland Trade c. 1696–1706." In R.P.T. Davenport-Hines and Jonathan Liebenau (eds.), *Business in the Age of Reason*. London: Frank Cass.

Rabin, Dana. 2014. "Empire on Trial: Slavery, Villeinage and Law in Imperial Britain." In John McLaren and Shaunnagh Dorsett (eds.), *Legal Histories of the British Empire: Laws, Engagements and Legacies*. New York: Routledge.

Raven, James. 2004. "The Book as a Commodity." In Michael F. Suarez (ed.), *The Cambridge History of the Book in Britain*, Vol. 5: 1695–1830. Cambridge: Cambridge University Press.

Robarts, Leslie M.M. 2009. "Draper, Somerset" and "Tonson, Jacob." In Annette Landgraf and David Vickers (eds.), *The Cambridge Handel Encyclopedia*. Cambridge: Cambridge University Press, 194, 644.

Sharp, Buchanan. 1988. "Common Rights, Charities and the Disorderly Poor." In Geoff Eley and William Hunt (eds.), *Reviving the English Revolution: Reflections and Elaborations on the Work of Christopher Hill*. London: Verso.

Snape, John. 2017. "The 'Sinews of the State': Historical Justifications for Taxes and Tax Law." In Monica Bhandari (ed.), *Philosophical Foundations of Tax Law*. Oxford: Oxford University Press.

Spencer, Jane. 1996. "Women Writers and the Eighteenth-Century Novel." In John Richetti (ed.), *The Cambridge Companion to the Eighteenth-Century Novel*. Cambridge: Cambridge University Press.

Sugarman, David and Warrington, Ronnie. 1996. "Land Law, Citizenship, and the Invention of 'Englishness': The Strange World of the Equity of Redemption." In John Brewer and Susan Staves (eds.), *Early Modern Conceptions of Property*. London: Routledge.

Twining, William. 2000. "The Ratio Decidendi of the Prodigal Son." In Katherine O'Donovan and Gerry R. Rubin (eds.), *Human Rights and Legal History*. Oxford: Oxford University Press.

Underdown, David. 1985b. "The Taming of the Scold: The Enforcement of Patriarchal Authority in Early Modern England." In Anthony John Fletcher and J. Stevenson (eds.), *Order and Disorder in Early Modern England*. Cambridge: Cambridge University Press.

Wolf, Edwin. 1979. "The Prodigal Son in England and America: A Century of Change." In Joan D. Dolmetsch (ed.), *Eighteenth-Century Prints in Colonial America: To Educate and Decorate*. Williamsburg, VA: Colonial Williamsburg Foundation; Charlottesville; distributed by University Press of Virginia.

Wood, Gordon S. 2006. "The American Revolution." In Mark Goldie and Robert Wokler (eds.), *The Cambridge History of Eighteenth-Century Political Thought*. Cambridge: Cambridge University Press.

Wrightson, Keith. 1980. "Two Concepts of Order: Justices, Constables and Jurymen in Seventeenth-Century England." In John Brewer and John Styles (eds.), *An Ungovernable People? The English and their Law in the Seventeenth and Eighteenth Centuries*. London: Hutchinson.

Wrigley, E.A. 1981. "Marriage, Fertility and Population Growth in Eighteenth-Century England." In R.B. Outhwaite (ed.), *Marriage and Society*. London: Europa Publications.

Yale, David E.C. 1961. "An Essay on Mortgages and Trusts and Allied Topics in Equity." In David E.C. Yale (ed.), *Lord Nottingham's Chancery Cases*, Selden Society Vol. 79. London: B. Quaritch.

Yale, David E.C. 1965. "Essay Mortgages and Trusts," and "Introduction." In David E.C. Yale (ed.), *Lord Nottingham's Manual of Chancery Practice and Prolegomena of Chancery and Equity*. Cambridge: Cambridge University Press.

Yale, David. E.C. 2004. "Finch, Heneage, first earl of Nottingham (1621–1682), lord chancellor." *Oxford Dictionary of National Biography*.

Young, G.M. 1950. "The Liberal Mind in Victorian England." In *Last Essays*. London: Hart-Davis.

DISSERTATIONS AND THESES

Howell, Jean. 1996. "The Doctrine of Notice: An Historical Perspective." *The University of Manchester Working Papers*, No. 19, August 1996.

Masciola, Amy. 2003. "'I Can See by this Woman's Features that She is Capable of any Wickedness': Representations of Criminal Women in Eighteenth-century England." Ph.D. diss., University of Maryland.

JOURNAL ARTICLES

Bomford, David and Roy, Ashok. 1982. "Hogarth's Marriage à la Mode." *National Gallery Technical Bulletin*, 6: 44–67.

Bonfield, Lloyd. 1989. "The Nature of Customary Law in the Manor Courts of Medieval England." *Comparative Studies in Society and History*, 31(3): 514–534.

Capp, Bernard. 1977. "English Youth Groups and the Pindar of Wakefield." *Past & Present*, 76: 127–133.

Clay, C. 1981. "Property Settlements, Financial Provision for the Family, and Sale of Land by the Greater Landowners 1660–1790." *Journal of British Studies*, 21(1): 18–38.

Dabhoiwala, Faramerz. 1996. "The Construction of Honour, Reputation and Status in Late Seventeenth- and Early Eighteenth-Century England." *Transactions of the Royal Historical Society*, 6 (Sixth Series): 201.

Davis, Jennifer. 1984. "A Poor Man's System of Justice: The London Police Courts in the Second Half of the Nineteenth Century." *Historical Journal*, 27(2): 309–335.

Devereaux, Simon. 2003. "The Fall of the Sessions Paper: The Criminal Trial and the Popular Press in Late Eighteenth-Century London." *Criminal Justice History*, 18(1): 57–88.

Devereaux, Simon. 2007. "From Sessions to Newspaper? Criminal Trial Reporting, the Nature of Crime, and the London Press, 1770–1800." *The London Journal*, 32(1): 1–27.

Edelstein, Dan. 2014. "Enlightenment Rights Talk." *Journal of Modern History*, 86: 530–565.

Forbes, T.R. 1988. "A Jury of Matrons." *Medical History*, 32(1): 23–33.

Gorsky, Martin. 1994. "James Tuckfield's 'Ride': Combination and Social Drama in Early Nineteenth-Century Bristol." *Social History*, 19(3): 319–338.

Hamburger, Philip. 1983. "The Conveyancing Purposes of the Statute of Frauds." *The American Journal of Legal History*, 27(4): 354–385.

Hanfling, Oswald. 2003. "Learning about Right and Wrong: Ethics and Language." *Philosophy*, 78(303): 25–41.

Hay, Douglas. 1998. "Patronage, Paternalism, and Welfare: Masters, Workers, and Magistrates in Eighteenth-Century England." *International Labor and Working-Class History* 53: 27–48.

Hejeebu, Santhi. 2005. "Contract Enforcement in the English East India Company." *The Journal of Economic History*, 65(2): 496–523.

Hitchcock, Tim, Crymble, Adam and Falcini, Louise. 2014. "Loose, Idle and Disorderly: Vagrant Removal in Late Eighteenth-century Middlesex." *Social History*, 39(4): 509–527.

Hufton, Olwen. 1984. "Women Without Men: Widows and Spinsters in Britain and France in the Eighteenth Century." *Journal of Family History*, 9: 355–376.

Ibbetson, David. 1982. "Assumpsit and Debt in the Early Sixteenth Century: The Origins of Indebitatus Count." *Cambridge Law Journal*, 41(1): 142–161.

Kent, D.A. 1989. "Ubiquitous But Invisible: Female Domestic Servants in Mid Eighteenth-Century London." *History Workshop Journal*, 28: 111–128.

King, Peter. 1984. "Decision-Makers and Decision-Making in English Criminal Law, 1750–1800." *The Historical Journal*, 27: 26–49.

King, Peter. 1989. "Gleaners, Farmers and the Failure of Legal Sanctions in England 1750–1850." *Past & Present*, 125(1): 116–150.

King, Peter. 2004. "The Summary Courts and Social Relations in Eighteenth Century England." *Past & Present*, 183(1): 125–172.

King, Peter. 2007. "Newspaper Reporting and Attitudes to Crime and Justice in Late-Eighteenth-and early-Nineteenth-Century London." *Continuity and Change*, 22(1): 73–112.

King, P. 2013. "Ethnicity, Prejudice, and Justice: The Treatment of the Irish at the Old Bailey, 1750–1825." *The Journal of British Studies*, 52: 390–414.

Koskenniemi, Martii. 2009. "The Advantage of Treaties: International Law in the Enlightenment." *Edinburgh Law Review*, 13: 27–67.

Langbein, John. 1978. "The Criminal Trial before the Lawyers." *The University of Chicago Law Review*, 45: 263–316.

Langbein, John. 1983. "Shaping the Eighteenth-Century Criminal Trial: A View from the Ryder Sources." *The University of Chicago Law Review*, 50: 1–136.

Langbein, John H. 1996. "Historical Foundations of the Law of Evidence: A View from the Ryder Sources." *Columbia Law Review*, 96: 1168–1202.

Lasch, Christopher. 1974. "The Suppression of Clandestine Marriage in England: The Marriage Act of 1753." *Salmagundi*, 26: 90.

Laurence, Anne. 2008. "The Emergence of a Private Clientele for Banks in the Early Eighteenth Century: Hoare's Bank and Some Women Customers." *Economic History Review*, 61(3): 565–586.

Law, C.M. 1972. "Some Notes on the Urban Population in the Eighteenth Century." *Local Historian*, 10: 13–26.

Lobban, Michael. 1997. "Contractual Fraud in Law and Equity, c1750–c1850." *Oxford Journal of Legal Studies*, 17(3): 441–476.

McKenzie, Andrea. 2003. "Martyrs in Low Life? Dying 'Game' in Augustan England." *Journal of British Studies*, 42: 167–205.

Mayall, David. 1992. "The Making of British Gypsy Identities, c.1500–1980." *Immigrants and Minorities*, 11(1): 21–41.

Mayall, David. 1997. "Egyptians and Vagabonds: Representations of the Gypsy in Early Modern Official and Rogue Literature." *Immigrants and Minorities*, 16(3): 55–82.

Mellinkoff, Ruth. 1973. "Riding Backwards: Theme of Humiliation and Symbol of Evil." *Viator*, 4: 153–176.

Minchinton, W.E. 1951. "The Beginnings of Trade Unionism in the Gloucestershire Woollen Industry." *Trans. Bristol and Glos. Archaeological Soc.*, 70: 134–135.

O'Connell, Lisa. 2011. "'By Ordinance of Nature': Marriage, Religion and the Modern English State." *Parergon*, 28(2): 149–166.

Oldham, J.C. 1985. "On Pleading the Belly: A History of the Jury of Matrons." *Criminal Justice History*, VI: 1–64.

Oldham, James. 2004. "Law-making at Nisi Prius in the Early 1800s." *Journal of Legal History*, 25: 221–247.

Panek, Jennifer. 2013. "Community, Credit and the Prodigal Husband on the Early Modern Stage." *ELH*, 80(1): 61–92.

Piggott, J. 1869. "Antiquities of Leominster: The Ducking Stool." *Notes and Queries*, 4th series, 4 (July 17): 61.

Pink, Andrew. 2015. "Solomon, Susanna and Moses: Locating Handel's Lost Librettist." *Eighteenth-century Music*, 12 (2): 211–222.

Quinlan, Daniel C. and Shackleford, Jean A. 1994. "Economy and English Families 1500–1850." *Journal of Interdisciplinary History*, 24(3): 431–463.

Radford, Ursula. 1933. "The Loyal Saddler of Exeter." *Transactions of the Devon Association*, 65: 227–235.

Razell, Peter E. 1965. "Population Change in Eighteenth Century England: A Reinterpretation." *Economic History Review*, 18(2): 312–332.

Rollison, David. 1981. "Property, Ideology and Popular Culture in a Gloucestershire Village, 1660–1740." *Past & Present*, 93: 70–97.

Schmidt, A.J. 1990. "The Country Attorney in Late Eighteenth-Century England: Benjamin Smith of Horbling." *Law and History Review* 8(2): 237–271.

Seal, Graham. 1988 "Tradition and Agrarian Protest in Nineteenth Century England and Wales." *Folklore*, 99(2): 146–169.

Shesgreen, Sean. 1976. "Hogarth's Industry and Idleness: A Reading." *Eighteenth-Century Studies*, 9(4): 569–598.

Singleton, Robert. R. 1970. "English Criminal Biography, 1651–1722." *Harvard Library Bulletin*, 18: 63–83.

Snell, Keith D.M. 2003. "The Culture of Local Xenophobia." *Social History*, 28(1): 1–30.

Spector, Céline. 2015. "The 'Mouthpiece of the Law'? The Different Figures of the Judge in *The Spirit of Laws.*" *Montesquieu Law Review*, 3: 87–102.

Staves, S. 1994. "Chattel Property Rules and the Invention of Englishness 1600–1800." *Law and History Review*, 12(1): 123–153.

Steintrager, James. A. 2001. "Monstrous Appearances: Hogarth's Four Stages of Cruelty and the Paradox of Inhumanity." *The Eighteenth Century*, 42(1): 59–82.

Storch, Robert D. 1982. "Popular Festivity and Consumer Protest: Food Price Disturbance in the Southwest and Oxfordshire in 1867." *Albion*, 14(3): 209–234.

Suggett, Richard. 1996. "Festivals and Social Structure in Early Modern Wales." *Past & Present*, 152: 79–112.

Taylor, Carole. 1984. "Handel and Frederick, Prince of Wales." *Musical Times*, 125(1692): 89.

Thompson, Edward P. 1971. "The Moral Economy of the English Crowd in the Eighteenth Century." *Past & Present*, 1: 76–136.

Wahrman, Dror. 1992. "National Society, Communal Culture: An Argument about the Recent Historiography of Eighteenth-Century Britain." *Social History*, 17(1): 43–72.

Wallis, Patrick. 2008. "Apprenticeship and Training in Pre-Modern England." *Journal of Economic History*, 68(3): 832–861.

Wells Roger. 1977. "The Revolt of the South-West, 1800–1801: A Study in English Popular Protest." *Social History*, 2(6): 713–744.

Wind, Barry. 1997. "Hogarth's Industry and Idleness Reconsidered." *Print Quarterly*, 14(3): 235–251.

Wood, Andy. 1997. "The Place of Custom in Plebeian Political Culture: England, 1550–1800." *Social History*, 22(1): 46–60.

NEWSPAPER ARTICLES

Bickley, A.C. 1902. "Some Notes on a Custom at Woking, Surrey." *Home Counties Magazine*, iv. 25–29.

CD BOOKLET NOTES

King, Robert. 2001. "The Coronation of King George II, 1727." CD booklet note, Hyperion CDA67286.

McCreesh, Paul. 1999. "Recording Handel's *Solomon*." CD booklet note, Deutsche Grammophon 459 689-2.

Smith, Ruth. 1999. "Ideal and Reality: The Libretto of *Solomon*." CD booklet note, Deutsche Grammophon 459 689-2.

Vickers, David. 2007. "'Let the loud Hosannahs rise': Handel's Solomon." CD booklet note, Harmonia Mundi France HMC 901949.50.

ONLINE RESOURCES

Backscheider, Paula R. 2010. "Haywood, Eliza." *Oxford Dictionary of National Biography*. Oxford: Oxford University Press (accessed June 6, 2017).

Battestin, Martin C. 2008. "Fielding, Henry (1707–1754)." *Oxford Dictionary of National Biography*. Oxford: Oxford University Press (accessed November 22, 2017).

Beattie, J.M. 2013. online edn, Sept 2013. "Garrow, Sir William (1760–1840)." *Oxford Dictionary of National Biography*. Oxford: Oxford University Press (accessed June 6, 2017).

Brayne, Charles. 2008. "Taverner, William." *Oxford Dictionary of National Biography*. Oxford: Oxford University Press (accessed June 6, 2017).

Davies, Owen. 2007. "Talk of the Devil: Crime and Satanic Inspiration in Eighteenth-Century England." University of Hertfordshire http://hertsacademiaedu/OwenDavies (accessed November 27, 2015).

Donnachie, Ian. 2004. "Malcolm, Sarah (c.1710–1733)." *Oxford Dictionary of National Biography*. Oxford: Oxford University Press (accessed June 6, 2017).

McConnell, Anita. 2004. "Newland, Abraham (1730–1807)." *Oxford Dictionary of National Biography*. Oxford: Oxford University Press (accessed June 6, 2017).

Miles, Ellen G. 2008. "Hudson, Thomas (*bap*. 1701–1779)." *Oxford Dictionary of National Biography*. Oxford: Oxford University Press (accessed November 21, 2017).

Miller, David Philip. 2008. "Barrington, Daines (1727/8–1800)." *Oxford Dictionary of National Biography*. Oxford: Oxford University Press (accessed June 6, 2017).

Rosen, F. 2014. "Bentham, Jeremy (1748–1832)." *Oxford Dictionary of National Biography*. Oxford: Oxford University Press (accessed June 6, 2017).

Smith, E.A. 2004. "Scott, John, first earl of Eldon (1751–1838)." *Oxford Dictionary of National Biography*. Oxford: Oxford University Press (accessed June 6, 2017).

PUBLIC LECTURE

Spector, Céline. 2012. "Commerce, Liberty and Empire in The Spirit of the Laws." Public Lecture delivered at the University of Warwick, March 14.

VOCAL SCORE

Bärenreiter. 2014. *Händel Solomon: Oratorio in three Acts HWV 67*. Edited by Andreas Köhs. Bärenreiter Kassel: Basel, London and elsewhere.

INDEX

abolitionism 141–3
absolutism 5, 6
accessible justice 133–6
Achenwall, Gottfried 87
Acts of Union 8, 11
Addison, Joseph 115
adultery 28, 67–8
agreements. *See* legal agreements
agricultural disputes 17
Allen, William 140
American War of Independence 5, 6
Andrews, Malcolm xii
Andrews, Robert 114
Anne, Queen of England 4, 35, 39
anti-semitism 8
apprenticeships 18, 20, 71, 79
Aquinas, Thomas 3
Archenholz, Johann W. von 130
Armstrong, John 57
arranged marriages 60–1
Ashby, Matthew 36
assizes 130
Astell, Mary 116–17, 118
Aufklärung 3, 4
Austen, Jane
   Emma 60
   Mansfield Park 68
   Persuasion 13
   Pride and Prejudice 12, 58, 62, 63
   Sense and Sensibility 68
Austin, John 3

Bach, Johann Sebastian 3
Bailey, Joanne 60
Bank of England 169
Barber, Francis 143
Barrington, Daines 7
barristers 148
Bearcroft, Edward 145
Beattie, J. M. 7
Beccaria, Cesare 11
Beggar's Opera (John Gay) 1, 3, 9, 13, 14, 64, 84, 137, 169
Bentham, Jeremy 11, 67, 68

Bill of Rights 4, 9, 35, 85
Birmingham 5
Black, Jeremy 146
Black Act 9, 10
black history 2
   slavery 7, 8, 11, 140–4, 165
Blackstone, Sir William 2, 35, 97, 133, 144, 156, 158
Bolingbroke, Henry St John, Viscount Bolingbroke 34, 35
Bonfield, Lloyd 17
Boscawen, William 133
Boswell, James 7, 13
Boulton, Matthew 5
Bow Street magistrates 134, 137
Boyce, William 37
Brewer, John 2, 34
British Constitution 11
   ancient and modern ideas of constitution 34
   centrality of law 49–52
   Crown and Parliament 35
   cultural significance 33–4
   embodiments of constitutional values 46–9
   equal treatment under law 38, 100, 105, 130
   Handel's *Solomon* 39–52
   known laws 36
   monarchy 35, 39, 52
   property rights 6, 7, 35–6, 85
   right to litigate 36–7
   rule of law 9, 128
   separation of powers 35, 85
British values 6, 7
Brougham, Henry, 1st Baron 150
Brown, Laura 110
Brown, Martin 158
Burke, Edmund 6, 105
Burn, Richard 133
Burney, Frances (Fanny) 7, 62
Burns, Robert 9
Butler, Samuel 27
Byng, Admiral John 13, 31
Byron, William, 5th Baron 130

INDEX

Campbell's Reports 148, 169
Canning, Elizabeth 101–4, 135, 136
Capp, Bernard 18
Care, Henry 11
Carrol, John 91
cartoons 12
Castlereagh, Robert Stewart, Lord Castlereagh 6, 14
Catholics 6, 50, 100, 163
Centlivre, Susanna 58
centralization 9
Chancery 16, 59, 111, 154–5
Cheek, Frances 98–9
Chicken, Edward 66
Child, Josiah 118
Church of England 5, 8, 36
  Archbishop of Canterbury 47, 48
  clergy 22, 139
  ecclesiastical courts 16
  marriage 63–7
Cibber, Colley 115
Clare, John 9, 19
Clark, William 102
Clarke, Daniel 127, 144
Clarkson, Thomas 141, 142
Clayton, Sir Robert 108, 111
clergy 22, 139
Cobbett, William 18
codification 53, 67, 68, 69
coffee houses 73–6, 79–80, 113
collective action 21
collectivism 4, 86
colonies 6, 7
  transportation to 10, 102
commerce 7–8, 39, 71
  East India Company 45, 72, 77, 78–9, 81, 118
  finance 76–7, 80–1
commercial law 11
  agreements 72–9, 85
  companies 80–1
common land 9
common law 10, 16, 17, 20, 21, 36, 43, 51, 111
communication networks 72–3, 88
company law 80–1
Congreve, William 63, 64
consideration 85
constitution. *See* British Constitution
context 89, 144
contracts. *See* legal agreements
Cook, Captain James 7
Cook, Hera 62

courts 16, 36–7
  assizes 130
  Chancery 16, 59, 111, 154–5
  King's Bench 145, 146, 148, 149, 150, 153, 154
Covent Garden Theatre 41
coverture 111, 113, 114, 116
Cowper, William 49
Crabbe, George 62
credit 76–7, 110–11
crime genre 136–9, 165
criminal justice 9–11, 13
  'bloody code' 91, 94
  celebrity criminals 136–7
  corruption 137, 139
  investigation and reporting of crime 134–5, 137–9
  mirror on society 137–9
  prevention and reform 139
criminal trials
  caseload 150
  emotions and sensibilities 98–100
  equality before the law 100, 105
  explanations and excuses 94–8
  high-profile trials 128–30
  juries 94, 95, 97, 98–9, 131, 156–9
  outsiders 100, 101, 105
  popular perceptions 93–4
  procedure 91–3
  reputation 96, 97, 105
  rights of the accused 92
  Sarah Malcolm 89–91
  theatricality 128–31
  verdicts 89
  women 100–5
crowds: violence and unrest 10, 23, 24, 127, 129–30, 131, 139–40
Cruikshank, George 80
cultural context 89, 144
cultural history xi–xii, 89
cultural norms 54, 57–8, 59, 61, 123
culture 2
Cumberland, Prince William Augustus, Duke of 5
customary practices 17, 20, 21, 22, 23, 25

Dabhoiwala, Faramerz 5
Darwin, Erasmus 5, 57
Davis, Jennifer 15
Dawes, Manassaw 99–100
Day, Thomas 60
death penalty 9–11, 13, 91, 94, 99, 127, 128, 136, 137, 144
  pleading pregnancy 10, 157–8, 159

debt 77, 113
Defoe, Daniel 13, 73, 118, 124, 125, 165, 167, 168
   Colonel Jack 138
   History of the remarkable life of John Sheppard 136, 137
   Moll Flanders 55, 63, 95–6, 114, 138
   pilloried 132
   Roxana 55, 66, 107, 108, 109–10, 111, 113, 114, 116
Delany, Mary 46
devil 81–2
Dickens, Charles 154
divine law 2, 3, 12, 14
Divine Right of Kings 6, 8
divorce 67, 68
doctrine of consideration 85
D'Oench, Ellen 118
Donnelly, John Jr. xi
Draper, Somerset 41
ducking 23, 25, 26, 29, 31
Dundas, Henry, Earl of Melville 128
Durnford, Charles 145, 148

Eagan, James 132
East, Edward 145, 148
East India Company 45, 72, 77, 78–9, 81, 118
Eastman, William 127
ecclesiastical courts 16
Edelstein, Dan 72, 73
Edgeworth, Maria 60, 62
Eldon, Sir John Scott, Lord Eldon 155, 159
Ellenborough, Edward Law, 1st Earl of 148, 149, 150, 169
empiricism 3, 4
employment contracts 18, 79–80
enclosures 9, 12, 22
encroachment 19
Engelsing, Rolf 73
Enlightenment 1, 3–4, 7
   Aufklärung 3, 4
   law and culture 11–14
   law of nations 86–7, 88
   Scotland 5
Entick v. Carrington 9, 36
entitlements 15, 17
equality before the law 38, 100, 105, 130
equity law 16, 17, 22, 111–12, 113, 120, 122, 125
Erskine, Thomas 148–9
Espinasse, Isaac 148
Euston, Lady Charlotte Maria Waldegrave, Countess of 129

executions 9–11, 13, 91, 94, 99, 127, 129, 136, 137, 144
   pleading pregnancy 10, 157–8, 159

Farquhar, George 115
Fawkes, Guy 30, 31
felony 9–10, 94, 95
Ferrers, Laurence Shirley, 4th Earl of 128, 130
Ferrier, Susan 60, 61, 67, 68
festivities 30–1
Fielding, Henry 73
   Joseph Andrews 12, 13, 62, 63, 65
   Life and death of Jonathan Wild the Great 138
   Tom Jones 57, 61, 64, 65
   Westminster magistrate 7, 34, 103
Fielding, Sir John 7, 133, 134, 139
finance 76–7, 80–1
   mortgages 107–12, 122
Finch, Heneage, 1st Earl of Nottingham 111
Fisher, Michael 167
Fitz-Adam, Adam 28
Fitzgerald, Norton 96
Fleet marriages 64–5
folk heroes 136–7
food riots 139–40
foreclosure 111–13, 118, 120, 122, 124, 125
foreign policy 87
Foundling Hospital 47, 60
Fox, Charles James 119
Foyster, Elizabeth 67
Franklin, Benjamin 5
Frasi, Giulia 42
fraud 122
Frederick, Prince of Wales 41, 47, 52
Freemasons 39
free will 85
French revolution 5
Fuller, William 132

Gainsborough, Thomas 12, 114
Galli, Caterina 42
Garrow, William 7, 11, 148, 169
Garton, John 97
Gascoyne, Sir Crisp 102
Gay, John (*The Beggar's Opera*) 1, 3, 9, 13, 14, 64, 84, 137, 169
General Post Office 72
George I of England 4
George II of England 4, 5, 35, 41, 46, 47
George III of England 5, 8, 11, 146, 147
Gibbs, Vicary 148
Giben, John 101–2

Gibson, William 132
Gillray, James 12
gleaning 21, 22
Glorious Revolution 4, 7, 8, 35, 39, 41, 51, 85
Goldsmith, Oliver 12, 17
Gordon riots 5, 164
Grantham, Richard 96
Greuze, Jean-Baptiste 83–4
Grevil, Thomas 102
Grey, Jemima, Marchioness Grey 50
Gronamann, Sibilla 43
Grose's *Classical Dictionary* 26, 27
gypsies 100, 101, 102, 104, 167

Hall, Virtue 101, 102
Hamilton, Elizabeth 56, 69
Handel, George Frideric
   Alexander Balus 36, 43, 47
   Coronation Anthems 47
   Joshua 39
   Judas Maccabaeus 11, 36, 39
   L'Allegro, Il Penseroso, ed Il Moderato 36
   naturalization 37
   oratorios 39–40, 41
   portrait 38
   residence in London 37–8
   Samson 48
   Solomon 33–52
   Susanna 39, 43, 47, 48
   Whig sympathies 37, 41
Hanoverian kings 4–5, 6, 34, 48
Hardwicke, Philip Yorke, 1st Earl of 35, 47, 48, 50, 52, 59, 112, 121
Harrington, James 36
Harris, Ellen 36, 46
Harrison, Lloyd 17
Harwood, Richard 96
Hatchett, William 124
Hawker, Essex 30
Hawkins, John 38
Hay, Douglas 59, 91
Haydn, Joseph 160
Hayek, Friedrich August von 4, 8
Haywood, Eliza 111, 125
   City Jilt 107, 123–4
   History of Jemmy and Jenny Jessamy 67
   History of Miss Betsy Thoughtless 55, 58, 64, 67, 68
Henry VIII, King of England 49
Herring, Thomas 48
Herrup, Cynthia 89
Hicks, Anthony 34

highwaymen 133, 136, 137
Hill, John 105
Hilton, Margaret 158
history 2
Hobbes, Thomas 86
Hogarth, William 111, 125
   Credulity, superstition, and fanaticism 135
   Execution of the Idle Apprentice 131
   Four Stages of Cruelty 116, 117, 137
   Harlot's Progress 54, 55, 56
   Hudibras encounters the Skimmington 27
   Industry and Idleness 116
   Marriage a la Mode 58, 82–4
   Portrait of Sarah Malcolm 89, 90
   Rake's Progress 58, 118, 119, 120
Hoppit, Julian 11
Hume, David 2, 4, 5, 6, 9, 36, 86, 87, 88, 143
Humphries, Polly 57
Hunt, Henry 140
Hunt, Margaret 54, 56
Hunter, David 34, 50
Huntington, William 32

Inchbald, Elizabeth 57
indigenous peoples 7
Ingram, Martin 23
Ingrassia, Catherine 123, 124
Inister, John 102
insularity 19
insurance contracts 75
intellectual property 9
international relations 2, 3, 72–3
   treaties 9, 86–7, 88
Ireland 8

Jacob, Giles 113, 133
Jacobite Rising 10, 11, 45
Jacobites 4, 6, 132
James I of England 4, 8, 51
James II of England 4, 51, 85
Jews 8, 37, 38, 50, 100
John, King of England x
Johnson, Charles 115
Johnson, Samuel 13, 14, 41, 143
joint stock companies 80, 81
Jones, Sir William 7
juries 94, 95, 97, 98–9, 131, 156–9
   "jury of matrons" 157–8
justice 15. *See also* criminal justice
   accessibility 133–6
   customary practices 17, 20, 21, 22, 23, 25
   entitlements 15, 17
   legal pluralism 16–17

owning justice 131–3
popular justice 24–32, 127, 144
punishment 9–11, 13, 18, 22–32, 131
restorative justice 133
righting wrongs 128–31
Justices of the Peace 16–17, 22

Kant, Immanuel 4
Kenyon, Sir Lloyd 150, 151–2
King, Peter 16, 21, 97, 167
King, William 27
King's Bench 145, 146, 148, 149, 150, 153, 154
Kingston, Elizabeth Chudleigh, Duchess of 129
Kirwan, Eleanor 158

labourers 18, 19–20
Landau, Norma 22
Langbein, John 92, 94, 150
Langford, Paul 12
Law, Edward, 1st Earl of Ellenborough 148, 149, 150, 169
law, rules of 2
law of nations 2, 3, 72–3
treaties 9, 86–7, 88
law reports 145, 148
legal agreements 71–2, 88
binding force 63, 64, 77, 85, 86, 88
commerce 72–9
companies 80–1
doctrine of consideration 85
employment contracts 18, 79–80
international treaties 86–7, 88
marriage contracts 82–4
rational self 81–2
religious attitudes 81–2
social contract 86
theoretical foundations 85
will theory 85
legal codes 53, 67, 68, 69
legal pluralism 16–17
legal profession 7, 12, 148–52
inefficiency and uncertainty 153–6
legal systems 8–11
legislation 9
Legrand, Pierre xi
Lemmings, David 2, 12, 37, 147
Lewis, Thomas 141
libertinage 54
liberty 7
Lillo, George 14

Lisle, David 141
Lloyd's Coffee House 75, 76
local attachments 18
Locke, Hew x
Locke, John 3, 4, 6, 67, 72, 86
London 5, 7
London Corresponding Society 139
Lord Chancellor, office of 47
Loughlin, Martin 40
Louis XIV of France 5, 6
Lowe, Thomas 47
luxury 8

Mably, Gabriel Bonnot de 86
McClelland, J. S. 49
McCreesh, Paul 40
MacLaine, Gentleman James 133, 136
Madan, Martin 99
Magna Carta x, xi
Malcolm, Sarah 89–91, 105
Mandeville, Bernard 3, 97
manorial courts 17
Mansfield, William Murray, 1st Earl of 11, 141
marriage
affection 58–9
age 61–3
arranged marriages 60–1
clandestine marriages 64–5
codification 67, 68, 69
contracts 82–4
cultural norms 54, 57–8, 59, 61
divorce 67, 68
elopement 67, 68
legal and religious requirements 63–6
marital relations 26–30, 67–8
marriage market and mortgages 123–5
profligate husbands 113–18
regulation 53
relationships outside 54–7
religious ideals 54
romantic love 60
social status and equality 57–60
women's rights 54, 60
Marten, James 67
Martens, Georg Friedrich 87
Marvell, Andrew 26
medical profession 157, 158
Mellinkoff, Ruth 26
Melton, Frank T. 111
Mendes, Moses 37, 38, 39
Millar, Andrew 5
miscarriage of justice 13–14

Moer, John 96
Mohun, Charles, 4th Baron 130
monarchy
    British Constitution 35, 39, 52
    coronation oath 46
    Divine Right of Kings 6, 8
    loyalty 48
    prerogative of judgment 51
Montesquieu, Charles-Louis Secondat, Baron de 2, 3, 5, 8, 35, 39, 45, 51
    Persian Letters 36, 50
    The Spirit of the Laws 41, 42, 50, 162
moralizing tales 115
Morell, Thomas 11, 37
mortgages 107–12, 122, 123–5
Moser, J. J. 87
Mozart, Leopold 7
Mozart, Wolfgang Amadeus 7
murder 10, 89, 94
Murphy, Christian 158

Napoleon 12
Napoleonic wars 5, 6
natural law 2, 3, 14, 51, 86, 87, 88
"Nelsonian blindness" 160
Newgate prison 7, 13, 89, 91, 93, 136
Newland, Abraham 169
newspapers 145–59
Newton, Sir Isaac 3
novels 113, 165
Nozick, Robert 4, 6
Nussbaum, Felicity 101

O'Bryen, Dennis 147
Old Bailey 135, 137, 147, 148, 150, 156
Oldham, James 169
oratorios 39–40, 41
Otis, James 160

Paine, Thomas 9, 17, 31, 34, 66–7, 92, 105
Palliser, Sir Charles 32
parishes 18–19, 22
Peake, Thomas 148
Penlez, Bosavern 144
Pepusch, John Christopher 1
Peterloo Massacre 10, 12, 14, 140
Phillips, Mark Salber 2
philosophers 5
pickpockets 23
pillory 131–2
Pink, Andrew 37
Pitt, William, the Younger 10, 12

Plaxton, John 97
Plough Monday 30, 31
politics 4–8
poor laws 116
Pope, Alexander 9, 135
Pope, Dudley 11
popular justice 24–32, 127, 144
popular press 145–59
    "reading revolution" 73
population 17–18
Porteous, George 27
Poser, Norman S. 11
positive law 2, 8, 9
postal system 72–3, 88
pragmatism 4, 86
pregnancy 10, 54, 55, 56, 157–8, 159
Priestley, Joseph 5
print culture 91, 93–4, 113–14, 133, 135
prisons
    model prisons 139
    Newgate 7, 13, 89, 91, 93, 136
prodigal sons 118–21, 123
profligate husbands 113–18
property offenses 10, 94
property rights 3, 6, 7, 9, 35–6, 85
    foreclosure 111–13, 118, 120, 122, 124, 125
    landed wealth 108, 109, 113
    marriage market 123–5
    mortgages 107–12, 122, 123–5
    prodigal sons 118–21, 123
    profligate husbands 113–18
Protestantism 3, 4, 36, 41, 46, 50
Prussia 3–4
public interest 9
Pulteney, William 135
punishment 9–11, 13, 18, 22–32, 131
    death penalty 9–11, 13, 91, 94, 99, 127, 128
Purcell, Henry 50
Purchas, Edward 97

radical orators 10, 32, 140
Ramsay, Allan 102, 103
Randall, Adrian 22
Rann, 16 string Jack 136, 137
rational self 81–2
Rawls, John 4
Ray, Martha 57
"reading revolution" 73
reason 81
Reinhold, Henry 48

religious bigotry 144
religious toleration 6, 8
"Republic of Letters" 73
reputation 96, 97, 105
restorative justice 133
reward posters 134
Reynolds, Frances 143
Ricarby, Latus 97
Rich, Edward, 6th Earl of Warwick 130
Rich, John 41
Richardson, Samuel 57, 61, 63, 64, 73, 114
Riding, Jacqueline 10
riots 10, 139, 140, 144
ritual punishments 30, 31
Roberts, William 96
Robertson, John 1
Robespierre, Maximilien 6
Rochefoucauld, François de la 92
Rogers, Nicholas 59
romantic love 60
Romilly, Sir Samuel 11
Rooke, Deborah W. 45
Rosen, Lawrence xi
"rough music" 25, 27, 28, 29, 31, 32, 140
Rousseau, Jean-Jacques 11, 60, 83, 86, 87, 88
Rowlandson, Thomas 66, 121
Rubenhold, Hallie 55
Rubens, Peter Paul 44
Rubin, Dana 12, 135
"Rule Britannia" 12
rule of law 9, 128
Ryder, Sir Dudley 98, 99, 166

satire 1
Savage, Richard 124
Savigny, Friedrich Carl von 85
Sayre, Stephen 128
Schmitt, Carl 40
Scotland 4
    Act of Union 8, 11
    Enlightenment 5
Scott, Sir John, Lord Eldon 155, 159
secularism 1, 5
self-interest 3, 4, 86, 87–8
Sen, Amartya 4
"sensibility" 98–100, 166
separation of powers 35, 85
sex 5
sexual agency 123, 124
sexual transgressions 22, 54–6
    adultery 28, 67–8
Shackleton, Robert 35

shaming processions 25–30
Sharp, Granville 141, 143
Shebbeare, John 58
Sheffield, John 71, 80
Shelley, Percy Bysshe 14
Sheppard, Jack 136, 137
Sheridan, Frances 65
Sheridan, Richard Brinsley 67
silk weavers 20, 26, 127
skimmingtons 25, 26, 27, 28, 30
slavery 7, 8, 11, 140–4, 165
Smith, Adam 3, 4, 5, 6, 9, 10, 88
    Wealth of Nations 87
Smith, Charlotte 58, 67
Smith, Ruth 33, 34, 41, 46, 51
Smith, Thomas 92
Smollett, Tobias 12, 64
    The Expedition of Humphrey Clinker 58, 66, 138
smuggling 10, 11
Snell, Kevin 19
social contract 86
social mobility 107, 111, 112, 125
social norms 53, 54, 57–8, 59, 61, 123
Sokol, Mary 68
Somersett, James 141
speculation 80
Spencer, John 121
Squires, Mary 101–5
stang riding 25, 29
Stapylton, Robert 141
Starke, Thomas 71, 80
Statute of Artificers 18, 20
Stebbing, Henry 58
Steele, Richard 115
Stephenson, Robert 97
Stewart, Robert, Lord Castlereagh 6, 14
Stokes, George 132
Strahan, William 5
Strong, Jonathan 141
Stuart cause 4–5, 8
Swanston, Hamish 49
Swift, Jonathan 13, 26, 36, 73

Taverner, William 117–18
    The Artful Husband 107, 109, 124–5
    The Artful Wife 109, 115–16, 124
taxation 6, 9
Tey, Josephine 136
theater 115
theft 96
Thomas, Keith 54

Thompson, E. P. 9, 17
Thomson, James 35
Thurlow, Edward, 1st Baron 57
Times (The) 145–59
Toft, Mary 135, 136
toleration 6, 8
Tonson, Jacob and Richard 41
Tories 5, 7, 10, 35, 139
Towneley, Francis 10
transportation of convicts 10, 102
treaties 9, 86–7, 88
trial by jury 156–9. *See also* criminal trials
Turner, James Grantham 54
Turpin, Dick 136
Tyburn 13

Underhill, Nicholas 47
"United Kingdom" 8

vagrancy 18
verdicts 89
Vickery, Amanda 54
Voltaire, François-Marie Arouet 3, 5, 9, 13–14

wage rates 20
Wahrman, Dror 22
Walpole, Edward 57
Walpole, Sir Robert 35, 137
War of Austrian Succession 39
War of Spanish Succession 5, 9
Wats, John 81
Watt, James 5
Wedgwood, Josiah 5
Weitzman, Steven 39
Wells, Susannah 101
Wenham, Jane 81
Whigs 1, 4, 7, 10, 35, 37, 41, 119, 137–8
wife beating 28, 29

Wilberforce, William 143
Wild, Jonathan 137, 138–9
Wilkes, John 140
William, Prince of Orange 4
Williams, Raymond 2
Williams, Thomas 82
will theory 85
witchcraft 24, 25, 81, 165
Wollstonecraft, Mary 6, 60
women's rights 6–7, 43, 60
    commercial activity 118
    criminal trials 100–5
    marital relations 26–30, 67–8
    marriage 54, 60, 123–5
    profligate husbands 113–18
    sexual agency 123, 124
women writers 124
Wood, Andy 22
Wood, Thomas 133
workers 18, 19–20
wrongs. *See also* justice
    cultural context 144
    elasticity of the concept of wrongfulness 127–8
    mirror on society 137–9
    protest and riot 139–40
    redefining wrongs 140–3
    righting wrongs and performing justice 128–31
    slavery 140–3
    trials (*see* criminal trials)

Yonge, Sir George 142
Yorke, Charles 50, 163
Yorke, Philip, 1st Earl of Hardwicke 35, 47, 48, 50, 52, 59, 112, 121

Zong (slave ship) 11, 141